Hospitality Security Services

HOSPITALITY SECURITY SERVICES

Neelam Singh

CENTRUM PRESS
NEW DELHI-110002 (INDIA)

CENTRUM PRESS

H.O.: 4360/4, Ansari Road, Daryaganj,
New Delhi-110002 (India)
Tel: 23278000, 23261597, 23255577, 23286875

B.O.: No. 1015, Ist Main Road, BSK IIIrd Stage,
IIIrd Phase, IIIrd Block, Bengaluru-560085 (INDIA)
Tel: 080-41723429

Email: centrumpress@gmail.com
Visit us at: www.centrumpress.com

Hospitality Security Services

First Edition, 2013

ISBN 978-93-81460-05-4

PRINTED IN INDIA

Printed at Balaji Offset, Delhi.

Contents

Preface

Until recently, managers and property owners in western democracies took it easy in matters of safety, security, and emergency management, economizing in the process. Following 9/11 and its aftermath, they can no longer afford this luxury. Business is "not" run as usual. A scramble to correct the situation leads many to adopt stop-gap measures, appointing only a limited number of managers and employees to provide some sort of safety measure, resulting in dangerous and misleading assumptions of effective organization and control. Incomplete planning and organization can cost many lives and lead to business loss. Managing emergencies and providing safety and security to guests, customers, employees, owners, and the property itself, requires informed and thorough planning and organization across the board, with the active involvement of all departments and employees. This responsibility cannot be relegated to only a few people in the organization. And these subjects cannot be considered as a "separate" field, but become an integral part of all operational functions. A Safety and Security Committee must be selected (appointed or elected by the management team), based on the ability of its members to plan, communicate, train, coordinate, delegate, implement, supervise, and control the many aspects related to the prevention and management of safety, security and emergency situations pertinent to the organization.

Hotels are required to provide reasonable care to ensure that guests have a safe and secure stay. Hotels are not required to guarantee guest security. You are responsible for your personal security and property. While in the room, keep the door closed and engage the dead bolt and privacy latch or chain. A limited number of hotel emergency keys can override the dead bolt locks. To ensure privacy use the latch or chain! Hoteliers provide guest room "safes" for the convenience of guests. However, these containers are not as durable as bank safes and can be breached. Furthermore, the Housekeepers Liability Laws provide that if guest property is not in the "care, custody and control of the hotel," the hotel is not liable. Guests should always place money or valuables in the safe deposit box at the front desk of the hotel. When leaving the guest room, ensure that the door properly closes and is secured. Make a mental note of how your property was left; avoid leaving valuables in plain view or in an unorganized manner. A number of hotel employees enter the room each day to clean, repair and restock the room. Although most hotel employees are honest and hardworking, a few succumb to the temptation of cash or jewellery left unprotected. If you determine that an item is missing, conduct a thorough search prior to reporting the incident to hotel security. Do not expect to receive a copy of the security report, as it is an internal document. The incident should be reported to the local police, the Regional Security and Consular Officers at the U.S. Embassy, and your insurance carrier. Hotel security can provide a letter verifying that you reported property missing.

Prior to travelling, it is recommended that you copy all credit cards, passport, air tickets and other documents to facilitate reporting loss and replacing them. While travelling abroad, secure these documents in the room safe deposit box and carry copies of your passport and visa. Request housekeeping make up your room while you are at breakfast, rather than leave a "Please Service This Room" sign on the door knob. This sign is a signal to criminals that the room is unoccupied. If you are required to use parking stickers in your auto, be sure that it does not indicate your name or room number.

This book deals with the fundamental and basic information of subject and the selection of contents makes it an appropriate textbook for the students.

—Author

1

Hospitality Security Management

Introduction

From the earliest times, thieves and robbers often subjected travelers to attacks. Outside of walled cities and castles travelers could usually find shelter and protection only in wayside inns. From this practice grew the principle that innkeepers were responsible for providing their guests not only food and lodging, but also security and protection against criminal attack.

While the duty of innkeepers to protect their guests is somewhat different today than it once was, lodgings, including gaming casinos often with attached or integrated hotels, still owe a responsibility to their guests and other invitees. And guests continue to be at risk today! Criminals often look at lodgings as attractive targets filled with unsuspecting potential victims, most of whom will leave town soon after being robbed or victimized.

While some cities, counties and states may require specific security measures at lodging properties (or casinos), in those jurisdictions not having such requirements, the legal responsibility owed to their guests by lodging management requires the operator to "exercise reasonable care" in identifying potential crime risks, and to take reasonable measures to prevent those crimes, or to warn guests against them. In general, the greater the likelihood of future crime or injury, the greater the innkeeper's responsibility to defend or warn against it.

Foreseeability

Determining what crime is "reasonably foreseeable" requires a thorough review of the facts in each particular instance. Some states use the "prior similar crimes" test, which analyzes previous crimes on the property. How similar the crimes must be and how recent their prior occurrence are matters usually determined by the judge in each case, often based on prior court decisions in that state.

Other states use the "totality of the circumstances" standard, which examines other factors in addition to any prior similar crimes on the property. Such factors can include:

- *Nature and operation of the facility:* For example, gaming casinos by their nature invite guests to bring large amounts of cash. Security for a roadside inn has some different considerations than a resort facility that attracts more affluent vacationers, typically to a larger, more spread-out property.
- *Location of the lodging facility:* Some cities have higher crime rates than others, and within most all cities some areas have higher crime rates than the average for that city. Being located in or near one of those "high crime" cities or areas may increase the crime risk to a specific lodging property.
- *Actual past crimes on the property:* These are frequently one of the best means of predicting future crimes, since what has occurred already is likely to recur if changes in security or other conditions haven't been made.
- Security problems created by the facility's design or layout, for example, "blind spots," where criminals may loiter or hide, and broken lines of sight that reduce visibility by staff and guests. Both problems may increase specific crime risks.
- *Alcoholic beverage service on the property:* Alcohol not only tends to reduce inhibitions, but it also reduces alertness and wariness—a situation many criminals like to exploit.
- *Crimes at similar nearby properties.* While properties generally compete against each other for business, they should be cooperating in the common fight against crime. The type

of crime that occurs on one property usually occurs or impacts all similar nearby properties.

Many other factors may also be applicable to assessing crime foreseeability, and many are specific to a given property and its unique operation or to its surrounding area. A professional security consultant can help identify them.

Reasonable Care Security

Almost any lodging facility, depending on its location and the nature of its operation, should utilize some or all of the following security measures:

- *Screening and background checks of employees:* This is a basic step for all lodging security. Many lodging employees have some access to guestrooms, guests and their belongings, or to confidential information about the guests or about facility security. If the staff is untrustworthy, most other security measures will fail.
- Adequate doors and locking hardware—the most basic of precautions. If the guest room door, its frame and its hardware are insufficient to resist moderate force—guests are at risk. Doors should be solid-core wood or metal. Likewise, providing appropriate locking devices is crucial. The standard, especially in larger lodgings, is evolving toward the use of electronic locks that can (and should) be changed immediately when a guest departs or when a key is reported lost. Where traditional metal keys are used, an effective key control and monitoring program is essential. All guestroom entry doors should be equipped with a minimum of two locks, one of them a dead bolt, and should be self-closing and self-locking. Entry doors should be equipped with a wide-angle peephole viewer in the door. A window adjacent to the door that permits viewing of visitors before opening the door will also serve the same purpose. Sliding balcony-type doors should be equipped with secondary locking devices, such as a "charley bar" and a through-the-door pin to prevent lifting the door from its track.
- Appropriate levels of lighting for all areas of risk, including parking lots and garages. Many criminals

prefer to commit their crimes in darkness, thus avoiding detection, possible identification, and incarceration. Appropriate lines of sight. Shrubs, which often provide concealment or interfere with lines of sight, should be not higher than 18 inches above ground. Tree branches should be trimmed so that they hang not lower than eight feet above the ground. Doing so enhances employees' ability to see, and guests are more able to perceive potential dangers at a distance.

- Appropriate security equipment, such as cameras and alarms. Depending on their size, layout, staffing and crime risk, properties may utilize security equipment to supplement manpower. Management should not only select and install appropriate equipment for the tasks, but it must also maintain it and promptly repair it if it fails.

  Note: Dummy cameras or false or misleading signage about cameras or monitoring should *never* be used.

- *Appropriate staffing for security duties:* In small properties, a night clerk monitoring the lobby and front desk may be all that is necessary, although some locations may require bullet-resistant materials for the clerk's protection, depending on the risk of armed robbery or sexual assault. In larger or more spread-out properties, or those with certain crime histories, or which have specific risks such as bar or casino operations, patrols by in-house or contract security officers may be required to monitor activities. By their observable, uniformed presence, such officers also act to deter criminal offenders.

- *Appropriate training for staff:* Security is the responsibility of all staff members; however, they can't properly perform that duty unless they are trained and made individually responsible for it. This is especially true of those who have specific daily security duties, such as managers and supervisors, front-desk clerks, bellhops and security personnel. But maids, maintenance personnel, servers and others should have clear reporting or other security duties spelled out in their job descriptions. It is important that such duties be spelled out not only in the individual's job description, but, most importantly, also in their performance evaluation. That which is monitored and graded tends to get done!

- *Appropriate record-keeping:* Maintaining records reflecting adherence to security procedures is critical for management to detect deviations from procedures, make corrections, and defend against future claims of negligent security. As one federal agency is fond of saying about training, "If it wasn't documented, it didn't occur." Security incidents should always be documented so that management can review the issues and take appropriate corrective actions.
- *Periodic risk assessments by management:* To know its risks and effectively plan to manage them, management of any facility should periodically assess not only its own crime experience, but also that of similar nearby lodgings (or casinos, or resorts), and any actual or potential changes impacting its operation. For example, is the property attracting more female business travelers or airline flight crews, either of which may be attractive targets for thieves or sexual predators? Or, is the property planning to host a jewelry trade show, or is it hosting increasing numbers of foreign visitors who may be unfamiliar with the local area, its customs, language, and its crime? All these factors and more can change the crime risk for a lodging facility.

Gaming Casinos

Casinos often appear to have dozens or even hundreds of cameras protecting their guests; however, in many cases the majority of those cameras are utilized (by law) only to ensure the integrity of the games, not for general security purposes. As a result some customers may be lulled into a false sense of security. To be effective and reasonable, a casino property must provide security for both the games and its business invitees (customers).

Because of the actual or perceived availability of "easy money," casinos pose special security risks. Additionally, the availability and consumption of large amounts of alcoholic beverages, which in many cases are "free," increase those risks. Not only do alcoholic beverages tend to reduce inhibitions in many people, they also tend to lessen their alertness and their awareness of potential crime or assault. Being in strange surroundings away from their familiar environment, such customers are more likely to become crime victims than they would in their familiar home area.

Casino management should devote adequate attention to securing all areas of the casino and its services. For example, garages and parking lots are favorite stalking areas for robbers, rapists and carjackers. Dimly lit walkways to remote housing units, and isolated unmonitored hallways are also favored stalking and assault locations.

Because of the heightened risks and the many venues in which they will have to operate, casino property security officers and guard forces should be screened and trained to a much higher level than most security personnel. They should be certified on any weapons they are authorized by management to carry or use; should be trained in non-lethal force; trained in customer relations; and trained in techniques for verbally defusing situations before they become violent. Casinos, by their very nature, tend to attract criminals. Because of their increased crime risk, guard staffing should be higher in casinos than in stand-alone hotels or nightclubs. Prepared management, coupled with sufficient visible and adequately trained security personnel, can help prevent casinos from becoming a "crime hot spot."

Parking Lot and Garage Security

Security professionals have long known that locations where people and their valuables are together—such as in parking lots and garages—are often favorite targets of criminals.

That fact, well known among security professionals and police, was confirmed by a study conducted by Liability Consultants, Inc. of Sudbury, Massachusetts. The study of more than 1,000 premises security liability lawsuits between 1992 and 2001 revealed that in almost one-third of all the cases reviewed, the basis of the lawsuit was a murder, rape, robbery or assault that occurred in a parking lot or garage. Those parking facilities included those such as might be found at an office building, motels and apartments, plants, retail stores and shopping centers, plus, pay-for-park lots and garages open to the general public. The study also found that jury awards or pretrial settlements to the plaintiffs in the lawsuits averaged between approximately $1 million for assaults and $2.75 million for homicides.

So, can owners provide "reasonable" parking lot and garage security for their customers and employees against these type crimes? In a word, Yes! (but it takes work)

Some cities and counties may mandate specific security measures to be used at parking lots and garages. Where such laws or regulations are not in effect, the general national standard of care for owners/operators of such facilities is "reasonable care" for the facility at that time and place, as in reasonable to a judge or jury. That means first identifying the likely security threats and crime risks, then implementing reasonable and appropriate security measures to counter those risks-and maintaining them as appropriate.

Garages and Covered Parking Facilities

In many garages, access to the garage can be controlled or closely monitored. A parking attendant can view the occupants of cars entering and leaving, and a closed circuit television (CCTV) camera can record license numbers and drivers' faces ... both major deterrents to many criminals.

However, ground-level pedestrian doors located out of sight of the parking attendant should not be accessible from the exterior of the building, or at least should be monitored by CCTV. Nor should there be any openings in the building walls (within 15 feet above the ground) through which a person could enter. Where possible, vehicle entry and exit should be limited to a single monitored entry, or to adjacent entry and exit points.

Because garages and parking lots contain valuable vehicles and their contents, plus the car occupants who also represent potential targets and victims-both are frequent favored "hunting grounds" for robbers and thieves. The threat to persons and property in covered/enclosed parking garages can be even higher than in open lots, because isolated floors and locations often make effective surveillance or monitoring difficult. However, adequate lighting and the use of CCTV monitoring can reduce (*but not eliminate*) the crime risk. Adequate lighting not only helps people recognize and avoid dangers, but also in many cases deters criminals by creating in them the fear of detection, identification and apprehension.

Note: If the CCTV cameras are not monitored live and instead only recorded for later review and prosecution, prominent signage should state this so that customers do not rely, to their detriment, on cameras that they think are being monitored and will produce immediate help.

When CCTV is used, good-quality color cameras that can, in enclosed garages, operate in low light along with high-resolution color monitoring/recording systems are essential. Digital recording is preferred. Black-and-white cameras and monitors usually offer poor detail definition, a critical issue when attempting to identify suspects or potential problems. A penny saved here may equal many thousands or millions of dollars lost later!

For safety and security, I recommend interior garage lighting should be a minimum of six footcandles (60 lux) on the pavement (with approximately the same level measured 1.5 m or five feet above the pavement) with an average uniformity ratio of not greater than 4:1. This level should be maintained throughout the garage, 24 hours per day, as sunlight seldom enters garage interiors, and cannot be relied upon for lighting. A minimum of 10 footcandles (100 lux) is recommended at pedestrian entry/exit points, over driving lanes, stairwells and elevator lobbies (out to a 30' radius from the elevator doors). Energy-efficient metal-halide lighting provides reasonable color rendition for CCTV and direct viewing. Interior walls and ceilings should be painted with a glossy or semi-glossy white paint to increase light reflection.

This also increases the ability of parkers to observe movement and potential threats. Pillars and ramp corners should be painted in contrasting (striped) colors for driving safety. Transitional lighting at the vehicle entry/exit points should lighted for eye adaption when going into the structure from the street, or vice versa. Garage owners/operators should discuss their specific needs with a lighting engineer.

Rooftop parking open to the sky should be illuminated to at least three footcandles, as specified below for surface parking lots.

Where possible, interior and exterior stairwells should be visible, either through the use of no walls on the stairwells, or glass or "see-through" type walls. This "open" approach deprives criminals of a place to hide and assault their victims, while providing customers early warning of potential danger and the ability to possibly be heard if they shout for help. In either case, the stairwells should be well lit.

Emergency call boxes, "panic alarms" and intercom systems often have large, red mushroom-shaped buttons. When pushed, the buttons activate an intercom connected to a security office or the parking garage attendant, who can provide directions or summon aid. When a CCTV camera also monitors the alarm box or station, the parking attendant or security officer can view the scene to assess the situation and more accurately respond. Boxes should be mounted five feet above surface to ensure visibility, but also comply with any ADA requirements. High visibility signage or lights at a six or seven foot height also increase their visibility.

Uniformed security officers on *continuous* patrol of all the levels of a garage, while costly, can also be a significant deterrent to criminals, and a reassurance to customers and employees. A patrol tour tracking system should be used to ensure that all patrolling officers are, in fact, patrolling as required. Security officers can also be used for customer escorts to their cars, but sufficient officers and other employees should be available so that no customer must wait more than 15-minutes for an escort. No security officer should be away from their patrol rounds for more than 15-minutes.

Many of the measures recommended here for garages might, depending on their specific configuration and needs, be used on surface parking lots. When making changes in garages, owners and operators should ensure that they are in compliance with ADA requirements and any local fire, safety and security codes.

Surface Parking Lots

Similar approaches can be used with surface parking lots. If the lot can be surrounded by a "see-through" fence, that is ideal.

If not, lesser demarcation of the lot boundaries with partial fencing, low hedges, planters or shrubs, etc. can provide a psychological barrier to criminals, and a clear indication of where the "private" property begins.

Where appropriate, the use of a parking lot attendant can also serve as a deterrent *if* the attendant is able to view the lot. With no CCTV for remote viewing on most large lots, and with the attendant's booth usually facing out toward the street, and the attendant's head often stuck in a book or portable TV, many attendants can't and don't see much of anything. As a result, they don't provide much, if any, security. This needs to be considered in planning.

A key element of security in most surface parking lots is visibility—for employees, customers, and passers-by. Within the lot, any trees and shrubs should not obstruct viewing. Tree branches and leaves should be not lower than 10 feet above the lot surface, and interior shrubs and bushes should not be higher than 18 inches above ground or curb so as not to obstruct vision, or provide concealment for a robber or rapist. Perimeter shrubs used as a barrier, with or without an adjacent fence, should not exceed 36" in height.

A significant part of visibility is lighting. Lighting should enable parkers and employees to note individuals or movement at night at a distance of 75 feet or more, and to identify a human face at approximately 30 feet, a distance that will allow them, if necessary, to take defensive action or avoidance while still at a safe distance. For safety and security, I recommend a minimum maintained illumination of not less than three footcandles (30 lux) throughout open surface parking lots. This will also provide adequate illumination for driving purposes. Energy-efficient metal-halide lighting offers good color recognition. The lighting should be controlled on and off - by a timer, or preferably, but a photo-electric sensor so that, whatever time it gets dark, the light go on.

This brief article cannot hope to answer all security related questions on parking lots with thousands of different configurations and operating requirements. It does, however, provide an introduction to those security measures and approaches that will help owners and operators provide a reasonable level of security at their property.

If in doubt about these issues, it is recommended that operators or owners consult with a professional independent security consultant, and/or their attorney.

Human resources development, employment and globalization in the hotel, catering and tourism sector.

Human resources is a term used to describe the individuals who make up the workforce of an organization, although it is also applied in labor economics to, for example, business sectors or even whole nations. Human resources is also the name of the function within an organization charged with the overall responsibility for implementing strategies and policies relating to the management of individuals (i.e. the human resources). This function title is often abbreviated to the initials "HR".

Human resources is a relatively modern management term, coined as late as the 1960s. The origins of the function arose in organizations that introduced 'welfare management' practices and also in those that adopted the principles of 'scientific management'. From these terms emerged a largely administrative management activity, coordinating a range of worker related processes and becoming known, in time, as the 'personnel function'. Human resources progressively became the more usual name for this function, in the first instance in the United States as well as multinational or international corporations, reflecting the adoption of a more quantitative as well as strategic approach to workforce management, demanded by corporate management to gain a competitive advantage, utilizing limited skilled and highly skilled workers.

Purpose and Role

In simple terms, an organization's human resource management strategy should maximize return on investment in the organization's human capital and minimize financial risk.

Human resource managers seek to achieve this by aligning the supply of skilled and qualified individuals and the capabilities of the current workforce, with the organization's ongoing and future business plans and requirements to maximize return on investment and secure future survival and success.

In ensuring such objectives are achieved, the human resource function is to implement an organization's human resource requirements effectively, taking into account federal, state and local labor laws and regulations; ethical business practices; and net cost, in a manner that maximizes, as far as possible, employee motivation, commitment and productivity.

Key Functions

Human Resources may set strategies and develop policies, standards, systems, and processes that implement these strategies in a whole range of areas. The following are typical of a wide range of organizations:

- Maintaining awareness of and compliance with local, state and federal labor laws
- Recruitment, selection, and on boarding (resourcing)
- Employee record-keeping and confidentiality
- Organizational design and development
- Business transformation and change management
- Performance, conduct and behavior management
- Industrial and employee relations
- Human resources (workforce) analysis and workforce personnel data management
- Compensation and employee benefit management
- Training and development (learning management)
- Employee motivation and morale-building (employee retention and loyalty)

Implementation of such policies, processes or standards may be directly managed by the HR function itself, or the function may indirectly supervise the implementation of such activities by managers, other business functions or via third-party external partner organizations. Applicable legal issues, such as the potential for disparate treatment and disparate impact, are also extremely important to HR managers.

Management Trends and Influences

In organizations, it is important to determine both current and future organizational requirements for both core employees and the contingent workforce in terms of their skills/technical abilities, competencies, flexibility etc. The analysis requires consideration of the internal and external factors that can have an effect on the resourcing, development, motivation and retention of employees and other workers.

External factors are those largely outside the control of the organization. These include issues such as economic climate and current and future labor market trends (e.g., skills, education level, government investment into industries etc.). On the other hand, internal influences are broadly controlled by the organization to predict, determine, and monitor—for example—the organizational culture, underpinned by management style, environmental climate, and the approach to ethical and corporate social responsibilities.

Major Trends

To know the business environment an organization operates in, three major trends must be considered:

1. *Demographics:* the characteristics of a population/ workforce, for example, age, gender or social class. This type of trend may have an effect in relation to pension offerings, insurance packages etc.
2. *Diversity:* the variation within the population/workplace. Changes in society now mean that a larger proportion of organizations are made up of "baby-boomers" or older employees in comparison to thirty years ago. Advocates of "workplace diversity" simply advocate an employee base that is a mirror reflection of the makeup of society insofar as race, gender, sexual orientation etc.
3. *Skills and qualifications:* as industries move from manual to more managerial professions so does the need for more highly skilled graduates. If the market is "tight" (i.e. not enough staff for the jobs), employers must compete for employees by offering financial rewards, community investment, etc.

Individual Responses

In regard to how individuals respond to the changes in a labor market, the following must be understood:

- *Geographical spread:* how far is the job from the individual? The distance to travel to work should be in line with the pay offered, and the transportation and infrastructure of the area also influence who applies for a post.

- *Occupational structure:* the norms and values of the different careers within an organization. Mahoney 1989 developed 3 different types of occupational structure, namely, craft (loyalty to the profession), organization career (promotion through the firm) and unstructured (lower/ unskilled workers who work when needed).
- *Generational difference:* different age categories of employees have certain characteristics, for example, their behavior and their expectations of the organization.

Framework

Human Resources Development is a framework for the expansion of human capital within an organization or (in new approaches) a municipality, region, or nation. Human Resources Development is a combination of training and education, in a broad context of adequate health and employment policies, that ensures the continual improvement and growth of both the individual, the organization, and the national human resourcefulness. Adam Smith states, "The capacities of individuals depended on their access to education". Human Resources Development is the medium that drives the process between training and learning in a broadly fostering environment. Human Resources Development is not a defined object, but a series of organized processes, "with a specific learning objective" (Nadler, 1984) Within a national context, it becomes a strategic approach to inter sectoral linkages between health, education and employment.

Structure

Human resources development is the structure that allows for individual development, potentially satisfying the organization's, or the nation's goals. Development of the individual benefits the individual, the organization—and the nation and its citizens. In the corporate vision, the Human Resources Development framework views employees as an asset to the enterprise, whose value is enhanced by development, "Its primary focus is on growth and employee development...it emphasizes developing individual potential and skills" (Elwood,

Olton and Trott 1996) Human Resources Development in this treatment can be in-room group training, tertiary or vocational courses or mentoring and coaching by senior employees with the aim for a desired outcome that develops the individual's performance. At the level of a national strategy, it can be a broad inter-sectoral approach to fostering creative contributions to national productivity.

Training and Development

At the organizational level, a successful Human Resources Development program prepares the individual to undertake a higher level of work, "organized learning over a given period of time, to provide the possibility of performance change" (Nadler 1984). In these settings, Human Resources Development is the framework that focuses on the organization's competencies at the first stage, training, and then developing the employee, through education, to satisfy the organization's long-term needs and the individual's career goals and employee value to their present and future employers. Human Resources Development can be defined simply as developing the most important section of any business, its human resource, by attaining or upgrading employee skills and attitudes at all levels to maximize enterprise effectiveness.

The people within an organization are its human resource. Human Resources Development from a business perspective is not entirely focused on the individual's growth and development; "development occurs to enhance the organization's value, not solely for individual improvement. Individual education and development is a tool and a means to an end, not the end goal itself" (Elwood F. Holton II, James W. Trott Jr). The broader concept of national and more strategic attention to the development of human resources is beginning to emerge as newly independent countries face strong competition for their skilled professionals and the accompanying brain-drain they experience.

Recruitment and Selection

Applicant recruitment and employee selection form a major part of an organization's overall resourcing strategies, which identify and secure people needed for the organization to survive and succeed in the short- to medium-term. Recruitment activities need to be responsive to the increasingly competitive market to secure suitably qualified and capable recruits at all levels. To be effective, these initiatives need to include how and when to source the best recruits, internally or externally. Common to the success of either are: well-defined organizational structures with sound job design, robust task and person specification and versatile selection processes, reward, employment relations and human resource policies, underpinned by a commitment for strong employer branding and employee engagement and onboarding strategies.

Internal recruitment can provide the most cost-effective source for recruits if the potential of the existing pool of employees has been enhanced through training, development and other performance-enhancing activities such as performance appraisal, succession planning and development centres to review performance and assess employee development needs and promotional potential.

Increasingly, securing the best quality candidates for almost all organizations relies, at least occasionally if not substantially, on external recruitment methods. Rapidly changing business models demand skill and experience that cannot be sourced or rapidly enough developed from the existing employee base. It would be unusual for an organization to undertake all aspects of the recruitment process without support from third-party dedicated recruitment firms.

This may involve a range of support services, such as: provision of CVs or resumes, identifying recruitment media, advertisement design and media placement for job vacancies, candidate response handling, shortlisting, conducting aptitude testing, preliminary interviews or reference and qualification verification. Typically, small organizations may not have in-house resources or, in common with larger organizations, may not possess the particular skill-set required to undertake a specific recruitment assignment. Where requirements arise, these are referred on an ad hoc basis to government job centres or commercially-run employment agencies.

Except in sectors where high-volume recruitment is the norm, an organization faced with sudden, unexpected requirements for an unusually large number of new recruits often delegates the task to a specialist external recruiter. Sourcing executive-level and senior management as well as the acquisition of scarce or 'high-potential' recruits has been a long-established market serviced by a wide range of 'search and selection' or 'headhunting' consultancies, which typically form long-standing relationships with their client organizations. Finally, certain organizations with sophisticated HR practices have identified a strategic advantage in outsourcing complete responsibility for all workforce procurement to one or more third-party recruitment agencies or consultancies. In the most sophisticated of these arrangements the external recruitment services provider may not only physically locate, or 'embed', their resourcing team(s) in the client organization's offices, but work in tandem with the senior human resource management team in developing the longer-term HR resourcing strategy and plan.

Other Considerations

Despite its more everyday use, terms such as "human resources" and, similarly, "human capital" continue to be perceived negatively and may be considered insulting. They create the impression that people are merely commodities, like office machines or vehicles, despite assurances to the contrary.

Modern analysis emphasizes that human beings are not "commodities" or "resources", but are creative and social beings in a productive enterprise. The 2000 revision of ISO 9001, in contrast, requires identifying the processes, their sequence and interaction, and to define and communicate responsibilities and authorities. In general, heavily unionized nations such as France and Germany have adopted and encouraged such approaches. Also, in 2001, the International Labour Organization decided to revisit and revise its 1975 Recommendation 150 on Human Resources Development. One view of these trends is that a strong social consensus on political economy and a good social welfare system facilitates labor mobility and tends to make the entire economy more productive, as labor can develop skills and experience in various ways, and move from one enterprise to another with little controversy or difficulty in adapting. Another view is that governments should become more aware of their national role in facilitating human resources development across all sectors. Which includes following:

Trans-national Labor Mobility

An important controversy regarding labor mobility illustrates the broader philosophical issue with usage of the phrase "human resources". Governments of developing nations often regard developed nations that encourage immigration or "guest workers" as appropriating human capital that is more rightfully part of the developing nation and required to further its economic growth.

Over time, the United Nations have come to more generally support the developing nations' point of view, and have requested significant offsetting "foreign aid" contributions so that a developing nation losing human capital does not lose the capacity to continue to train new people in trades, professions, and the arts.

Ethical Management

In the very narrow context of corporate "human resources" management, there is a contrasting pull to reflect and require workplace diversity that echoes the diversity of a global customer base. Such programs require foreign language and culture skills, ingenuity, humor, and careful listening. These indicate a general shift through the human capital point of view to an acknowledgment that human beings contribute more to a productive enterprise than just "work": they bring their character, ethics, creativity, social connections and, in some cases, pets and children, and alter the character of a workplace. The term corporate culture is used to characterize such processes at the organizational level.

When the ILO Governing Body created the ILO Industrial Committee for the Hotel, Restaurant and Tourism Sector, which subsequently became the Committee for the Hotel, Catering and Tourism Sector, the sector included:

(a) hotels, boarding houses, motels, tourist camps, holiday centres;

(b) restaurants, bars, cafeterias, snack bars, pubs, night clubs, and other similar establishments;

(c) establishments ... for the provision of meals and refreshments within the framework of industrial and institutional catering (for hospitals, factory and office canteens, schools, aircraft, ships, etc.);

(d) travel agencies and tourist guides, tourism information offices;

(e) conference and exhibition centres.

Statistics are being organized according to the International Standard Industrial Classification of all Economic Activities (ISIC), the latest edition of which is ISIC Rev. 3. In that classification, the sectors most relevant for the ILO definition of the sector are Hotels and restaurants (division 55) 2 and Activities of travel agencies and tour operators, Tourist assistance activities (class 6304).

Other organizations concerned with tourism, including governments, intergovernmental organizations and NGOs, often use much broader definitions of the term than that used by the ILO. They subsume under it all services and products consumed by tourists, including transport. In the ILO denomination of the sector, the part referring to "tourism" only covers travel agencies and tour operators.

Hotels and catering, including restaurants, are considered by most organizations to belong to the "tourism characteristic industries" and therefore subsumed under tourism, although in some countries only a small part of their services is for tourists. However, the fact that the ILO definition of the sector thus differs considerably from the concept of tourism used by other organizations does not prevent most concerns about the development of tourism from being shared by those organizations. One such concern is the sector's potential to provide employment. Nevertheless, the ILO's focus on labour issues is unique as it includes all working and employment conditions in the HCT sector.

Changing Consumer Preferences

Today, new consumers are influencing the pace and direction of underlying changes in the industry. The "new tourists" are more experienced travellers. Changes in consumer behaviour and values provide the fundamental driving force for the new tourism. The increased travel experience, flexibility and independent nature of the new tourists are generating demand for better quality, more value for money and greater flexibility in the travel experience.

The new consumers also reflect demographic changes–the population is ageing, household size is decreasing and households have greater disposable income.

Changing lifestyles of the new tourists are creating demand for more targeted and customized holidays. A number of lifestyle segments–families, single parent households, "empty nesters" (i.e. couples whose children have left home), doubleincome couples without children–will become prevalent in tourism, signalling the advent of a much more differentiated approach to tourism marketing.

Changing values are also generating demand for more environmentally conscious and nature-oriented holidays. Suppliers will therefore have to pay more attention to the way people think, feel and behave than they have done hitherto.

Within the context of international expansion and market cooperation, companies have had recourse to a number of competitive methods which merit attention. The growing number of alliances is changing industry structures and the level of competition has shifted from the individual company level to alliance groups level. The last five years have witnessed nine major mergers and acquisition transactions in the international hotel market-place. For example, Hilton and Hilton International have merged their sales forces, integrated their logos and marketing efforts, and shared their reservation systems in a strategic alliance considered to be the largest since 1996. Hilton has also allied with Patriot American Hospitality for market expansion. Starwood has established a strategic alliance with Discovery Hotel Group in Asia to open Four Points Hotels in China.

Choice International has done the same with Flag International in Asia. 40 There are other goals and objectives which strategic alliances can fulfil in order to assist multinational hotel firms in strengthening their market positions, improving partnership relations and supplying diversified products and quality services to their customers. These goals and objectives include: acquisition of new information and communication technology (Hyatt and Starwood with Microsoft's Expedia, Hyatt with MSN network, Carlson and Bass with WizCom to link to global distribution systems); distribution of products and cross-marketing between food-service providers and hotels (Ramada with Bennigan's Restaurants, Marriott, Hilton, Bass with Pizza Hut); distribution and cross-promotion of bank credit cards and financial services between banks and hotels (Bass Hotels and Resorts with Visa and American Express, Marriot with Visa and Chase Manhattan's processing system, Hilton, Starwood, and Accor with American Express); consolidation of transportation and hotel services (Carlson and Bass Hotels and Resorts each with more than 20 airlines, Marriott with United Airlines, Starwood with British Airways and Alitalia, and Shangri-la with Canadian Airlines); co-promotion of hotels and films and media (Marriott, Choice Hotels and Cendant with new films, Bass with ESPN and Discovery Channel, and Best Western with Sci-Fi Channel and E-Entertainment Channel).

Impact of New Technology on Skills Requirements

Information and communications technology (ICT) systems which integrate the power of the Internet, customer relationship management and supply chain management in a seamless, one-source destination site, allow a variety of operations – product selection, ordering, fulfilment, tracking, payment and reporting – to be performed with one easy-to-use tool. 8 By cutting out one or more layers of the purchasing structure, these systems yield cost savings by putting the buyer in some instances into direct contact with the producer. They also have employment implications, as intermediaries find that their share of the market is shrinking, with inevitable reductions in labour requirements upstream of the HCT sector. Technology which facilitates on-line hotel, restaurant and theatre reservations or travel arrangements will have an impact in terms of staff reductions on the front-desk hotel staff who used to perform those functions. This technology also calls for a different range of skills from employees. Although systems designers, aware of the rapid turnover among front-desk staff, are working on products that are easier to operate and thus reduce training time for new recruits, the technology is changing so fast that knowledge becomes obsolete ever more quickly. Training will therefore become a continuous need and the remaining jobs will require greater skills.

Many hotels are examining the possibility of installing personal computers in their guest rooms, and some have indeed already done so. This allows customers to use hotel rooms as their offices. Increasing numbers of business guests are also travelling with their own portable computers. Hyatt International Hotels are an example of how new job profiles may be created as a result of this technology. The group has introduced "technology concierges" in their deluxe properties worldwide. These specialist employees, known within the group as "compcierges", are trained to help guests to set up their mobile communications equipment, to explain how to use the in-room technology, hook up laptop computers, provide support in accessing e-mail or the Internet, and so on.

They may also help to locate local retailers that service computers and stock software. While technological expertise is essential, the emphasis is on service; all the team members come from a hospitality background and have in addition received the training needed to become electronic troubleshooters. ICT equipment installed in hotels also requires maintenance and planning departments, making this a new field with job creation potential, although such work may largely be subcontracted to outside operators.

Swissotel has established an ICT department employing ten people, which is now an independent, profitable element of the company. The Carlson Hospitality Group also has a knowledge technologies division, which was created to ensure the smooth operation of the reservation and customer information systems installed in the group's 600 hotels throughout the world. The new technology is also being used by a number of companies as a means of raising skills levels. Domino's Pizza has developed interactive, learner-centrad programmes to guide young employees through the steps involved in making a pizza. Computer-based coaches will soon be available to guide employees through all stages of customer relations. Companies will invest in these new techniques to fulfil their training needs.

Hotel managements are studying technologies which will reduce the attention which guests require from hotel staff. These include: electronic key cards which will open doors and act as credit cards for all on-site purchases; management systems which record the time guests are likely to check out, so that room service may be programmed more efficiently; and cleaning staff equipped with hand-held computers, linked to the hotel's property management system (PMS), so that information can be centralized and constantly updated in real time. The Canadian Regional Office of the Hotel Employees and Restaurant Employees International Union (HEREIU) has expressed concern that such systems will allow hotel companies to computerize almost all everyday front-office operations. Where customers can make their own reservations via the Internet, they could replace switchboard operators altogether. HEREIU further maintains that new in-room technologies such as video check-out systems will replace front-line workers, while electronic keys will be able to tell the PMS exactly how long each employee has spent cleaning a room, and may thus tend to promote an aggressive productivity policy.

The International Union of Food, Agricultural, Hotel, Restaurant, Catering, Tobacco and Allied Workers' Associations (IUF) notes that placing the emphasis on time-saving and labour-saving technologies also means that the pace of work is faster, and argues that in reality, "labour-saving" and "time-saving" are inclined to mean reductions in the numbers of workers. In the IUF's view, the ultimate consequence of time-and-attendance computer software, which provides information on guest arrivals and departures so that workers can be dispatched to their duties immediately, is the dehumanization of work.

(a) New Technologies in Restaurants

New technologies will also result in structural changes in restaurant kitchens. Use of the "sous-vide" technique, where food that has been totally or partially preprepared or precooked is supplied directly to the restaurant, means that a large number of cooking operations can now be outsourced to independent suppliers or to centralized, chain-based kitchens. New methods of food preservation, such as freezing, drying, irradiation, and vacuum and modified-atmosphere packing, enhance the shelf life of products and further reduce last minute operations. On the other hand, new types of equipment have given the baking process in restaurant kitchens a new lease of life. Suppliers of pre-prepared dough cooperate with the manufacturers of specialized ovens so that restaurant staff are required to do nothing more than place the dough in the ovens, activate the appropriate computer programme and remove the bread when it is ready. But the tendency of these innovations is to transform restaurant kitchens into assembly lines, with fewer staff members, since both the simple repetitive tasks, such as vegetable preparation, and the more complex, last minute operations, will be outsourced.

Both the HEREIU and the IUF argue that "regenerated preprocessed foods" require fewer skills of kitchen staff and result in the loss of many kinds of food preparation and cooking jobs in the industry. The IUF also points to a devaluation in wages as a result of the deskilling of the remaining jobs. These arguments are difficult to refute, since most of these technologies provide savings in terms of staffing levels. On the other hand, the technologies could open up crucial empowerment possibilities, freeing staff to deal more attentively with customers, thus enhancing the profile of the establishment.

(b) New Technologies and Travel Agencies

Access to on-line booking via the Internet is causing traditional travel agents considerable problems. It will soon be possible to reserve travel tickets using new mobile phone technology, without the need for a computer. A recent survey carried out by the International Air Transport Association (IATA) revealed that some 37 per cent of travellers worldwide had used electronic tickets, while in the United States, 50 per cent of travellers expected to use such tickets by the end of 2000. Some travel agents are responding to this situation by adopting a more entrepreneurial attitude, charging customers a fee instead of the traditional commission earned on a ticket price.

However, while agents may retain business contracts, they are likely to lose individual customer business for simple trips, and this drop in trade will have an impact on employment levels in the branch. Other agencies see the future in strengthening their role as consultants capable of planning complicated trips involving numerous and varied travel means and stopoffs. However, while the human element will not disappear, it will probably diminish with the spread of 24-hour "warehouse" travel agents (much as 24-hour banking has developed) which allow customers to call and make their bookings at any time.

Salaries and Wages

According to a 1996 survey by the European Foundation for the Improvement of Living and Working Conditions covering 15 European Union countries, working conditions within the industry included a number of potentially problematic areas, such as irregular working hours, frequent work on Sundays, wages without a fixed basic element in 25 per cent of cases, widespread absence of overtime payments and wage levels generally 20 per cent below the European Union average. The following national examples from Europe and North America are illustrative:

- In Switzerland, despite an agreement of 1 January 1999 covering all hotel and restaurant employees, HCT workers had average monthly earnings of Sw.frs.3,394 for an effective working week of 42.8 hours, while monthly pay in the economy as a whole averaged Sw.frs.5,000.
- In the United Kingdom, average weekly wages for full-time manual, hotel and catering jobs were £225.80 for men and only £170.80 for women in 1998, while national average wages for manual workers were £328.00 for men and £211.00 for women.
- In New Orleans in the United States, the Hospitality, Hotels and Restaurant Organizing Council (HOTROC) has stated that an average hotel housekeeper earns US$5.48 an hour, which places most hotel workers and their families 20 per cent below the federal poverty level. In this connection it should be noted that hotel workers in New Orleans are the only non-unionized hospitality workers in a major United States tourist and convention destination.
- In Canada, average weekly earnings increased by 5 per cent in the accommodation sector between 1998 and 1999, but food and beverage earnings lag far behind, having risen by only 1.9 per cent, in line with inflation. The average weekly wage in Canada in accommodation is Can$309.14, and in food and beverage Can$221.30. These wages should be viewed against the national average wage of Can$582.85 a week. Such comparisons

do not give a complete picture of the wage structure in the industry. For one thing, comparisons between HCT sector wages established by law or collective agreements and national averages may not fully account for the real wages in those branches where tips or gratuities account for a sizeable proportion of employees' earnings. These are not always declared for tax purposes, nor are they always known by the employer, and may thus represent a net, tax-free source of income. Secondly, comparisons need to be made with similar occupations of equivalent skill and training levels in other sectors, but the statistical basis for doing so is often lacking.

Some comparative data are provided in the tables in Appendix 2. They are taken from the few countries where sufficient information is available. The figures suggest that hotel and restaurant workers earn less than workers in socially comparable occupations, and that the differential tends to be higher in developing countries, and higher for the occupations requiring higher skills and responsibilities.

Changing forms of Remuneration

Basic wages reflect competitive labour markets, collective agreements and national laws. Variable pay is emerging as a way to reward employees whose performance enhances the success of an establishment. As a strategy, this idea is not yet common in the sector, but it is beginning to take hold. In the United States, Rodeway Inn International, at Orlando, and Motel Properties, Inc. have both developed successful techniques to reward employees above their basic salaries, based on a monthly assessment scheme.

Job and Income Stability and Staff Turnover

Turnover figures vary from region to region within countries, but the overall picture is alarming. In the United States, according to a 1998 study, 21 annual turnover in 1997 was running at 51.7 per cent for line-level employees, 11.9 per cent for supervisory levels, and 13.5 per cent for property managers. The study shows that the turnover rate for the managerial levels is far lower than for line employees. In Asia, rates of around 30 per cent annually are quoted, rising to more than 50 per cent in Hong Kong, China (possibly owing to the construction of numerous hotels, creating a more competitive labour market). In the United Kingdom, a study carried out by the Institute of Personnel and Development in 1997 found a national turnover rate in the sector of 42 per cent, second only to the retail trade, with a rate of 43.5 per cent and far in advance of construction, where the rate was 25 per cent.

In the fast food sector, in both Europe and the United States, turnover rates as high as 300 per cent are reported. It should be noted, however, that turnover figures do not separate out non-standard, part-time jobs from full-time posts. Many employees, such as college students, are not interested in permanent positions.

2

Human Resource Development

Introduction

The traditional constraints of the hotel, catering and tourism industry – long, antisocial working hours, low pay, unstable, seasonal employment, low job status, etc. – make employment within the industry appear unattractive to many. A study carried out in 1996 in Germany found that employment in the hotel and catering trade was not the first choice for nine out of ten employees, while only one employee in seven was satisfied with the trade as a choice of career. Nevertheless, the industry does attract some people either on a short-term basis or for a long-term career.

The immediate and most obvious consequences of such a situation are the difficulty of recruiting suitable staff and high staff turnover; both these effects are costly to the industry. There is therefore a perceived need for human resource development, to raise the profile of the industry, increase productivity and provide decent, sustainable employment within the sector.

Estimating Labour Productivity

A wide range of technological developments in service in hotels may be affecting productivity. Integrated management systems are enabling hotel companies to computerize day-to-day reception operations. Clients are thus able to make their own reservations via the Internet, while electronic in-room installations make it possible to settle accounts from the hotel room. This technology will also make it possible to monitor the productivity of personnel, while new techniques in food preparation and storage are reducing the skills needed in the kitchen and the time required for food preparation. Hotels are therefore seeking new ways to measure service delivery that take into account customer satisfaction and return visits, rather than sticking to a narrow "input/output" system.

In Europe, tourist-related activities account on average for 5.5 per cent of GDP in all European Union Member States and for a total of 9 million employees, representing 6 per cent of the total workforce. The precise percentages vary from country to country. According to WTTC simulated figures, the tourism industry's labour force represents about 3 per cent of the world's total labour force and produces about 4 per cent of total world GDP. The industry can therefore not be regarded as labour intensive throughout.

The most striking thing to note regarding labour productivity in the different regions is the gap between Europe's average of about US$47,000 per employee and the overall average of US$22,000. The performance of the Caribbean (around US$28,000) is also impressively higher than average. In the hotel industry in developing countries there may be on average up to three people employed for each hotel bed, while in developed countries the inverse is true, with one person employed for up to three or even four hotel beds. However, figures of this sort can be affected by the range of services provided by a hotel: an establishment surrounded by a leisure complex, health resort or spa will naturally employ more ancillary workers. Labour productivity in hotels has increased over the last ten years by about 1 per cent per year. In the United States, the number of employees per 100 hotel rooms sold has declined from 81 in 1986 to 75 in 1997.

The same productivity growth applies to the entire HCT sector whose GDP, according to WTTC simulated figures, has been growing by about 3 per cent per year, whilst employment in the industry has grown by only about 2 per cent per year. Labour productivity in restaurants is hard to measure. Since only 50-60 per cent of all restaurant employees worldwide are full-time workers, the information available hardly allows us to establish absolute productivity ratios.

Hospitality Services

The concept of hospitality exchange, also known as "accommodation sharing", "hospitality services" (short "hospex"), and "home stay networks", "home hospitality" ("hoho"), refers to centrally organized social networks of individuals, generally travelers, who offer or seek accommodation without monetary exchange. These services generally connect users via the internet.

History

In 1949, Bob Luitweiler founded the first hospitality service called Servas Open Doors as a cross national, nonprofit, volunteer run organization advocating interracial and international peace. In 1965, John Wilcock set up the Traveler's Directory as a listing of his friends willing to host each other when traveling. In 1988, Joy Lily rescued the organization from imminent shutdown, forming Hospitality Exchange. In 1970 Jimmy Carter (then US President) announced the formation of Friendship Force International which has chapters in 57 countries today. In 2000, Veit Kuhne founded Hospitality Club, the first Internet-based service. In 2004, Casey Fenton started Couch Surfing, now the largest hospitality exchange organization.

How they Work

Generally, after registering, members have the option of providing very detailed information and pictures of themselves and of the sleeping accommodation being offered, if any. The more information provided by a member improves the chances that someone will find the member trustworthy enough to be their host or guest. Names and addresses may be verified by volunteers. Members looking for accommodation can search for hosts using several parameters such as age, location, sex, and activity level.

Home stays are entirely consensual between the host and guest, and the duration, nature, and terms of the guest's stay are generally worked out in advance to the convenience of both parties. No monetary exchange takes place except under certain circumstances (e.g. the guest may compensate the host for food). After using the service, members can leave a noticeable reference about their host or guest.

Instead of or in addition to accommodation, members also offer to provide guide services or travel-related advice. The websites of the networks also provide editable travel guides and forums where members may seek travel partners or advice. Many such organizations are also focused on "social networking" and members organize activities such as camping trips, bar crawls, meetings, and sporting events.

Some networks cater to specific niche markets such as students, activists, religious pilgrims, and even occupational groups like police officers.

Benefits : Monetary Savings

As these networks provide accommodation at no charge, monetary savings can be significant.

Local Contact

Hospitality exchange gives travelers the chance to experience what life is like for people living in other places. In addition, making interpersonal connections and fostering understanding of different cultures may in the long run also be important to international relations. During hospitality exchanges, hosts may show off their local knowledge and exciting places "off the tourist map". Not only may travelers get a distinct experience, but they will also get a feel for the everyday lives of local residents.

Reciprocity

The concept behind Hospitality services is based on the pay it forward philosophy, gift economy, and reciprocal altruism.

Drawbacks : Lack of Guarantee

There is no contractual agreement between users in these systems. Reservations are made, but if they are for some reason broken, there is no higher authority to which one could plead for a refund or other compensation.

The only repercussion will be the poor rating you give that user and your only consolation will be that your warning will deter others from visiting or hosting them. For those who feel insecure unless their travel arrangements are written in stone before departure, this system will not be comforting.

Potential Interpersonal Conflict or Awkwardness

There is a chance that guest and host will not get along. Perhaps there will be scheduling or ideological conflicts. Maybe you will find that hosts or visitors have misrepresented themselves. Perhaps the experience will not live up to your expectations. Intense interpersonal communications in advance and a flexibility once you have arrived is your best bet. These experiences require additional planning and courtesy towards the demands of your host. Thus, your living conditions, length of stay, and overall experience will be circumscribed by the living conditions you enter into.

Digital Divide and Demographic Segregation

As use of these services generally requires access to the internet and knowledge of the English language, the sample population found in searches of these databases is really much less diverse than a geographical representation of worldwide users might suggest.

Security

Staying in someone's house, or inviting people into your house leaves open the possibility of being taken advantage of.

Home Hospitality in Scouting

In the Scout Movement, home hospitality (hoho) refers to Scouts living for a few days with a host Scouting family to experience everyday life in that community. This often takes place before or after a jamboree and is usually organized by the organization running the jamboree.

Example Networks

There are countless websites that serve the idea of hospitality service, with new ones appearing as this phenomenon becomes more popular. While this page is not intended to be a directory listing, here is a small sample of the well-established and long-standing networks:

- *Couch Surfing:* A very active network with over 2 million members in more than 200 countries
- *Hospitality Club:* A very active network with over 550,000 members in more than 200 countries

- *Servas International:* human rights and global peace oriented since 1949. A relatively small network now with over 16,000 members with a very long history.
- *Friendship Force International:* A network of chapters worldwide which concentrates on building understanding across cultures.

Specialized Networks

Some networks offer specialized hospitality services.

- Lesbian and Gay Hospitality Exchange International
- Warm Showers - Hospitality network for touring cyclists
- *Dachgeber:* Hospitality network for touring cyclists in Germany with about 3000 members
- *Pasporta Servo:* for Esperanto speakers
- *WWOOF:* "Worldwide Opportunities on Organic Farms", help on the property is exchanged for food, accommodation, education and cultural interaction
- *Freagle:* "Free Camping, worldwide!" - Uniting Outdoor Lovers Through Hospitality and Mutual Help.
- *HelpX:* "Help Exchange", help is exchanged for food, accommodation, experience and cultural interaction
- *Homeshare International:* charitable organization providing exchange of housing for help in the home
- *Ridester:* ride sharing for travelers in USA
- *Jewgether:* a hospitality network that connects Jewish people from all around the world and helps Jewish travelers find a place to stay.

Service Quality of Hospitality Industry

The domination of the service sector today is confirmed by the fact that 70% of the world GDP is realized in the service sector. The same sector sees the concentration of 70% of workforce. In order to ensure and keep the quality expected by today's customer/tourist, we need to differentiate two aspects of quality in general with particular attention to tourism, namely: design quality and the quality of conformity with design.

The design quality is a concept implying the presentation of products/services directed to the needs of the clients. The hotel company can satisfy the demands of the client (tourist) only if they are included in its design, i.e. in order to do that, his demands need to be included or "built into" the product/service of the hotel. The hotels do market research in order to determine who their customers are and which of their demands require special attention.

The quality of conformity with the design completes the first aspect because it represents the level to which the product/service meets the demands of the market. The quality represents the satisfaction of the client's needs and in order to achieve it and keep it in time, we not only need a continuous research into the demands of the clients but also of our own capabilities. Such an approach would ensure the pursuing of constant improvements according to the demands of the clients.

The harsh competition on tourist market requires the development of a new approach to management known as TQM – Total Quality Management. When introducing the quality management system, hotel companies use various approaches adapted to their business conditions. The following part of the paper describes the most common service quality measurement criteria, in particular the model of internal service quality and the SERVQUAL model.

Review of the Literature

Service quality is a way to manage business processes in order to ensure total satisfaction to the customer on all levels (internal and external). It is an approach that leads to an increase of competitiveness, effectiveness and flexibility of the entire company.

Benefits arising from a high quality are reflected in a more competitive positioning on the market, but also in a better business result. This statement can be proved by measuring the increase of profitability and market share. The results of a research carried out in the USA on a sample of 2600 companies in the period between 1987 and 2002, show a direct connection between the level of quality of goods and services and their financial performances. As a matter of fact, it was observed that all indicators of success of a company, like market share, return on investments, property turnover coefficient, show significantly more value in companies with a higher level of goods and services.

The efficiency of the whole system is possible only if we monitor and analyze the demands of the customers, as well as define and control the process and implement constant improvements. Quality is a complex term, made up of several elements and criteria.

All quality elements or criteria are equally important in order to obtain one hundred percent quality. If only one element of quality is missing, the complete quality of product or service is impossible to obtain. Besides the mentioned general elements of quality, the product or service have to satisfy specific elements of quality, according to the demands of the profession in their pertaining activity.

Today quality is the result of growing and increasingly diverse needs of the consumers, along with a highly increasing competition, market globalization and the development of modern technology. Problems in service quality measurement arise from a lack of clear and measurable parameters for the determination of quality. It is not the case with product quality since products have specific and measurable indicators like durability, number of defective products and similar, which make it relatively easy to determine the level of quality.

The most important characteristics of services, separating them neatly from products, are the impossibility to separate production from consumption; the impossibility to store services; their non material quality; transience and heterogeneity.

The impossibility to separate production from consumption and the impossibility to store services implicitly includes a simultaneous production and consumption, which is characteristic for most services. Since the services are performances, ideas or concepts rather than objects, they cannot be seen in the same way as products and are, therefore, characterized by their being immaterial.

Furthermore, it is impossible to preserve services, which raises the issue of harmonizing offer and demand for services. The same service can be provided by different persons in an institution, and each of them might provide it in their own way so that heterogeneity also counts among characteristics of services that differentiate them from products.

The quality system is based on principles such as commitment of the management, focus on the customers, employees and facts, constant improvement and cooperation of all the participants to the process. Research carried out in 101 companies in the service provision field (Zemke, Schaff, 1989) show the following results:

> *"Managers are "obsessed" with listening to the changeable wishes, needs and expectations of their customers, and the wish to respond to them.*
>
> *"A solidly defined strategy of servicing "inspired by consumers" is created by managers in their companies, and transferred to the staff.*
>
> *"Managers develop and maintain a* customer-friendly *system of providing services.*
>
> *"Managers look for, and then inspire and develop staff that is in direct contact with consumers.*

Two basic approaches to service quality have been identified in the early nineties of the twentieth century. The first approach is "technical" and product oriented, while the second approach is customer related. These two approaches have been recognized as results of managerial efforts to consider the aspect of quality when providing services from two angles: on one hand, the manager tends to abide by the set standards, while on the other, he wishes to satisfy the customer. The first approach is production oriented and tends to the consistency of service by impeding or minimizing the influence of the personnel directly involved in providing a service.

The service providing process is defined as a standard performance. The role of the staff providing services is reduced to the realization of the defined performance and the staff's discretion, i.e. its influence on the performance itself is minimized. In that way we can achieve maximum efficiency. Such a "product based" approach to the process of service provision is the result of the managerial view on this process as a series of elements that require a trained coordination and control, while the service itself is strictly standardized. The "product based" approach is contradictory to the aspirations of the consumers to be treated as individual people with marked personal tendencies and expectations. Besides, such an approach, "industrial" and cliche, is in contrast with the wish of the consumer to find warm and friendly manners when *consuming* the service.

The second approach is consumer oriented. Expectations are the basis for satisfaction. After consuming the service, they compare their earlier expectations with experience. Results can range from satisfaction to dissatisfaction. The consumer anticipates the service standards in his expectations. Wilkie claims: "The seed of the consumer's dissatisfaction is sown in the pre-purchase stage, before reaching the decision to purchase." According to this, the consumer creates his own, individual *benchmark,* and the rating of his satisfaction is the result of his after purchase state.

Normann, the creator of the concept "moment of truth", points out that the first generation of researchers in the field of service sector management, had the task to determine the specificities of the services as opposed to other sectors, which paved the way for the second generation of researchers who focused on the relations in the service industry, the behaviour when providing service and service design, with the aim to optimize the "moment of truth".

On the basis of the above exposed thesis, the understanding of service quality is based on the *paradigm of service*. In that sense, the service sector company manager looks for a "balance between the human factor and technology, between expenses and profit and, after all, between quality and productivity" (Gummesson, 1993).

The organization has to strive for success. When the set goals are achieved, we set other goals, striving for higher levels of product, processes and service efficiency. Accepting the concept of constant improvement means changing the management style. A total quality cannot be a program of changes with a set duration, it is a continuous, constant process. The questions set before the organization are the following: How do you keep up the constant striving for new improvement? What kind of measures and revisions of the business process do you have to use? How do you convince the employees that the business success and survival of the organizations can only occur if all employees accept constant actions to improve all their activities in the organizations? A successful organization constantly identifies and tackles the causes of problems or potential problems that employees have in doing their jobs. For that reason every employee has to be trained to identify such problems. The management and the employees must work together on implementing suitable corrective and preventive measures.

Each business process is subject to variability. Process variability is considered a normal phenomenon that is usually counted on. Parameter variability in the field of transformation of incoming values into outcoming values of the process affects the variability of the entire business process. For example, a lack of a specific product on the supplies market may require a substitution with another product of similar characteristics. Departure from the usual process (*variability*) can affect the quality of meals as results of a process, the timing of a process cycle, expenses of process quality, the level of satisfaction of the consumer/user with the process result.

Each episode of variability and a departure from the optimal process does not necessarily have a negative impact on the quality level of the process results. However, if the process is moving away from its optimal course so much as to get close to the acceptable limit or it has surpassed the limit, cost incur due to poor quality. The process becomes too expensive, jeopardizing the quality of the results and thus seriously risking dissatisfaction on the part of the client/consumer, in other words, it becomes irrational.

Service Quality Measurement in Hotel Industry

In order to achieve rationality the models of business excellence also, in a way, determine whether the criteria have been met, but the evaluation of business excellence is based not only on the fulfillment of the set criteria but also on the determination of the level up to which the criteria have been fulfilled (systems of points).

When analyzing the quality of service it is desirable to analyze the largest possible number of companies supplying the same type of service. As we already mentioned, if a company carries out a research and finds that the results are negative, it can interpret this information in the wrong way and conclude that it provides services in a totally wrong way. On the other hand, when analyzing a large number of companies, it is possible to compare data and obtain a realistic picture of the position of an individual company compared to others regarding quality.

The upper part of the model includes phenomena tied to the consumer, while the lower part shows phenomena tied to the supplier of services. The expected service is the function of earlier experiences of the consumer, their personal needs and oral communication. Communication with the market also influences the expected service.

Experienced service, here called perceived service, is the result of a series of internal decisions and activities. The management's perceptions of the consumer's expectations is the guiding principle when deciding on the specifications of the quality of service that the company should follow in providing service.

If there are differences or discrepancies in the expectations or perceptions between people involved in providing and consuming services, a "service quality gap" can occur. Since there is a direct connection between the quality of service and the satisfaction of clients in hotel industry, it is important for the company to spot a gap in the quality of service.

The first possible gap is the knowledge gap. It is the result of the differences in managing knowledge and their real expectations. This gap can lead to other gaps in the process of service quality and is, among other things, caused by:

> *"incorrect information in market researches and demand analysis;*
>
> *"incorrect interpretations of information regarding expectations;*
>
> *"lack of information about any feedback between the company and the consumers directed to the management;*
>
> *"too many organizational layers that hinder or modify parts of information in their upward movement from those involved in contact with the consumers.*

The second possible gap is that of standard. It is the result of differences in managing knowledge of the client's expectations and the process of service provision (delivery).

This gap is the result of:

" mistakes in planning or insufficient planning procedures;

"bad management planning;

"lack of clearly set goals in the organization; and

"insufficient support of the top management to service quality planning.

The management can be right in evaluating the client's expectations and develop business methods to satisfy these expectations, without the employees being correct in providing service. For example, a restaurant can order the waiters to serve the customers in two minutes after they sit at the table. Nevertheless, the waiters can ignore that specification and talk between them on the side. The fourth possible gap is the communication gap arising when there is a difference between the delivered service and the service that the company promised to the clients via external communications.

The reasons are:

"the planning of communication with the market is not integrated with the services;

"lack or insufficient coordination between traditional marketing and procedures;

"organizational performance not in keeping with the specifications, while the policy of communication with the market abides by the given specifications; and

"tendency to exaggerate in accordance with exaggerated promises.

Should any of the mentioned gaps arise, the "service gap" will also appear because the real service will not satisfy the client's expectations. Hotel companies try to detect the "service gap" with survey questionnaires. Gap analysis is the fill conductor for the management to find the causes of problems regarding quality and to find suitable ways to remove such gaps. For this reason the first four gaps are also called organizational or internal gaps. The conceptual model of service quality presented the frame for the development of a model of internal service quality – INSQPLUS. The authors of INSQPLUS model saw the need to add a 5th gap in the model of internal service quality – the rating gap, because it is necessary to have supervision over control, or better, the evaluation of service delivery before its consumption.

Although there are several models (scales) for the measurement of service quality and the satisfaction of customers, they are often too generalized or ad hoc, and as such hard to apply in the hotel industry. As opposed to TQM, which began before all in companies that dealt with products, due to the specificities of services (the basic are: impalpability, inseparability from provider and receiver of service, impossibility of storage), a specific concept called SERVQUAL (Services Quality Model) was created.

The SERVQUAL model offers a suitable conceptual frame for the research and service quality measurement in the service sector. The model has been developed, tested and adapted during various researches in cooperation with the Marketing Science Institute from Texas and numerous companies operating in the service sector. The model is based on the definition of quality as a comparison of the expected and the obtained as well as a consideration of gaps in the process of service provision. SERVQUAL is based on the client's evaluation of service quality. The described concept is based on the gap between expectations and perception of the clients. Service quality represents a multidimensional construction.

The choice of the most important characteristics was an issue dealt with in various ways. One of these is a logical attempt to work out a list of desirable attributes from the basic needs of the clients. A variant of a scale containing desirable characteristics of services, known as SERVQUAL scale, is currently quite popular in literature. It was developed in marketing circles with the aim to measure service quality (Bakoviae, Lazibat). In the original SERVQUAL instrument, Parasuraman et al. (1985) define service quality through ten dimensions which they sum up in five in 1988:

1. Reliability,
2. Assurance,

3. Tangibles,
4. Empathy,
5. Responsiveness.

Each of the listed dimensions has different features. Just like dimensions have different influence on the final service quality, so do these features have different influence on the grading of success of a single dimension. Despite its popularity and wide application, SERVQUAL is exposed to numerous criticisms, from both the conceptual and the operational aspect.

Theoretical criticism:

> *"pattern objections: SERVQUAL is based rather on an affirmation pattern than on the pattern of understanding; it does not manage to tie in with proved economical, statistical and psychological theories.*
>
> *"Gap model: there is little evidence that the consumer evaluates service quality in the sense of perception – expectation gaps.*
>
> *"Direction to the process: SERVQUAL is directed to the process of service delivery and not to the result of service experience.*
>
> *"Dimensionality: the five dimensions of SERVQUAL are not universal; the number of dimensions that encompass service quality is connected to the context; there is a high degree of inter-correlation between RATER dimensions. RATER is a mnemonic acronym where R = reliability, A = assurance, T = tangibles, E = empathy and R = responsiveness. Operative criticism:*
>
> *"Expectations: the term of expectations has multiple meanings; in evaluating services consumers use standards instead of expectations; SERVQUAL cannot measure the absolute expectations of service quality.*
>
> *"Content of the elements: four out of five elements cannot encompass the variability inside each dimension of service quality.*
>
> *"Moment of truth: the consumer's rating of the service can vary from one to the next moment of truth.*
>
> *"Polarity: the reverse polarity of the scale elements causes wrong reactions.*

"Scale grading: Likert's scale with 7 ratings is inadequate.

"Dual administration: dual administration of instruments causes boredom and confusion.

The most important criticism of SERVQUAL was the usage of gap analysis results (difference between expectations and perception of the received service) in measuring service quality (Cronin and Taylor, 1992, 1994). Comparing the expectation-perception gaps with perception only, called SERVPERF, Cronin and Taylor concluded that measurement of service quality based only on perception was enough.

Servqual Model in Croatian Hotel Industry

The Faculty for Tourist and Hospitality Management in Opatija constructed an empirical model for the measurement of service quality in hotel industry on the model of hospitality on the Opatijska Riviera. Its use shall be simple and effective in hotel practice.

The aims of the research were:

(a) Evaluate expectations and perceptions of hotel guests on the studied sample,

(b) Evaluate and calculate the SERVQUAL gap,

(c) Test the reliability of the SERVQUAL model in hotel industry,

(d) Determine the dimensions of service quality in hotel industry by applying the method of factor analysis.

From a practical point of view, the research intended to test the adapted SERVQUAL model for the measurement of service quality of hotel guests (Markoviae: 2005). The survey among hotel guests was carried out in 16 hotels on Opatijska Riviera (in Opatija, Lovran and Mosaeenieka Draga) during Christmas and New Year Holidays 2001/2002, in the period from Dec 28, 2001 to Jan 8, 2002.

The SERVQUAL gap was calculated on the basis of what is shown in image. It represents the difference between the average ratings of perceptions and the average expectations ratings. The wider the gap, the greater the difference between expectations and perception.

The need for the application of SERVQUAL model in hotel industry is confirmed by the fact that, in the observed sample, hotel managers do not know the expectations of their guests because the dimensions of service quality they consider most important, do not match those that are most important for the clients, which is confirmed by the total SERVQUAL gap.

Conclusion

SERVQUAL can be widely applied, not only in science but also in practice in various services. The aim of the scientists is to work out and test useful instruments for managers in order to help them determine those organizational variables (policy, staff, structure, technology, processes) that will guarantee the best service quality with minimal costs. This methodology can assist hotel managers in assessing the position of the hotel regarding its competition and strategic and operative decision-making. In hotel industry, service quality, as an extremely subjective category, is crucial to the satisfaction of the client. It is therefore imperative for managers in hotel industry to apply the SERVQUAL model for the measurement of service quality in their own hotel company, in order to satisfy the guest's expectations and ensure a position on the growing global tourist market.

The results of the quantitative application of SERVQUAL instrument show that this model can provide managers with useful information for the assessment of expectations and perception of hotel guests, with the aim of learning about gaps in individual service quality dimensions need for the application of SERVQUAL model in hotel industry is confirmed by the fact that, in the observed sample, hotel managers do not know the expectations of their guests because the dimensions of service quality they consider most important, do not match those that are most important for the clients, which is confirmed by the total SERVQUAL gap. To sum up, this article tend to clarify the SERVQUAL model as not only provider to the managers with a clear picture of the quality of the provided service, but also helping in discovering the needs, wishes and expectations of the guests. The same is analyzed by determining the characteristics of service quality that are most important for guests. We can say that it helps managers in setting the standards for the provision of services in the hospitality industry.

3

Organizational Culture in Hospitality Services

Listening to Feedback Helps Hotels Improve

There's nothing like an attentive staff to keep guests happy. And effective management of guest feedback is crucial to guest satisfaction.

Guest comments are a chance to do better next time, said Cathy Forbes, g.m. at the Best Western Auburn Inn in Auburn, Ind.

"Too often, people in the industry take it as a personal criticism instead of an opportunity to change," she said. "If you're not listening to your customers, someone else will."

Responding to guests' comments is at the heart of guest services, according to hoteliers. And sometimes, the comments can reinforce an idea.

"I had been after the owner for king beds and in-room coffee makers," Forbes said. "Seventy-five percent of the decision was based on guest comment cards."

Focus Hospitality Services, the owner and operator of the 52-room Auburn Inn, developed a point-based tracking system for guest feedback about amenities.

At the Four Seasons Atlanta, individual guest preferences are tracked with the property-management system, said Michael Sharlet, director of rooms.

"If you ask us once, that's the last time you should have to ask," he said.

The hotel always asks if there is any other service the guest would like to see added. Sharlet said a guest suggested a coffee maker be in the room, and just like a genie, the hotel granted the caffeinecraver's wish.

"We placed a coffee Omaker in the room," Sharlet said. "[The guest] was completely wowed."

To address guests' needs on a larger scale, the Four Seasons has an "I need it now" kit.

"It has more than 100 essentials at the concierge [desk], available 24 hours a day," Sharlet said. Matthias Kammerer, v.p. and g.m. of the Sonesta Beach Resort Key Biscayne (Fla.), reads guest comment cards as they are received. Trends are tracked on a monthly basis.

"Last year we had an interesting trend," he said. "We did not have Fox News channel in the TV lineup. I received personal phone calls from people that felt very strongly about the Fox channel. It was an extremely political year and there came a point where we said, 'Maybe this is something to look at.' We added the channel."

Kammerer said it doesn't take a high-tech system to respond to guest comments and concerns.

"It's a straightforward, simple system," he said. "There are systems where feedback can be collected in an electronic form, but how many times does that go down? Then you postpone reading and reacting to them for that reason. It's simply important to listen to guests."

The resort listened to guests about their Internet access preferences, as well.

"Another item we got feedback on was Internet access in rooms," Kammerer said. "We did charge for it separately. There was a regular trickle of guest feedback, so we said, 'Let's address it.' We upgraded the whole system. We went wireless in August and [we were] free of charge as of Dec. 1."

Guest feedback is an important component for success at a hotel, Kammerer said.

"There's no point in hiding guest comment cards in a folder," he said. "We prominently display them. We want feedback."

The Auburn Inn also took the wireless leap after listening to guests' comments.

"Everybody was going to wireless," Forbes said. "It was a matter of whether we could afford not to."

Response time is key at the Four Seasons Atlanta, Sharlet said.

"We react very quickly to guest feedback," he said. "If something comes out of an interaction at the desk, it's a matter of putting it in the PMS and alerting the manager."

Guest comment cards are reviewed as they arrive at the executive offices at the Four Seasons.

"It's a daily way of life," Sharlet said. "They are reviewed at the executive office by the g.m., myself and the food-and-beverage director."

At the daily operations meeting with department heads, all guest comments are reviewed with the staff.

"Anything that requires being addressed, we respond to it immediately," Sharlet said. "It's never more than 24 hours out."

The hotel also uses Guest Ware to track all types of guest feedback.

"We use it to look at recurring requests," he said. "It helps us grow and stay focused on what's most important to the guests."

All Four Seasons hotels offer curbside check-in for regular guests, Sharlet added.

"The biggest thing the business traveler was looking for was efficient check-in," he said. "If it's a regular guest, on their ninth visit we introduce the curbside check-in so they are prepared for it for the 10th stay. Everything is on file. The doorman has keys waiting for you. Guests love that."

Job Design Management

Job design is the specification of task activities, usually repeated on a regular basis, associated with each particular job.

a. Task activities need to be grouped in reasonably logical ways for each job.

b. The way the jobs are configured influences employee motivation.

Work specialization is the degree to which the work necessary to achieve organizational goals is broken down into various jobs.

In Work specialization the tasks in an organization are divided into separate jobs. Another term for this is *division of labor.*

1. Work specialization can be traced back to the writings of Adam Smith.
2. Work specialization was seen as a way to make the most efficient use of workers' skills because workers would be placed in jobs according to their skills and paid accordingly.
3. Other advantages of work specialization included improvement in employees' skills at performing a task, more efficient employee training, and encouragement of special inventions and machinery to perform work tasks.
4. Work specialization was viewed as a source of unending productivity improvements. And it was— up to a certain point.
5. The human diseconomies from work specialization included boredom, fatigue, stress, lowered productivity, poor quality of work, increased absenteeism, and higher job turnover.

B. There are four approaches to job design.

1. Job simplification is the process of configuring or designing jobs so that job holders have only a small number of narrow, repetitive, activities to perform.
   a. The concept of job simplification was championed by economist Adam Smith and by Frederick Taylor
   b. Training new workers becomes relatively easy and workers become almost interchangeable.
   c. The advantage is that major production efficiencies may be gained.
   d. The disadvantages are that, if carried too far, job satisfaction may be destroyed by narrow, repetitive,

boring jobs and the firm may become too inflexible to serve customers with varying needs.

Types of Departmentalization

Departmentalization is the clustering of individuals into units and units into departments and larger units in order to facilitate achieving organizational goals.

1. An organization design is an overall pattern of departmentalization.
2. There are four major patterns of departmentalization.
   a. The functional structure groups jobs into units based upon similarity of expertise, skills, and work activities, e.g., marketing, accounting.
   b. The divisional structure groups jobs into units according to the similarity of products or markets.
   c. The hybrid structure combines aspects of both the functional and divisional forms, with some jobs grouped into departments by functions and other grouped by products or markets.
   d. The matrix structure superimposes a horizontal set of divisional reporting relationships onto a hierarchical functional structure.

Assessing Structural Alternatives

A. Each of the four most common types of departmentalization has major advantages and disadvantages.

B. Functional structure is a type of departmentalization in which positions are grouped according to their main functional (or specialized) area.

   1. Typical functional form of organization has several major advantages.
   2. The functional form of organization has several major advantages.
      a. In-depth development of expertise is encouraged.
      b. Employees have clear career paths within their function.
      c. Resources are used more efficiently.

d. Economies of scale may be possible because of specialized people and equipment.

e. Intradepartmental coordination is facilitated.

f. Specialized technical competencies may be developed and may constitute a competitive advantage.

3. The functional form of origination has several disadvantages.

a. Response time on multifunctional problems may be slow due to coordination problems.

b. Major issues and conflicts between departments may have to be resolved by top management, with resultant delays.

c. Bottlenecks due to sequential tasks.

d. Over specialization may lead to a restricted view of the department's and the organization's needs.

e. Performance may be difficult to measure because several functions are responsible for organizational results.

f. Managers may be trained too narrowly in a single department.

4. The functional form of departmentalization is more appropriate under certain circumstances.

a. The organization is small or medium-sized.

b. There is a limited number of related products or services, or a relatively homogeneous set of customers or clients.

c. The organization is large and diverse, but the environment is stable. C Divisional structure is a type of departmentalization in which positions are grouped according to similarity of products, services, or markets.

1. Divisional structures are also called "self-contained structures" because each division contains the major functional resources it needs to pursue its own goals with little or no reliance on other divisions.

2. The three major forms of divisional structure differ according to the rationale for forming the divisions.

a. Product divisions are divisions created to concentrate on a single product or service or at least a relatively homogeneous set of products or services.

b. Geographic divisions are divisions designed to serve different geographic areas.

c. Customer divisions are divisions set up to service particular types of clients or customers. 3. Divisional structure has several major advantages.

a. Divisions can react quickly to changes in the environment.

b. Coordination across functions is simplified.

c. Each division can focus upon serving its customers.

d. The division's goals can be emphasized.

e. Performance is more easily measured.

f. Managers can be trained in general management skills.

4. Divisional structure has several disadvantages.

   a. Duplication of resources in each division often occurs.

   b. In-depth expertise may be sacrificed.

   c. Divisions may compete for limited resources.

   d. Expertise across divisions may not be shared.

   e. Innovations may be restricted to single divisions.

   f. Divisional goals may take priority over overall organizational goals.

5. The divisional structure is likely to be used in large organizations where substantial differences exist among products or services, geographic areas, or customers served.

D. Hybrid structure is a form of departmentalization that adopts parts of both functional and divisional structures at the same level of management.

   1. Hybrid structures are adopted by large organizations to gain the advantages of functional and divisional structures.

a. Functional departments are created to take advantage of resource utilization efficiencies, economies of scale, or in-depth expertise.

b. Divisional departments are usually created to benefit from a stronger focus on products, services, or markets.

2. The hybrid structure has several advantages.

a. Corporate and divisional goals can be aligned.

b. Specialized expertise and economies of scale can be achieved in major functional areas.

c. Adaptability and flexibility may be achieved in handling diverse product or service lines, geographic areas, or customers.

3. The hybrid structure has several disadvantages.

a. Conflict may arise between departments and divisions.

b. Hybrid organizations tend to develop excessively large staffs in the corporate-level functional departments.

c. There may be a slow response to exceptional situations requiring coordination between a division and a corporate functional department.

4. The hybrid structure is best used under particular conditions.

a. The organization faces environmental uncertainty best met by a divisional structure.

b. The organization requires functional expertise and/or efficiency.

c. The organization has sufficient resources to justify the structure.

E. A matrix structure is a type of departmentalization that superimposes a horizontal set of divisional reporting relationships onto a hierarchical functional structure.

1. An organization with a matrix structure has a functional and a divisional structure at the same time.

2. Employees who work in a matrix organization report to two "bosses," thus, the unity-of-command principle is violated.
3. Organizations that adopt a matrix structure usually go through several identifiable structural stages.
   a. Stage 1 is a traditional structure, usually a functional structure, which follows the unity-of-command principle.
   b. Stage 2 is a temporary overlay in which managerial integrator positions are created to handle issues of finite duration that involves coordinating across functional departments.
   c. Stage 3 is a permanent overlay in which the managerial integrator positions become permanent. d. Stage 4 is a mature matrix, in which matrix bosses have equal power.
4. As an organization passes through the matrix stages, horizontal integration increases at the cost of greater administrative complexity. The matrix form of organization has several advantages.
5. The matrix form of organization has several advantages.
   a. Decision making can be decentralized.
   b. Horizontal coordination is strengthened.
   c. Environmental monitoring is improved.
   d. Responses to environmental changes are quickly made.
   e. Functional specialists can be added to or resigned to projects as needed.
   f. Support systems can be allocated to projects as needed.
6. Matrix designs have several disadvantages.
   a. Administrative costs are increased.
   b. Lines of authority and responsibility may not be clear to individual employees.
   c. Possibilities of conflict are increased.

d. Individuals can become preoccupied with internal relations at the expense of clients and project goals.

e. All decisions may become group decisions, leading to gross inefficiency.

f. Reactions to change may be slowed if interpersonal skills are lacking or top management fights for control.

7. Matrix designs are usually appropriate when the following three conditions are met:

   a. The considerable pressure from the environment that necessitates a simultaneous and strong focus on both functional and divisional dimensions.

   b. The demands placed on the organization are changing and unpredictable, making it important to have a large capacity for processing information and coordinating activities quickly.

   c. There is pressure for shared resources.

8. Research indicates some of the factors that may be necessary to the success of a matrix systems

   a. The organizational culture may need to be changed to support collaboration.

   b. Managers may need special training, especially in interpersonal relations.

F. Of particular interest are two new types of organizational structure that have recently emerged: the Process structure and the networked structure.

1. A process structure is a type of departmentalization which groups positions into process team which are given beginning-to-end responsibility for that process or that specified work flow. The process structure is sometimes called the horizontal organization.

2. The networked structure is a form of organizing in which many functions are contracted out to other independent firms and coordinated through the use of information technology networks. Sometimes the networked structure is called the virtual corporation because it performs as virtually one corporation.

4

Security and Alarm Management

Security is the degree of protection against danger, damage, loss, and crime. Security as a form of protection are *structures and processes that provide or improve security as a condition.* The Institute for Security and Open Methodologies (ISECOM) in the OSSTMM 3 defines security as "a form of protection where a separation is created between the assets and the threat". This includes but is not limited to the elimination of either the asset or the threat. Security as a national condition was defined in a United Nations study (1986), so that countries can develop and progress safely.

Security has to be compared to related concepts: safety, continuity, reliability. The key difference between security and reliability is that security must take into account the actions of people attempting to cause destruction.

Different scenarios also give rise to the context in which security is maintained:

- With respect to classified matter, the condition that prevents unauthorized persons from having access to official information that is safeguarded in the interests of national security.
- Measures taken by a military unit, an activity or installation to protect itself against all acts designed to, or which may, impair its effectiveness.

Perceived Security Compared to Real Security

Perception of security may be poorly mapped to measurable objective security. For example, the fear of earthquakes has been reported to be more common than the fear of slipping on the bathroom floor although the latter kills many more people than the former. Similarly, the perceived effectiveness of security measures is sometimes different from the actual security provided by those measures. The presence of security protections may even be taken for security itself. For example, two computer security programs could be interfering with each other and even cancelling each other's effect, while the owner believes s/he is getting double the protection.

Security theater is a critical term for deployment of measures primarily aimed at raising subjective security in a population without a genuine or commensurate concern for the effects of that measure on—and possibly decreasing—objective security. For example, some consider the screening of airline passengers based on static databases to have been Security Theater and Computer Assisted Passenger Prescreening System to have created a *decrease* in objective security.

Perception of security can also increase objective security when it affects or deters malicious behavior, as with visual signs of security protections, such as video surveillance, alarm systems in a home, or an antitheft system in a car such as a Lo Jack, signs.

Since some intruders will decide not to attempt to break into such areas or vehicles, there can actually be less damage to windows in addition to protection of valuable objects inside. Without such advertisement, a car-thief might, for example, approach a car, break the window, and then flee in response to an alarm being triggered. Either way, perhaps the car itself and the objects inside aren't stolen, but with *perceived security* even the windows of the car have a lower chance of being damaged, increasing the financial security of its owner(s).

However, the nonprofit, security research group, ISECOM, has determined that such signs may actually increase the violence, daring, and desperation of an intruder This claim shows that perceived security works mostly on the provider and is not security at all.

It is important, however, for signs advertising security not to give clues as to how to subvert that security, for example in the case where a home burglar might be more likely to break into a certain home if he or she is able to learn beforehand which company makes its security system.

Categorizing Security

There is an immense literature on the analysis and categorisation of security. Part of the reason for this is that, in most security systems, the "weakest link in the chain" is the most important. The situation is asymmetric since the 'defender' must cover all points of attack while the attacker need only identify a single weak point upon which to concentrate.

Security Concepts

Certain concepts recur throughout different fields of security:

- *Assurance:* assurance is the level of guarantee that a security system will behave as expected
- *Countermeasure:* a countermeasure is a way to stop a threat from triggering a risk event
- *Defense in depth:* never rely on one single security measure alone
- *Exploit:* a vulnerability that has been triggered by a threat-a risk of 1.0 (100%)
- *Risk:* a risk is a possible event which could cause a loss
- *Threat:* a threat is a method of triggering a risk event that is dangerous
- *Vulnerability:* a weakness in a target that can potentially be exploited by a threat security

Security Management in Organizations

In the corporate world, various aspects of security were historically addressed separately - notably by distinct and often noncommunicating departments for IT security, physical security, and fraud prevention. Today there is a greater recognition of the interconnected nature of security requirements, an approach variously known as holistic security, "all hazards" management, and other terms.

Inciting factors in the convergence of security disciplines include the development of digital video surveillance technologies and the digitization and networking of physical control systems. Greater interdisciplinary cooperation is further evidenced by the February 2005 creation of the Alliance for Enterprise Security Risk Management, a joint venture including leading associations in security (ASIS), information security (ISSA, the Information Systems Security Association), and IT audit (ISACA, the Information Systems Audit and Control Association).

In 2007 the International Organisation for Standardization (ISO) released ISO 28000 - Security Management Systems for the supply chain. Although the title supply chain is included, this Standard specifies the requirements for a security management system, including those aspects critical to security assurance for any organisation or enterprise wishing to management the security of the organisation and its activities. ISO 28000 is the foremost risk based security system and is suitable for managing both public and private regulatory security, customs and industry based security schemes and requirements.

Private Police

Private police are law enforcement bodies that are owned and/or controlled by non-governmental entities.

These can be firms to which the government contracts out police work (e.g. the 1975–1977 Oro Valley, Arizona-Rural/Metro contract, the 1980 Reminderville, Ohio-Corporate Security contract, the 1976 Indian Springs, Florida-Guardsmark contract, and the 1976 Buffalo Creek, West Virginia-Guardsmark contract). Or, they can be officers who contract with various firms to patrol the area, as in the case of the San Francisco Patrol Specials.

A specific type of private police is company police, such as the specialized railroad police or mall security. In some cases, private police are sworn in as government employees in order to ensure compliance with the law, as in the Kalamazoo, Michigan-Charles Services contract, which lasted 3½ years. Private police services are sometimes called "Subscription-Based Patrol."

Private security firms in the U.S. employ more security guards, patrol personnel and detectives than the U.S. federal, state and local governments combined, fulfilling many of the beat-patrol functions once thought central to the mission of public police. It has been argued that the private police market furnishes tangible evidence about what people want but are not receiving from public police. The growth of private policing is a phenomenon that is occurring all over the world. In Australia, private and public police have conventionally been considered parallel systems, with private security as very much the lesser or junior entity.

Private police typically focus on loss instead of crime; preventive methods rather than punishment; private justice (such as firing embezzlers or issuing no trespassing warnings to shoplifters) rather than public court proceedings; and private property rather than public property. Most do not have the ability to arrest civilians, unless they are also peace officers.

Definitions

"Policing" and "private policing" are somewhat elusive concepts. "Private sector" police have been described as "any individual or group involved with law enforcement or security, but lacking official police authority." At the core of the policing concept, though, is the combating of crime. Patrick Tinsley writes:

> *"Enforcement of law is a phenomenon that admits of infinite degrees and permutations. Take the case of a jewelry store. The theft of its wares is a crime under the law. But the jewelry store does not rely exclusively—or even primarily —on the majesty of the state's enforcement of that law for its own security. The jewelry store engages the services of manifold private protection outfits: it takes out an insurance policy on its gems, which are kept under a locked glass display case, which can only be opened by an employee, who is under the ever-vigilant eye of video monitoring equipment, and who watches the customers with the aid of convex mirrors, and keeps the store's cash in a locked vault, which is in a back room, which is in turn locked at closing time, and the store's alarm activated as the employees leave and the armed night watchmen arrive. All of these are provided by private companies in the business of providing "security," and all of which should give pause to those who consider the enforcement of law uniquely the franchise of the government."*

Examples

United States

In South Carolina, all Security Officers have the same authority and power to make an arrest as Sheriff's Deputies. Spring Valley HOA in Columbia, SC is a good example of this. Private Officers respond to calls for service, make arrests and use blue lights and traffic radar. They are Law Enforcement under state law, case law and AG's opinion, and are authorized by the state to issue Uniform Traffic Tickets to violators. Security Officers in some cases are also considered Police Officers.

In Boston, Massachusetts, more than 100 housing projects and low-income apartment buildings are patrolled by private security. One firm, Naratoone Security Corporation, fields 122 traditional security officers in those locations, as well as 43 "special police officers," who are armed and licensed by the Boston Police Department and have limited arrest powers.

South Africa

An increasing number of South Africans are using private security companies to protect themselves and their assets. The broad private security industry is employing over 200,000 security guards throughout the country, of which the guarding industry is the largest, with 125,000 guards working for approximately 3,200 security companies. Many of the larger South African private security companies have expanded their operations into other countries in Southern Africa. Private security companies have even involved themselves in political conflicts that are occurring on the subcontinent. In South Africa, private companies that make use of guards are regulated by a statutory body, the Security Officers' Board. The Board polices the regulations that govern the private security industry and sets minimum training standards for security guards.

Relationship to Anarcho-capitalism

Private police figures prominently in anarcho-capitalist theory and, along with advocacy of private defense agencies, dispute resolution organizations, and private production of law, distinguishes it from minarchism. Since complete privatization of the police function (with funding, control, ownership, etc. of all police forces passing to private entities) would eliminate the ability of the state to forcibly collect taxes, arguably the only way it could work would be within the context of a society in which all other services were privatized as well. Moreover, the state would lose the ability to intervene to enforce its concept of justice; this factor also tends to make it incompatible with the idea of a night watchman state that could take action to protect liberty.

History

In Great Britain, the police function was historically performed by private watchmen (existing from 1500 on), thief-takers, and so on. The former were funded by private individuals and organizations and the latter by privately-funded rewards for catching criminals, who would then be compelled to return stolen property or pay restitution.

In 1737, George II began paying some London and Middlesex watchmen with tax moneys, beginning the shift to government control. In 1750, Henry Fielding began organizing a force of quasi-professional constables. The Macdaniel affair added further impetus for a publicly-salaried police force that did not depend on rewards. Nonetheless, In 1828, there were privately financed police units in no fewer than 45 parishes within a 10-mile radius of London.

Perceived Advantages

One of the alleged benefits of such arrangements is the potential for competition. If government contracts out to a private police company, then different contractors may compete to offer the highest quality and/or lowest price.

If individual firms and households can choose their own police company, then competition may have even greater benefits for the citizens, as contractors seek to serve various niche markets. Under that system, individual citizens, firms, homeowners associations, etc. can choose a service that they perceive as providing the right quality/price mix for them, and concentrating on the security needs that are more important to them.

There is evidence that private police can provide services more cheaply than public police. The cost of San Francisco's private patrol specials is $25–30/hour, compared to $58/hour for an off-duty police officer. In Reminderville, Corporate Security outbid the Summit County Sheriff Department's offer to charge the community $180,000 per year for 45-minute response time emergency response service by offering a $90,000 contract for twice as many patrol cars and a 6-minute response time.

This system might also better prevent poor service and other abuses, as citizens could unilaterally fire their police company, rather than having to lobby the government to do so, an effort that many would be relatively disinclined to pursue, due to the uncertainty as to whether it would be successful, and the time consumed.

Homeowners associations and landlords would have a stronger incentive to monitor the activity of private police they hire for their neighborhood, as nearby neighborhoods with better or cheaper police services could gain a competitive advantage in attracting residents and remaining profitable. Reputation could be an additional safeguard, as companies that gain a poor reputation would likely have more difficulty attracting new customers.

The ability of people to sue private police could be another safeguard. Companies would have an incentive to carefully screen applicants and fire abusive employees, in order to avoid costly lawsuits that could cause their liability insurance premiums to rise.

Public police, by contrast, are covered by sovereign immunity in many situations; and in any case, the public police lack an owner whose potential to suffer financially from lawsuits would provide a strong incentive to take action. Theoretically, the citizens as a whole might be considered the "owner" of government; but the difference is that these owners lack a means of selling their investment if their fellow owners refuse to cooperate in taking action to avoid losses; and there is less potential for hostile takeover or bankruptcy to affect a change in control, as the government can simply raise taxes (or print money, in some cases) to compensate for financial losses.

There are the usual public choice issues involved that can thwart public sector reform, such as the fact that citizens realize their individual votes have little chance of affecting the outcome.

As Bruce L. Benson notes, "Many people are very concerned about what the government is doing for (or to) them, but they rationally choose not to invest in information about candidates or to vote because they recognize that the costs of doing so exceed the benefits."

Another advantage cited by Benson is that private police would have a contractual responsibility to protect their customers. In *Warren v. District of Columbia,* the court found that public police have no such responsibility. Thus, they cannot be sued if they fail to respond to calls for help, for instance.

James F. Pastor addresses such disadvantages by analyzing a number of substantive legal and public policy issues which directly or indirectly relate to the provision of security services. These can be demonstrated by the logic of alternative or supplemental service providers. This is illustrated by the concept of "para-police." Para-police is another name for private police officers. Many public safety agencies use auxiliary police officers, who are part-time sworn police officers. Some also use reserve police officers, who are hired on an "as needed" basis, with limited police powers. These officers are typically called to duty for special details or events. In contrast to auxiliary and reserve officers, private policing is a relatively new and growing phenomenon.

There are several key distinctions between these options. Briefly, the distinctions relate to the level of police powers associated with the officer, the training levels required for each officer, the funding sources for the service provision, and the contractual and liability exposures related to each supplemental arrangement. Each alternative or supplemental service has its own strengths and weaknesses. The use of private police, however, has particular appeal because property or business owners can directly contract for public safety services, thereby providing welcome relief for municipal budgets. Finally, private police functions can be flexible, depending upon the financial, organizational, political, and situational circumstances of the client.

Perceived Disadvantages

Problems within the industry include the possibility of criminals setting up their own firms, misuse of surveillance devices, the proliferation of weapons, and strained relationships between the public and private police.

Under anarcho-capitalism, taxpayers would not be forced to fund police services; these transactions would be voluntary. One argument against such a policy is that it would disadvantage the poor, who could not afford to spend much money on police. Thus, some more moderate libertarians favor issuing police vouchers to each citizen, granting them a certain amount of money to hire a private police company of their choice at taxpayer expense.

Murray Rothbard notes, "police service is *not* 'free'"; it is paid for by the taxpayer, and the taxpayer is very often the poor person himself. He may very well be paying more in taxes for police now than he would in fees to private, and far more efficient, police companies. Furthermore, the police companies would be tapping a mass market; with the economies of such a larger-scale market, police protection would undoubtedly be much cheaper."

Public police, by contrast, are limited in size by the political jurisdiction; although some local public police forces already contract with national private firms for specialty services, such as maintenance of communications equipment, for which it would not be economical for them to hire a full-time government employee.

Ultimately, some people see the potential for a "dual system" of policing—one for the wealthy and one for the poor—and others see the provision of private security as the primary protective resource in contemporary America.

In Florida, Critical Intervention Services patrols neighborhoods and has used lethal force before. They have limited power, like other private security agencies in the state, regulated by Florida Statute 493.

Mall Cop

A mall cop, also referred to as mall security, is a privatized shopping mall security officer charged with enforcing the rules and protecting the building, like a police force would for a government. They are sometimes referred to (normally in a derogative manner) as *"rent-a-cop"*. Mall of America has America's largest shopping mall security.

As with any large retail establishment, malls have a security group. Although the phrase "mall cop" is sometimes used to describe mall security, they tend to be private security agents (who, unless they are also peace officers, do not retain police power or the ability of arrest), and are often outsourced to an agency that specializes in retail security. Depending on jurisdiction, security agents found in malls may or may not retain certain rights (typically those related to the laws likely to be violated in a mall situation); often, mall security will maintain a relationship with the local police force. This may involve providing evidence to be used in prosecution, assisting in detention (although subject to local laws), or even the observation of a suspect.

Mall security tend to be strictly guided by local laws and ordinances; they are generally not charged with engaging in "dangerous" situations. This may extend to official policy requiring private security to acquiesce in the case of robbery; typically, the overall policy of the mall management is to maintain safety at all costs, and any sort of violence may be considered more damaging than money lost to robbery.

Security Guard

A security guard (or security officer) is a person who is paid to protect property, assets, or people. Security guards are usually privately and formally employed personnel. Often, security officers are uniformed and act to protect property by maintaining a high visibility presence to deter illegal and inappropriate actions, observing (either directly, through patrols, or by watching alarm systems or video cameras) for signs of crime, fire or disorder; then taking action and reporting any incidents to their client and emergency services as appropriate.

Since at least the Middle Ages in Europe, the term watchman was more commonly applied to this function. This term was carried over to North America where it was interchangeable with night-watchman until both terms were replaced with the modern security-based titles. Security guards are sometimes regarded as fulfilling a private policing function.

Functions and Duties

Many security firms and proprietary security departments practice the "detect, deter, observe and report" methodology. Security officers are not required to make arrests, but have the authority to make a citizen's arrest, or otherwise act as an agent of law enforcement at the request of a police officer, sheriff, and others.

In addition to the methodology mentioned above, a private security officer's primary duty is the prevention and deterrence of crime. Security personnel enforce company rules and can act to protect lives and property. In fact, they frequently have a contractual obligation to provide these actions. Security officers are often trained to perform arrest and control procedures (including handcuffing and restraints), operate emergency equipment, perform first aid, CPR, take accurate notes, write detailed reports, and perform other tasks as required by the contract they are serving.

Many security officers are required to go through additional training mandated by the state for the carrying of weapons such as batons, firearms, and pepper spray (e.g. the Bureau of Security and Investigative Services [1] in California has requirements that a license for *each* item listed must be carried while on duty). Some officers are required to complete police certification for special duties.

Positions are also set to grow in the U.S., with 175,000 new security jobs expected before 2016. In recent years, due to elevated threats of terrorism, most security officers are required to have bomb-threat training and/or emergency crisis training, especially those located in soft target areas such as shopping malls, schools, and any other area where the general public congregate.

One major economic justification for security personnel is that insurance companies (particularly fire insurance carriers) will give substantial rate discounts to sites which have a 24-hour presence; for a high risk or high value venue, the discount can often exceed the money being spent on its security program.

This is because having security on site increases the odds that any fire will be noticed and reported to the local fire department before a total loss occurs. Also, the presence of security personnel (particularly in combination with effective security procedures) tends to diminish "shrinkage," theft, employee misconduct and safety rule violations, property damage, or even sabotage. Many casinos hire security guards to protect money when transferring it from the casino to the casino's bank.

Security personnel may also perform access control at building entrances and vehicle gates; meaning, they ensure that employees and visitors display proper passes or identification before entering the facility. Security officers are often called upon to respond to minor emergencies (lost persons, lockouts, dead vehicle batteries, etc.) and to assist in serious emergencies by guiding emergency responders to the scene of the incident, helping to redirect foot traffic to safe locations, and by documenting what happened on an incident report.

Armed security officers are frequently contracted to respond as law enforcement until a given situation at a client location is under control and/or public authorities arrive on the scene.

Patrolling is usually a large part of a security officer's duties. Often these patrols are logged by use of a guard tour patrol system, which require regular patrols. The most commonly used form used to be mechanical clock systems that required a key for manual punching of a number to a strip of paper inside with the time preprinted on it.

Recently, electronic systems have risen in popularity due to their light weight, ease of use, and downloadable logging capabilities. Regular patrols are, however, becoming less accepted as an industry standard, as it provides predictability for the would-be criminal, as well as monotony for the security officer on duty.

Random patrols are easily programmed into these systems, allowing greater freedom of movement and unpredictability. Global positioning systems are also easing their way into the market as a more effective means of tracking officer movement and patrol behavior.

Personnel

Although security officers differ greatly from police officers, military personnel, federal agents/officers, and the like, Australia and the United States have a growing proportion of security personnel that have former police or military experience, including senior management personnel. On the other hand, some security officers, young people in particular, use the job as practical experience to use in applying to law enforcement agencies.

Types of Security Personnel and Companies

Security personnel are classified as either of the following

- "in-house" or "proprietary" (i.e. employed by the same company or organization they protect, such as a mall, theme park, or casino); formerly often called works police or security police in the United Kingdom
- "contract," working for a private security company which protects many locations.
- "Public Security," "Private Police Officers," or security police
- "Private Patrol Officers", vehicle patrol officers that protect multiple client premises.
- "Parapolice", aggressive firms that routinely engage in criminal investigation and arrests.

Industry terms for various security personnel include: security guard, security agent, security officer, safety patrol, private police, company police, security enforcement officer and public safety. Other job titles in the security industry include bouncer, bodyguards, executive protection agent loss prevention, alarm responder, hospital security officer, mall security officer, crime prevention officer, private patrol officer, and private patrol operator.

State and local governments sometimes regulate the use of these terms by law—for example, certain words and phrases that "give an impression that he or she is connected in any way with the federal government, a state government, or any political subdivision of a state government" are forbidden for use by California security licensees by Business and Professions Code Section 7582.26. So the terms "private homicide police" or "special agent" would be unlawful for a security licensee to use in California. Similarly, in Canada, various acts [2] specifically prohibits private security personnel from using the terms *Probation Officer, law enforcement, police,* or *police officer*.

Alberta and Ontario probibit the use of the term 'Security Officer' which is in widespread use in the United States for many decades. Recent changes to the act have also introduced restrictions on uniform and vehicle colours and markings to make private security personnel clearly distinctive from police personnel. Some sources feel that some of these restrictions are put in place to satisfy the Canadian Police Association.

There is a marked difference between persons performing the duties historically associated with watchmen and persons who take a more active role in protecting persons and property. The former, often called "guards," are taught the mantra "observe and report," are minimally trained, and not expected to deal with the public or confront criminals.

The latter are often highly trained, sometimes armed depending on contracts agreed upon with clientele, and are more likely to interact with the general public and to confront the criminal element. These employees tend to take pride in the title "Security Officer" or "Protection Officer" and disdain the label of "guard."

Ironically enough, there may be no relationship between duties performed and compensation—many mall "security officers" who are exposed to serious risks make less per hour than "industrial security guards" with less training and responsibility. However, there are now more positions in the security role that separate not just the titles, but the job itself. The roles have progressed and so have the areas for which security people are needed. All security jobs vary in pay and duties at present.

The term "agent" is particularly problematic in the security industry because it can describe not only a civil legal relationship between an employee and their employer or contractor ("agent of the owner" in California PC 602), but also describes a person in government service ("Special Agent Jones of the Federal Bureau of Investigation.") However we should then also consider the fact that this title is also made available to banking agents, loan agents and real estate agents.

Security "agents" found in loss prevention and personal or executive protection (bodyguards) typically work in plainclothes, without a uniform, and are usually highly trained to act lawfully in direct defense of life and/or property. There is also confusion with bail enforcement agents, or as they are popularly known "bounty hunters," who are sometimes regulated by the same agencies which regulate private security.

Security personnel are essentially private citizens, and therefore are bound by the same laws and regulations as the citizenry they are contracted to serve, and therefore are not allowed to represent themselves as law enforcement under penalty of law.

Licensing and Regulation

Australia

Any person who conducts a business or is employed in a security related field within Australia is required to be licensed. Each of the six states and two territories of Australia have separate legislation that covers all security activities. Licensing management in each state/territory is varied and is carried out by either Police, Attorney General's Department, Justice Department or the Department of Consumer Affairs.

New South Wales - (Police) Security Industry Act 1997 & Security Industry Regulation 2007; Victoria - (Police) Private Security Act 2004; Queensland - (Justice & Attorney-General) Security Providers Act 1993; South Australia - (Consumer & Business Affairs) Security and Investigation Agents Act 1995; Western Australia - (Police) Security & Related Activities (Control) Act 1996 & Security & Related Activities (Control) Regulations 1997; Tasmania - (Police) Security and Investigation Agents Act 2002; Northern Territory - (Justice) Private Security Act & Private Security (Security Officer/Crowd Controller/Security Firms/ Miscellaneous Matters) Regulations; Australian Capital Territory - (Regulatory Services) Security Industry Act 2003 & Security Industry Regulation 2003. All of this legislation was aimed to enhance the integrity of the private security industry.

All persons licensed to perform security activities are required to undertake a course of professional development in associated streams that are recognized nationally. This has not always been the case and the introduction of this aspect should regulate the educational standards/knowledge base expected so that the particular job can be competently undertaken.

Strict requirements are laid down as to the type of uniform and badging used by security companies. Uniforms or badging that may be confused with a police officer are not permitted similarly, the use of the title 'Security Police' or 'Private Detective' are unacceptable. Whilst the term security guard is used by companies, government bodies and individuals, the term security officer is deemed more suitable. 'Bouncers' are Crowd Controllers and Store Detectives are Loss Prevention or Asset Protection Officers.

Security Officers are not permitted to carry firearms, handcuffs or batons unless they have a legitimate requirement to do so and then only when working and have the appropriate subclass accreditation to their license.

Canada

In Canada, private security falls under the jurisdiction of Canada's ten provinces and three territories. All ten of Canada's provinces and one of its territories (the Yukon) have legislation that regulates the contract security industry. These eleven jurisdictions require that companies that provide security guard services and their employees be licensed. Most provinces in Canada regulate the use of handcuffs and weapons (such as firearms and batons) by contract security companies and their employees, either banning such use completely or permitting it only under certain circumstances.

Canada's federal laws also restrict the ability of security guards to be armed. For example, section 17 of *Firearms Act* makes it an offence for any person, including a security guard, to possess prohibited or restricted firearms (i.e. handguns) anywhere outside of his or her home.

There are two exceptions to this prohibition found in sections 18 and 19 of the Act. Section 18 deals with transportation of firearms while Section 19 deals with allowing persons to carry such firearms on their persons to protect their lives or the lives of other persons, or for the performance of their occupation (Armour Car Guards, Licensed Trappers), provided an Authorization to Carry (ATC) is first obtained.

British Columbia

Private security in the province of British Columbia is governed by two pieces of legislation: the *Security Services Act* and the *Security Services Regulation*. These laws are administered and enforced by the Security Programs and Police Technology Division of the Ministry of Public Safety and Solicitor General.

The legislation requires that guards must be at least 19 years old, undergo a criminal background check, and successfully complete a training course. As far as weapons, British Columbia law severely restricts their use by security guards. Section 11(1)(c) of the *Security Services Regulation* prohibits security personnel from carrying or using any "item designed for debilitating or controlling a person or animal", which the government interprets to include all weapons. As well, section 11 forbids private security from using or carrying restraints, such as handcuffs, unless authorized by the government. However, as in other parts of Canada, armoured car guards are permitted to carry firearms.

In the past, only personnel that worked for contract security, that is, security companies, were regulated in British Columbia. However, as of September 1, 2009, in-house security guards and private investigators came under the jurisdiction of the *Security Services Act* and *Security Services Regulation*. The same occurred to bodyguards and bouncers, effective November 1, 2009.

Europe

Armed private security are much rarer in Europe, and nonexistent in many countries, such as the United Kingdom, The Netherlands and Switzerland. In developing countries (with host country permission), an armed security force composed mostly of ex-military personnel is often used to protect corporate assets, particularly in war-torn regions.

As a requirement of the Private Security Industry Act 2001, the UK now requires all contract security guards to have a valid Security Industry Authority license. The licence must be displayed when on duty, although a dispensation may be granted for store detectives, bodyguards and others who need to operate without being identified as a security guard. This dispensation is not available to Vehicle Immobilisers. Licenses are valid for three years and require the holders to undergo formal training, and are also to pass mandatory Criminal Records Bureau checks. Licences for Vehicle Immobilisers are valid for one year. Armed guarding and guarding with a weapon are illegal.

In Finland, all contract security guards are required to have a valid license granted by police. Temporary license is valid for four months and normal license for five years. License requires a minimum 40-hour course for temporary license and 60 hours more for a normal license. Additionally a narrow security vetting is required.

The 40-hour course allows the carrying of a fixed-length baton and handcuffs, separate training and license is required for the security guard to carry pepper spray, extendable baton or a firearm. Rehearse of weapons usage is mandatory every year and is regulated by the Ministry of The Interior, to ensure the safe handling of pepper spray and such. In Finland, a security guard has the right to detain a person "red-handed", or seen committing a crime and the right to search the detained individual for harmful items and weapons. An individual who has been forcefully detained can only be released by the police. All companies providing security guarding services are also required to have a valid license from Ministry of the Interior.

In The Netherlands security guards Beveiligingsbeambte must undergo a criminal backgroundcheck by the local police department in the area where the private security company is located. To become a security guard in The Netherlands a person must complete the basic training level 2 Beveiliger, to complete the training a trainee must undergo a three month intership with a private security company that is licensed by the svpb, this is the board that controls security exams. A trainee guard must pass for his diploma within one year, if the trainee does not pass he is not allowed to work anymore until the trainee completes his training with a positive result, after a positive result a new ID can be issued and is valid for three years, after that the guard must undergo a backgroundcheck by the local police again.

Security guards in The Netherlands are not allowed to carry any kind of weapon or handcuffs. Every uniformed security guard in The Netherlands must have the V symbol on its uniform to ensure the public they are dealing with a private guard, this rule is mandatory by the Ministry of justice. Security uniforms may not look like similar to police uniforms, and may not contain any kind of rank designation, and the collor yellow or gold are not allowed to used because the Dutch police uses gold accents in their uniforms, also wearing a uniformcap is not longer allowed. Every new uniform design or addition must be approved by the ministry of justice before use. A patrol vehicle may not look like a police striped vehicle. The only private security guards that are allowed to carry firearms are those who work for the military or Dutch National bank (De Nederlandsche Bank) this is were the national gold reserve can be found.

Norway

In Norway security officers are called "Vektere", there are a couple of different types of vektere. You have the normal uniformed and/or civil-clothing officers who normally watch over private and semipublic properties. The government can also hire vektere in public places, like for instance the Parliament. The security officers at the Parliament has a little more power by the law than private security officers.

Security officers must undergo three weeks of coursing and internship. They are allowed to work for six months after one week of introduction course. It's also possible to take Security as a High School major, with 2 years of school and 2 years of trainee positions at private companies which will give the officer a certificate from the government. This certificate will make it easier to get a job, and slightly higher pay. It will also make it easier to get a job elsewhere in the security industry. The certificate can also be taken privately by security officers who have had a minimum of 5 years working experience.

In addition to normal "vektere" there also is a special branch for "Ordensvakter" which normally works as bouncers or security at concerts and similar types of events. Ordensvakter has to undergo an extra week of coursing and learn Technics on how to handle drunk people and people on different drugs. They also learn about the alcohol laws of Norway (who are rather strict). The local police in the police district has to approve each Ordensvakt. In the 1990s bouncers had a bad reputation, specially in Oslo for being to brutal and rough with people. And the police had no control over who worked as bouncers. After the government forced training and mandatory ID-cards for bouncers it has gotten much better. And the police of Oslo now even says that Ordensvakter are helping the police finding crime that otherwise would not be reported.

In 2007 several Securities officers harshly arrested a thief on Karl Johans Gate (the main street of Oslo). This was filmed with a mobile camera by some pedestrians and created a media storm on Security Officers taking the law in their own hands. When it later came to a fact that the thief attacked the security guards when they approached him the charges were dropped on the security guards. But the police said that they would be harsher in the criminal background checking of people working as Security Guards. Before 2007 security guards were checked when they applied for a job, but not while they were working. And the companies employing the guards got massive critic for not checking criminal records suffice, and some times not at all.

Now people in private security is being checked annually. And the police have the authority to withdraw the companies licence for operating if they do not send in lists of employees. The Police in Norway has later been widely criticized for not checking this properly, and when they do, Security Guards still work for months before anything is done. The big security company G4s stated after critic from the police about hiring criminals that they cannot do anything about the problem, because the police is the only instance who has the possibility to check the records.

Today it is around 15,000 people working within private security in Norway. For comparison the police have around 10,000 employees in total.

Notable companies operating in Norway:

- Securitas
- G4S
- Vakt service
- Hafslund infratek
- ISS A/S (formerly Personellsikring)
- ProSec – Professional Security (mainly event security)

Hong Kong

In Hong Kong, the term *Security Officer* refers to a senior staff member who supervises a team of security personnel. The staff who work under security officers' supervision are called *Security Guards.*

Legislation

Before 1 October 1996, private security personnel were regulated by the *Watchmen Ordinance* (Chapter 299). However, there were many problems with that system of regulation—for example, there were no restrictions as to whom may establish private security service companies to provide security services to a client. Also, there was no regulation of people whom may perform installation of security systems.

Some employers hired "caretakers" instead of security guards to avoid their responsibilities under the ordinance (in formal definition, "caretakers" are supposed to provide facilities management service, although security service, which provided to residential properties, takes some parts of facilities management service). As a result, the Hong Kong Government enacted a wholly new law, the *Security and Guarding Services Ordinance* (Chapter 460), to replace the *Watchmen Ordinance.*

According to the *Security and Guarding Services Ordinance*: No individual shall do, agree to do, or hold himself/herself out as doing, or as available to do, security work for another person unless he/she does so:

- under and in accordance with a permit; or
- otherwise than for reward.

Security work means any of the following activities:

- guarding any property;
- guarding any person or place for the purpose of preventing or detecting the occurrence of any offence; (Replaced 25 of 2000 s. 2)
- installing, maintaining or repairing a security device;
- designing for any particular premises or place a system incorporating a security device.

Security device means a device designed or adapted to be installed in any premises or place, except on or in a vehicle, for the purpose of detecting or recording- (Amended 25 of 2000 s. 2)

- the occurrence of any offence; or

- the presence of an intruder or of an object that persons are, for reasons of security, not permitted to bring onto the premises or place or any other premises or place.

Qualification

Any applicant who wishes to apply for a Security Personnel Permit (SPP) must:

- He/she have been living in Hong Kong for at least 5 years. (This requirement may have been changed)
- No criminal record.
- At least 18 years old when submitting his/her application.
- Have passed a mandatory 16 hour training course and have been granted a certificate of the course.
- If the applicant is over 65 years old, he/she must submit his/her health examination report.

Although the Security and Guarding Services Industry Authority (SGSIA) is the agency in charge of the security service industry, all applicants must submit their application and pay the fee by mail or in person to Hong Kong Police Force (License Section).

Permit

Security Personnel Permit was separated to four types: A, B, C, and D.

- Type A permit holder was permitted to work in a "single-block" residential building; they are not allowed to carry firearms. No age limit.
- Type B permit holder was permitted to work in any type of properties, but they also are not allowed carry firearms. The maximum age limit of this permit is 65.
- Type C permit holder was permitted to work as an armed guard. (Usually, they are members of the cash transport car crew.) The maximum age limit of this permit is 55.
- Type D permit holder was permitted to design, install, and repair security devices. No maximum age limit.

The permit is valid for five years. All holders must renew their permit before it expires, or they will lose their qualification to work, as such, until their permit is renewed. The type A and Type B security service are gradually combined with property management service, though the boundary between these two industries is unclear.

Power of Arrest

Security Guards in Hong Kong do not have special powers of arrest above that of the ordinary citizen, i.e. citizen's arrest, also known locally as the "101 arrest power." The Section 101 in the Criminal Procedure Ordinance addresses that arrest of an offender by a private citizen is allowed in certain circumstances if the offender is attempting an arrestable offense. Once arrested, the suspect must be delivered to a police office as soon as possible. An arrestable offence is defined as any crime carrying a sentence of more than 12 months imprisonment. No security personnel are allowed to search other person, nor are they allowed to get personal information from other people, with the exception of some specific circumstances.

Israel

In Israel, almost all security guards carry a firearm, primarily to prevent terror attacks. Security guards are common: they perform entrance checks at shopping malls, transportation terminals, government and other office buildings, and many stores. Many locations with a high number of visitors, such as the Jerusalem Bus Station, employ X-ray machines to check passenger's bags; in other places, they are opened and visually inspected. As of 2009, private security guards have also replaced official security forces at some checkpoints inside and on the border of the West Bank, as well as the crossings to Gaza.

Malaysia

In August 2007, Malaysia banned hiring of foreign security guards following a rape and murder of a student by a Pakistani security guard. Security guard companies need to apply to the Ministry of Internal Security.

South Africa

Security guards along with the rest of the private security industry are regulated under Act 56 of 2001, Private Security Industry Regulation Act.

United States

Private security guards have outnumbered police officers since the 1980s, predating the heightened concern about security brought on by the September 11, 2001, attacks. The more than 1 million contract security officers, and an equal number of guards estimated to work directly for U.S. corporations, dwarf the nearly 700,000 sworn law enforcement officers in the United States.

Most states require a license to work as a security officer. This license may include a criminal background check and/or mandated training requirements.

Most security officers do not carry weapons and have the same powers of arrest as a private citizen, called a "private person" arrest, "any person" arrest, or "citizen's arrest." If weapons are carried, additional permits and training are usually required. Armed security personnel are generally used to protect sensitive sites such as government and military installations, armored money transports, casinos, banks (or other financial institutions), nuclear power plants, etc. However, armed security is quickly becoming a standard for vehicle patrol officers and on many other non-government sites.

Security guard/officer continue to gain broader responsibilities. A growing trend is the increased use of private security to support services previously provided by police departments. James F. Pastor addresses substantive legal and public policy issues which directly or indirectly relate to the provision of security services. These can be demonstrated by the logic of alternative or supplemental service providers. The use of private police has particular appeal because property or business owners can directly contract for public safety services, thereby providing welcome relief for municipal budgets. Finally, private police functions can be flexible, depending upon the financial, organizational, political, and situational circumstances of the client.

Arizona Licensed security companies are required to provide eight hours of pre-assignment training to all persons employed as security guards before the employee acts in the capacity of a security guard. There is a state-mandated curriculum that must be taught, and subjects covered must include criminal law and laws of arrest, uniforms and grooming, communications, use of force, general security procedures, crime scene preservation, ethics and first response.

California

Security Guards are required to obtain a license from the Bureau of Security and Investigative Services (BSIS), of the California Department of Consumer Affairs. Applicants must be at least 18 years old, undergo a criminal history background check through the California Department of Justice (DOJ) and the Federal Bureau of Investigation (FBI), and complete a 40-hour course of required training. This required training is broken down into smaller training sections and time-lines. The first is 8-hours of BSIS-designed instruction on powers to arrest and weapons. Then, within 30 days of getting the individual officers license, they must receive 16-hours of training on various mandatory and elective courses. Finally, within 6-months of getting their license, they must receive an additional 16-hours of training on various mandatory and elective courses.

California security officers are also required to complete 8-hours of annual training on security-related topics, after the first, above mentioned 40-hours are complete.

The training and exam may be administered by any private patrol operator or by any of a large number of certified training facilities. This training can be classroom or online.

New Jersey As of 2006 all security personnel must undergo a state mandated certified training program. This law commonly referred to SORA is the state's effort to increase the quality of security personnel.

New Mexico As of 2008 all security guards must undergo FBI background checks and a certified training program. Guards who carry firearms must also undergo additional training with a firearm through an approved firearms instructor and pass a phycological exam. The security industry is regulated through New Mexico Regulation and Licensing Division.

Oklahoma Security officers in Oklahoma are licensed by CLEET (Council on Law Enforcement Education and Training). To be licensed as an unarmed officer an individual must be at least 18 years of age and undergo 40 hours of classroom training and pass criminal history checks. Armed guards must be 21 years of age, have another 40 hours of classroom training, qualify with their firearm and pass a psychological evaluation.

Pennsylvania No licensing requirements to be an unarmed security guard. However, armed security guards must undergo and successfully complete a 40 hour training course (including shooting range time) in order to be certified to carry weapons and on watch while on duty under the Lethal Weapons Training Act (commonly referred to as Act 235 certification). Certification involves qualifying on a pistol range, with firing of 50 rounds of ammo larger than a .380acp. You are also required to qualify on a shotgun. The certification is good for five years at which time an eight hour refresher course must be taken or the certification is revoked.

South Carolina All Security Officers have the same authority and power to make an arrest as Sheriff's Deputies, while on the property they are paid to protect. Most companies prohibit this authority by policy due to lack of confidence and liability fears. Private Officers may respond to calls for service, make arrests and use blue lights and traffic radar. They may also be specially authorized by the State Law Enforcement Division (SLED), to issue Uniform Traffic Tickets to violators. Security Officers are licensed or registered (as appropriate) by SLED for one year at a time. Training for unarmed officers is 8 hours, an additional 8 hours is required for a security weapons permit or a concealed security weapons permit. Additional hours are required to be documented for officers issuing public or private tickets as well as officers that will be using batons, pepper spray or tasers.

Virginia Security officers in Virginia are required to be licensed by DCJS (Department of Criminal Justice Services). To be licensed as an unarmed security officer one must go through 18 hours of classroom training from a licensed instructor in order to obtain this card and it must be done by the end of their 90 days after hire with a Security company. Every two years the card must be renewed, by completing an in service with a licensed instructor. To be licensed as an armed security officer one must complete an additional 16 hours of firearms training, 6 hours of training in conducting a lawful arrest, and qualification with the type and caliber of weapon they intend to carry. Firearms endorsements must be renewed annually by completing an in service and passing a firearms qualification. Licensed armed security officers are authorized under state code to arrest for any offense committed in their presence while they are on duty at the location they are hired to protect. They may also be granted the authority by the chief law enforcement officer in their jurisdiction to issue summons to appear in court for felonies and misdemeanors.

St Louis, Missouri Security officers are required to be licensed by the St Louis County Police or St Louis City Police. St Louis County Security Officer training is a two day class and yearly renewal class. Armed officers must shoot biannually to keep their "armed" status. County license is called a Metropolitan License meaning to is good for St Louis City and County. More Info for St Louis County License is available though the County website posted here: St Louis City Web site has all the info regarding licensing requirements due to fact they are the same in city and county. The City web site is posted here. Readers should note that this only apply to persons working in security in St Louis City or St Louis County

Security Officers and the Police

Security personnel are not police officers, unless they are security police, but are often identified as such due to similar uniforms and behaviors, especially on private property. Security personnel in the U.S. derive their powers from state laws, that allow them a contractual arrangement with clients that give them Agent of the Owner powers.

This includes a nearly unlimited power to question with the absence of probable cause requirements that frequently dog public law enforcement officers, provided that the security officer does not tread on the rights and liberties of others as guaranteed by the United States Constitution.

Some jurisdictions do commission or deputize security officers and give them limited additional powers, particularly when employed in protecting public property such as mass transit stations. This is a special case that is often unique to a particular jurisdiction or locale. Additionally, security officers may also be called upon to act as an agent of law enforcement if a police officer, sheriff's deputy, etc. is in immediate need of help and has no available backup.

Some security officers do reserve police powers and are typically employed directly by governmental agencies. Typically, these are sworn law enforcement personnel whose duties primarily involve the security of a government installation, and are also a special case.

Other local and state governments occasionally enter into special contracts with security agencies to provide patrol services in public areas. These personnel are sometimes referred to as "private police officers."

Sometimes police officers work as security personnel while not on duty. This is usually done for extra income, and work is particularly done in hazardous jobs such as bodyguard work and bouncers outside nightclubs.

Police are called in when a situation warrants a higher degree of authority to act upon reported observations that security does not have the authority to act upon, however, some states allow Licensed Security Officer the full arrest powers equal to that of a Sheriff Deputy.

In 1976, the Law Enforcement Assistance Administration's National Advisory Commission on Criminal Justice Standards and Goals reported:

> *'One massive resource, filled with significant numbers of personnel, armed with a wide array of technology, and directed by professionals who have spent their entire adult lifetimes learning how to prevent and reduce crime, has not been tapped by governments in the fight against criminality. The private security industry, with over one million workers, sophisticated alarm systems and perimeter safeguards, armored trucks, sophisticated minicomputers, and thousands of highly skilled crime prevention experts, offers a potential for coping with crime that can not be equalled by any other remedy or approach... Underutilized by police, all but ignored by prosecutors and the judiciary, and unknown to corrections officials, the private security professional may be the only person in this society who has the knowledge to effectively prevent crime.'*

In New York, the Area Police/Private Security Liaison program was organized in 1986 by the NYPD commissioner and four former police chiefs working in the private security industry to promote mutual respect, cross-training, and sharing of crime-related information between public police and private security.

Trends : Australia

Private Security personnel initially outnumbered police. From the Australian Bureau of Statistics Report in 2006 there were 52,768 full-time security officers in the security industry compared to 44,898 police officers. But since Security Industry Regulation Act 2007 it has dropped to less than half that.

UK

The trend in the UK at the time of writing (March 2008) is one of polarization. The market in Manned Guarding (the security industry term for the security guards most people are familiar with) is diverging toward two opposite extremes; one typified by a highly trained and well paid security officer; the other with security officers on or about minimum wage with only the minimum training required by law.

Within the "in-house" sector, where security personnel are not subject to licensing under the Private Security Industry Act 2001, the same divergence can be seen; with some companies opting for in-house security to maintain control of their standards, whilst others use it as a route to cheaper, non-regulated, security.

USA

Economist Robert B. Reich, in his 1991 book *The Work of Nations*, stated that in the United States, the number of private security guards and officers was comparable to the number of publicly paid police officers. He used this phenomenon as an example of the general withdrawal of the affluent from existing communities where governments provide public services.

Instead, the wealthy pay to provide their own premium services, through voluntary, exclusive associations. As taxpayer resistance has limited government budgets, and as the demand for secure homes in gated communities has grown, these trends have continued in the 1990s and 2000s.

In the aftermath of 9/11, the trend in the US is one of a quiet transformation of the role of security guards into first responders in case of a terrorist attack or major disaster. This has resulted in longer guard instruction hours, extra training in Terrorism tactics and increased laws governing private security companies in some states.

History

The *vigiles* were soldiers assigned to guard the city of Rome, often credited as the origin of both security personnel and police, although their principal duty was as a fire brigade. There have been night watchmen since at least the Middle Ages in Europe; walled cities of ancient times also had watchmen. A special chair appeared in Europe sometime in the late Middle Ages, called the watchman's chair; this unupholstered wooden chair had a forward slanting seat to prevent the watchman from dozing off during his watch.

Notable Security Guards

- The security guard Frank Wills detected the Watergate burglars, ultimately leading to the resignation of Richard M. Nixon as President of the United States.
- Christoph Meili, night guard at a Swiss bank, became a whistle blower in 1997. He told about the bank destroying records related to funds of Holocaust victims, whose money the bank was supposed to return to their heirs.
- In 1999, Pierlucio Tinazzi rescued 10 victims from the Mont Blanc Tunnel Fire, before dying while trying to rescue an 11th.
- In 2001, Gary Coleman, former child actor, was employed as a shopping mall security guard in the Los Angeles area. Whilst shopping for a bulletproof vest for his job, Coleman assaulted a female autograph collector. Coleman said he felt "threatened by her insistence" and punched her in the head. He was later charged for the assault and ordered to pay her $1,665 for hospital bills.
- Derrick Brun, an unarmed security guard employed by the Red Lake School District in Minnesota, was praised

by President Bush for his heroic role in protecting children during the 2005 Red Lake High School Massacre: "Derrick's bravery cost him his life, and all Americans honor him".

- In 2007, Matthew Murray fatally shot two and wounded two others at the Youth With A Mission retreat center in Arvada Colorado. A few hours later he fatally shot two others and wounded another three in the New Life Church parking lot. When Murray entered the church, he was met by armed security guard Jeanne Assam, who ordered him to drop his weapon. Assam shot and wounded Murray when he failed to comply. The pastor of New Life Church credited Assam with saving over 100 lives.

Unionization : Canada

Many security guards in Canada are unionized. The primary unions which represent security guards in Canada are the United Food and Commercial Workers (UFCW), Local 333, and the Canadian branch of the United Steelworkers (USW). In contrast to the legal restrictions in the United States, Canadian labor relations boards will certify bargaining units of security guards for a Canadian Labour Congress (CLC)-affiliated union or in the same union with other classifications of employees.

United States

In June, 1947, the United States Congress passed the Taft-Hartley Act placing many restrictions on labor unions. Section 9 (B) (3) of the act prevents the National Labor Relations Board (NLRB) from certifying for collective bargaining any unit which mixes security employees with non-security employees. This restricts the ability of security employees to join any union that also represents other types of employees.

They may be part of an independent, "security-only" union, not affiliated with any coalition of other types of labor unions such as the American Federation of Labor and Congress of Industrial Organizations (AFL-CIO). A union which also represents non-security employees may also represent and bargain on behalf of security employees with the employer's consent.

Two of the largest security unions are the Security, Police, and Fire Professionals of America (SPFPA) and the United Government Security Officers of America (UGSOA).

Security, Police, and Fire Professionals of America

In 1948 with the Taft-Hartley restrictions well into effect, the Detroit, Michigan area security guards of United Auto Workers (UAW) Amalgamated Local 114 were forced to break away and start a separate "Plant Guards Organizing Committee". The NLRB ruled that as an affiliate of the CIO, the committee was indirectly affiliated with production unions and therefore ineligible for certification under the new restrictions.

The committee was then forced to completely withdraw from the CIO and start the independent United Plant Guard Workers of America. By the 1990s, this union had evolved to include many other types of security officers and changed its name to the SPFPA.

United Government Security Officers of America

In 1992, the USGOA was formed. It specializes in organizing federal, state, and local government security officers, but since May, 2000 has been open to representing other types of security personnel as well.

Others

The Service Employees International Union (SEIU) has also sought to represent security employees, although its efforts have been complicated by the Taft-Harley Act because the SEIU also represents janitors, trash collectors, and other building service employees.

Hazards in the Industry

Security personnel often are exposed to physical and physiological trauma that can have lasting effects. This has always been an issue but the 21st century's more violent and angry culture combined with drug and alcohol related violence results in more instances of security personnel being physically or verbally abused.

Other contributing factors are high workload, long hours, low pay, boredom and disregard of industry standards by employers and clients e.g. break times, access to bathrooms and facilities ECT.

Another problem particularly in NSW Australia is the severe security officer shortage brought on by the rushed Security Industry Regulation Act 2007 (which has been nicknamed the Crimpers act). This act was approved by David Andrew Campbell who at the time was Minister for Illawarra and acting police commissioner and had signed the Act for both parties.

Watchman (law enforcement)

Watchmen were groups of men, usually authorized by a state, government, or society, to deter criminal activity and provide law enforcement. Watchmen have existed in various guises throughout the world and were generally succeeded by the emergence of formally organized policing.

Early Origins

An early reference to a watch can be found in the Bible where the Prophet Ezekiel states that it was the duty of the watch to blow the horn and sound the alarm. (Ezekiel 33:1-6)

The existence of watchmen have also been found in the Ottoman, Greek and Egyptian Empires.

The Roman Empire turned the role of a watchman into a profession by creating two organizations:

- the Praetorian Guard thus establishing a rank and file system with a Captain of the Guard.
- Vigiles, literally the watch.

Watchmen in England

By order of the King of England the Winchester Act Mandating The Watch. Part Four and the King commandth that from henceforth all Watches be made as it hath been used in past times that was to wit from the day of Ascension unto the day of St. Michael in every city by six men at every gate in every borough by twelve men in every town by six or four according to the number of inhabitants of the town. They shall keep the Watch all night from sun setting unto sun rising. And if any stranger do pass them by them he shall be arrested until morning and if no suspicion be found he shall go quit.

Later in 1279 King Edward I formed a special guard of 20 sergeants at arms who carried decorated battle maces as a badge of official office. By 1415 a watch was appointed to the Parliament of England and in 1485 King Henry VII established a household watch that became known as the Beefeaters.

From 1485 to the 1800s it was the Watch and Ward that acted as London's police force upholding and enforcing the laws of the land.

Watchmen in the United States of America

The first form of societal protection in the United States was based on practices developed in England. The City of Boston was the first settlement in the 13 colonies to establish a night watch in 1631. New York (then New Amsterdam) and Jamestown followed in 1658.

5

Security Vulnerabilities Persist in Hospitality Industry

When checking into a hotel and asked for a credit card for incidentals, or when prepaying online, do you honestly give it a second thought considering most hotels are big chains and well established? If you're among the majority of consumers, then no, you do not. However, recent breaches and a new study from Trustwave might make you pause in the future.

Earlier this week, Trustwave, a PCI vendor and Qualified Incident Response Assessor, issued an advisory on the results of 75 investigations for credit card compromise. The advisory, while lacking the names of clients who were investigated at their own request, highlighted some interesting observations. Presently, Trustwave's data shows over one million accounts at risk.

In the majority of investigations, the data held on the magnetic stripe was a complete loss, thanks to antiquated processing systems and technologies used. Since the outdated processing applications store the card's data completely, all an attacker needs to do is compromise the system or network and download the stored files. In addition, other similarities in the investigations, such as weak passwords or default passwords, insecure remote access, and improper firewall configurations, each led to a compromise at the hotel.

A spokesperson for the company told The Tech Herald that in each of the 75 confirmed breaches, there were two main methods for extracting data, which none of the businesses were able to prevent at the time of compromise. The first is, again, outdated processing applications. The fact they are so old means they're out of compliance with PCI, which is a regulation all hotels, motels, and hospitality operations are required to comply with. These applications simply store the data on the system. Once that system is compromised, the data is there for the taking.

The second is custom Malware. This Malware parses magnetic stripe data from volatile memory. Residing within the memory of the infected system, as it's used to record payment transactions, the Malware copies the information and offloads it to any number of destinations. Criminals often create databanks of captured information where they can access it at will. Trustwave said that, in many cases, systems deemed compliant with PCI at one time can fall victim to this type of attack because of issues created during configuration that allowed the Malware to infect the system.

Weak communications, when dealing with remote processing centers for credit card application or remote properties (as in the case of a hotel chain), as well as internal communications, is another avenue of compromise. While Trustwave did not break down how many of the 75 clients were breached by this method, some were, and it is a known risk. Earlier this year, Visa issued an alert that warns of Malware attacks on card data in transit.

Since most hotels have a centralized processing application for credit or debit card purchases, customers in the restaurant, gift shop or spa all face the same risk as those who used a card to simply pay for their room.

The fact that most hotel chains are connected via a larger network means that if one site is compromised, it isn't too much of a stretch to assume the other sites are compromised as well. The truth is, in cases like this, if one site is compromised then you can be sure the others are too—a point proven in the case of Wyndham Hotels and Resorts.

Earlier this year, Wyndham reported that sometime last July, criminals breached the network of a franchised Wyndham property and, because the franchise was linked to a central network, the criminals had access to 41 other properties and their systems.

According to reports at the time, the true scope of the damage was unknown, the hotel never revealed how many accounts were exposed, only Florida listed a figure. In a statement around the time of the disclosure, the Florida Attorney General said that almost 21,000 residents could have been affected by the Wyndham breach.

As a consumer, should you worry? No. Several regulations will prevent you from being liable for fraudulent charges by someone who stole your credit card. There are also stringent protections to help curb some of the pain of identity theft. The problem with most of these identity theft protections is that they still require a lot of hoop jumping.

So what can the hospitality industry do to prevent breaches? According to Trustwave, following the best practices is a start. For example, enforcing stronger passwords, proper egress filtering for the firewalls, and remote access enforcement, are just some of the things listed in its report.

While PCI is not 'end-all-be-all' security, it is the first step. Checklist security is only effective if followed completely, and added to by knowing your business and knowing what risks you face. Reliance on checklists alone will do you no good, as proven by the countless breaches that have occurred at PCI-certified businesses. Each business compromised, sticking only with the reported breaches from 2008 and 2009, was compliant at one point in time. However, what happens between the time of certification and the annual audit is what matters.

Access Control

Access control is a system which enables an authority to control access to areas and resources in a given physical facility or computer-based information system. An access control system, within the field of physical security, is generally seen as the second layer in the security of a physical structure.

Access control is, in reality, an everyday phenomenon. A lock on a car door is essentially a form of access control. A PIN on an ATM system at a bank is another means of access control. The possession of access control is of prime importance when persons seek to secure important, confidential, or sensitive information and equipment.

Item control or electronic key management is an area within (and possibly integrated with) an access control system which concerns the managing of possession and location of small assets or physical (mechanical) keys.

Physical Access

Physical access by a person may be allowed depending on payment, authorization, etc. Also there may be one-way traffic of people. These can be enforced by personnel such as a border guard, a doorman, a ticket checker, etc., or with a device such as a turnstile. There may be fences to avoid circumventing this access control. An alternative of access control in the strict sense (physically controlling access itself) is a system of checking authorized presence, see e.g. Ticket controller (transportation). A variant is exit control, e.g. of a shop (checkout) or a country.

In physical security, the term access control refers to the practice of restricting entrance to a property, a building, or a room to authorized persons. Physical access control can be achieved by a human (a guard, bouncer, or receptionist), through mechanical means such as locks and keys, or through technological means such as access control systems like the Access control vestibule. Within these environments, physical key management may also be employed as a means of further managing and monitoring access to mechanically keyed areas or access to certain small assets.

Physical access control is a matter of who, where, and when. An access control system determines who is allowed to enter or exit, where they are allowed to exit or enter, and when they are allowed to enter or exit. Historically this was partially accomplished through keys and locks. When a door is locked only someone with a key can enter through the door depending on how the lock is configured. Mechanical locks and keys do not allow restriction of the key holder to specific times or dates. Mechanical locks and keys do not provide records of the key used on any specific door and the keys can be easily copied or transferred to an unauthorized person. When a mechanical key is lost or the key holder is no longer authorized to use the protected area, the locks must be re-keyed.

Electronic access control uses computers to solve the limitations of mechanical locks and keys. A wide range of credentials can be used to replace mechanical keys. The electronic access control system grants access based on the credential presented. When access is granted, the door is unlocked for a predetermined time and the transaction is recorded. When access is refused, the door remains locked and the attempted access is recorded. The system will also monitor the door and alarm if the door is forced open or held open too long after being unlocked.

Access Control System Operation

When a credential is presented to a reader, the reader sends the credential's information, usually a number, to a control panel, a highly reliable processor. The control panel compares the credential's number to an access control list, grants or denies the presented request, and sends a transaction log to a database. When access is denied based on the access control list, the door remains locked. If there is a match between the credential and the access control list, the control panel operates a relay that in turn unlocks the door. The control panel also ignores a door open signal to prevent an alarm. Often the reader provides feedback, such as a flashing red LED for an access denied and a flashing green LED for an access granted.

The above description illustrates a single factor transaction. Credentials can be passed around, thus subverting the access control list. For example, Alice has access rights to the server room but Bob does not. Alice either gives Bob her credential or Bob takes it; he now has access to the server room. To prevent this, two-factor authentication can be used. In a two factor transaction, the presented credential and a second factor are needed for access to be granted; another factor can be a PIN, a second credential, operator intervention, or a biometric input.

There are three types (factors) of authenticating information:

- something the user knows, e.g. a password, pass-phrase or PIN
- something the user has, such as smart card
- something the user is, such as fingerprint, verified by biometric measurement

Passwords are a common means of verifying a user's identity before access is given to information systems. In addition, a fourth factor of authentication is now recognized: someone you know, where another person who knows you can provide a human element of authentication in situations where systems have been set up to allow for such scenarios. For example, a user may have their password, but have forgotten their smart card. In such a scenario, if the user is known to designated cohorts, the cohorts may provide their smart card and password in combination with the extant factor of the user in question and thus provide two factors for the user with missing credential, and three factors overall to allow access.

Credential

A credential is a physical/tangible object, a piece of knowledge, or a facet of a person's physical being, that enables an individual access to a given physical facility or computer-based information system. Typically, credentials can be something you know (such as number or PIN), something you have (such as an access badge), something you are (such as a biometric feature) or some combination of these items. The typical credential is an access card, key fob, or other key. There are many card technologies including magnetic stripe, bar code, Wiegand, 125 kHz proximity, 26 bit card-swipe, contact smart cards, and contactless smart cards. Also available are key-fobs which are more compact than ID cards and attach to a key ring. Typical biometric technologies include fingerprint, facial recognition, iris recognition, retinal scan, voice, and hand geometry.

Access Control System Components

An access control point, which can be a door, turnstile, parking gate, elevator, or other physical barrier where granting access can be electronically controlled. Typically the access point is a door. An electronic access control door can contain several elements. At its most basic there is a stand-alone electric lock. The lock is unlocked by an operator with a switch. To automate this, operator intervention is replaced by a reader. The reader could be a keypad where a code is entered, it could be a card reader, or it could be a biometric reader. Readers do not usually make an access decision but send a card number to an access control panel that verifies the number against an access list. To monitor the door position a magnetic door switch is used. In concept the door switch is not unlike those on refrigerators or car doors. Generally only entry is controlled and exit is uncontrolled. In cases where exit is also controlled a second reader is used on the opposite side of the door. In cases where exit is not controlled, free exit, a device called a request-to-exit (RTE) is used. Request-to-exit devices can be a push-button or a motion detector.

When the button is pushed or the motion detector detects motion at the door, the door alarm is temporarily ignored while the door is opened. Exiting a door without having to electrically unlock the door is called mechanical free egress. This is an important safety feature. In cases where the lock must be electrically unlocked on exit, the request-to-exit device also unlocks the door.

Access Control Topology

Access control decisions are made by comparing the credential to an access control list. This lookup can be done by a host or server, by an access control panel, or by a reader. The development of access control systems has seen a steady push of the lookup out from a central host to the edge of the system, or the reader. The predominate topology circa 2009 is hub and spoke with a control panel as the hub and the readers as the spokes. The lookup and control functions are by the control panel. The spokes communicate through a serial connection; usually RS485. Some manufactures are pushing the decision making to the edge by placing a controller at the door. The controllers are IP enabled and connect to a host and database using standard networks.

Types of Readers

Access control readers may be classified by functions they are able to perform:

- *Basic (non-intelligent) readers:* simply read card number or PIN and forward it to a control panel. In case of biometric identification, such readers output ID number of a user. Typically Wiegand protocol is used for transmitting data to the control panel, but other options such as RS-232, RS-485 and Clock/Data are not uncommon. This is the most popular type of access control readers. Examples of such readers are RF Tiny by RFLOGICS, ProxPoint by HID, and P300 by Farpointe Data.

- *Semi-intelligent readers:* have all inputs and outputs necessary to control door hardware (lock, door contact, exit button), but do not make any access decisions. When a user presents a card or enters PIN, the reader sends information to the main controller and waits for its response. If the connection to the main controller is interrupted, such readers stop working or function in a degraded mode. Usually semi-intelligent readers are connected to a control panel via an RS-485 bus. Examples of such readers are InfoProx Lite IPL200 by CEM Systems and AP-510 by Apollo.
- *Intelligent readers:* have all inputs and outputs necessary to control door hardware, they also have memory and processing power necessary to make access decisions independently. Same as semi-intelligent readers they are connected to a control panel via an RS-485 bus. The control panel sends configuration updates and retrieves events from the readers. Examples of such readers could be InfoProx IPO200 by CEM Systems and AP-500 by Apollo. There is also a new generation of intelligent readers referred to as "IP readers". Systems with IP readers usually do not have traditional control panels and readers communicate directly to PC that acts as a host. Examples of such readers are PowerNet IP Reader by Isonas Security Systems, ID08 by Solus has the built in webservice to make it user friendly, Edge ER40 reader by HID Global, LogLock and UNiLOCK by ASPiSYS Ltd, and BioEntry Plus reader by Suprema Inc.

Some readers may have additional features such as LCD and function buttons for data collection purposes (i.e. clock-in/clock-out events for attendance reports), camera/speaker/microphone for intercom, and smart card read/write support.

Access control readers may also be classified by the type of identification technology.

Access Control System Topologies

Serial Controllers: Controllers are connected to a host PC via a serial RS-485 communication line (or via 20mA current loop in some older systems). External RS-232/485 converters or internal RS-485 cards have to be installed as standard PCs do not have RS-485 communication ports. In larger systems multi-port serial IO boards are used, Digi International being one of most popular options. Advantages:

- RS-485 standard allows long cable runs, up to 4000 feet (1200 m)
- Relatively short response time. The maximum number of devices on an RS-485 line is limited to 32, which means that the host can frequently request status updates from each device and display events almost in real time.
- High reliability and security as the communication line is not shared with any other systems.

Disadvantages:

- RS-485 does not allows Star-type wiring unless splitters are used
- RS-485 is not well suited for transferring large amounts of data (i.e. configuration and users). The highest possible throughput is 115.2 kbit/s, but in most system it is downgraded to 56.2 kbit/s or less to increase reliability.
- RS-485 does not allow host PC to communicate with several controllers connected to the same port simultaneously. Therefore in large systems transfers of configuration and users to controllers may take a very long time and interfere with normal operations.
- Controllers cannot initiate communication in case of an alarm. The host PC acts as a master on the RS-485 communication line and controllers have to wait till they are polled.
- Special serial switches are required in order to build a redundant host PC setup.
- Separate RS-485 lines have to be installed instead of using an already existing network infrastructure.
- Cable that meets RS-485 standards is significantly more expensive than the regular Category 5 UTP network cable.

- Operation of the system is highly dependent on the host PC. In case the host PC fails, events from controllers are not retrieved and functions that required interaction between controllers (i.e. anti-passback) stop working.

Serial Main and Sub-controllers: All door hardware is connected to sub-controllers (a.k.a. door controllers or door interfaces). Sub-controllers usually do not make access decisions, and forward all requests to the main controllers. Main controllers usually support from 16 to 32 sub-controllers. Advantages:

- Work load on the host PC is significantly reduced, because it only needs to communicate with a few main controllers.
- The overall cost of the system is lower, as sub-controllers are usually simple and inexpensive devices.
- All other advantages listed in the first paragraph apply.

Disadvantages:

- Operation of the system is highly dependent on main controllers. In case one of the main controllers fails, events from its sub-controllers are not retrieved and functions that require interaction between sub controllers (i.e. anti-passback) stop working.
- Some models of sub-controllers (usually lower cost) have no memory and processing power to make access decisions independently. If the main controller fails, sub-controllers change to degraded mode in which doors are either completely locked or unlocked and no events are recorded. Such sub-controllers should be avoided or used only in areas that do not require high security.
- Main controllers tend to be expensive, therefore such topology is not very well suited for systems with multiple remote locations that have only a few doors.
- All other RS-485-related disadvantages listed in the first paragraph apply.

Serial Main Controllers & Intelligent Readers: All door hardware is connected directly to intelligent or semi-intelligent readers. Readers usually do not make access decisions, and forward all requests to the main controller. Only if the connection to the main controller is unavailable, the readers use their internal database to make access decisions and record events. Semi-intelligent reader that have no database and cannot function without the main controller should be used only in areas that do not require high security. Main controllers usually support from 16 to 64 readers. All advantages and disadvantages are the same as the ones listed in the second paragraph.

Serial Controllers with Terminal Servers: In spite of the rapid development and increasing use of computer networks, access control manufacturers remained conservative and did not rush to introduce network-enabled products. When pressed for solutions with network connectivity, many chose the option requiring less efforts: addition of a terminal server, a device that converts serial data for transmission via LAN or WAN. Terminal servers manufactured by Lantronix and Tibbo Technology are popular in the security industry.

Advantages:

- Allows utilizing existing network infrastructure for connecting separate segments of the system.
- Provides convenient solution in cases when installation of an RS-485 line would be difficult or impossible.

Disadvantages:

- Increases complexity of the system.
- Creates additional work for installers: usually terminal servers have to be configured independently, not through the interface of the access control software.
- Serial communication link between the controller and the terminal server acts as a bottleneck: even though the data between the host PC and the terminal server travels at the 10/100/1000Mbit/s network speed it then slows down to the serial speed of 112.5 kbit/s or less. There are also additional delays introduced in the process of conversion between serial and network data.

Network-enabled Main Controllers: The topology is nearly the same as described in the second and third paragraphs. The same advantages and disadvantages apply, but the on-board network interface offers a couple valuable improvements. Transmission of configuration and users to the main controllers is faster and may be done in parallel. This makes the system more responsive and does not interrupt normal operations. No special hardware is required in order to achieve redundant host PC setup: in case the primary host PC fails, the secondary host PC may start polling network controllers. The disadvantages introduced by terminal servers (listed in the fourth paragraph) are also eliminated.

IP Controllers: Controllers are connected to a host PC via Ethernet LAN or WAN.

Advantages:

- An existing network infrastructure is fully utilized, there is no need to install new communication lines.
- There are no limitations regarding the number of controllers (32 per line in case of RS-485).
- Special RS-485 installation, termination, grounding and troubleshooting knowledge is not required.
- Communication with controllers may be done at the full network speed, which is important if transferring a lot of data (databases with thousands of users, possibly including biometric records).
- In case of an alarm controllers may initiate connection to the host PC. This ability is important in large systems because it allows to reduce network traffic caused by unnecessary polling.
- Simplifies installation of systems consisting of multiple sites separated by large distances. Basic Internet link is sufficient to establish connections to remote locations.
- Wide selection of standard network equipment is available to provide connectivity in different situations (fiber, wireless, VPN, dual path, PoE)

Disadvantages:

- The system becomes susceptible to network related problems, such as delays in case of heavy traffic and network equipment failures.
- Access controllers and workstations may become accessible to hackers if the network of the organization is not well protected. This threat may be eliminated by physically separating the access control network from

the network of the organization. Also it should be noted that most IP controllers utilize either Linux platform or proprietary operating systems, which makes them more difficult to hack. Industry standard data encryption is also used.

- Maximum distance from a hub or a switch to the controller (if using a copper cable) is 100 meters (330 ft).
- Operation of the system is dependent on the host PC. In case the host PC fails, events from controllers are not retrieved and functions that required interaction between controllers (i.e. anti-passback) stop working. Some controllers, however, have peer-to-peer communication option in order to reduce dependency on the host PC.

IP Readers: Readers are connected to a host PC via Ethernet LAN or WAN.

Advantages:

- Most IP readers are PoE capable. This feature makes it very easy to provide battery backed power to the entire system, including the locks and various types of detectors (if used).
- IP readers eliminate the need for controller enclosures.
- There is no wasted capacity when using IP readers (i.e. a 4-door controller would have 25% unused capacity if it was controlling only 3 doors).
- IP reader systems scale easily: there is no need to install new main or sub-controllers.
- Failure of one IP reader does not affect any other readers in the system.

Disadvantages:

- In order to be used in high-security areas IP readers require special input/output modules to eliminate the possibility of intrusion by accessing lock and/or exit button wiring. Not all IP reader manufacturers have such modules available.
- Being more sophisticated than basic readers IP readers are also more expensive and sensitive, therefore they

should not be installed outdoors in areas with harsh weather conditions or high possibility of vandalism, unless specifically designed for exterior installation. A few manufacturers make such models.

- In the past, the variety of IP readers in terms of identification technologies and read range was much lower than that of the basic readers. However, with the advent of long range multi-technology readers such as those manufactured by Nedap, Sirit, and a few others, this is no longer so.

The advantages and disadvantages of IP controllers apply to the IP readers as well.

Security Risks

The most common security risk of intrusion of an access control system is simply following a legitimate user through a door. Often the legitimate user will hold the door for the intruder. This risk can be minimized through security awareness training of the user population or more active means such as turnstiles. In very high security applications this risk is minimized by using a sally port, sometimes called a security vestibule or mantrap where operator intervention is required presumably to assure valid identification.

The second most common risk is from levering the door open. This is surprisingly simple and effective on most doors. The lever could be as small as a screw driver or big as a crow bar. Fully implemented access control systems include forced door monitoring alarms. These vary in effectiveness usually failing from high false positive alarms, poor database configuration, or lack of active intrusion monitoring.

Similar to levering is crashing through cheap partition walls. In shared tenant spaces the divisional wall is a vulnerability. Along the same lines is breaking sidelights.

Spoofing locking hardware is fairly simple and more elegant than levering. A strong magnet can operate the solenoid controlling bolts in electric locking hardware. Motor locks, more prevalent in Europe than in the US, are also susceptible to this attack using a donut shaped magnet. It is also possible to manipulate the power to the lock either by removing or adding current.

Access cards themselves have proven vulnerable to sophisticated attacks. Enterprising hackers have built portable readers that capture the card number from a user's proximity card. The hacker simply walks by the user, reads the card, and then presents the number to a reader securing the door. This is possible because card numbers are sent in the clear, no encryption being used.

Finally, most electric locking hardware still have mechanical keys as a fail-over. Mechanical key locks are vulnerable to bumping.

The Need-to-know Principle

The need to know principle can be enforced with user access controls and authorization procedures and its objective is to ensure that only authorized individuals gain access to information or systems necessary to undertake their duties. See Principle of least privilege.

Computer Security

In computer security, access control includes authentication, authorization and audit. It also includes measures such as physical devices, including biometric scans and metal locks, hidden paths, digital signatures, encryption, social barriers, and monitoring by humans and automated systems.

In any access control model, the entities that can perform actions in the system are called *subjects*, and the entities representing resources to which access may need to be controlled are called *objects* (see also Access Control Matrix). Subjects and objects should both be considered as software entities and as human users. Although some systems equate subjects with *user IDs*, so that all processes started by a user by default have the same authority, this level of control is not fine-grained enough to satisfy the Principle of least privilege, and arguably is responsible for the prevalence of malware in such systems.

In some models, for example the object-capability model, any software entity can potentially act as both a subject and object.

Access control models used by current systems tend to fall into one of two classes: those based on capabilities and those based on access control lists (ACLs). In a capability-based model, holding an unforgettable reference or *capability* to an object provides access to the object (roughly analogous to how possession of your house key grants you access to your house); access is conveyed to another party by transmitting such a capability over a secure channel. In an ACL-based model, a subject's access to an object depends on whether its identity is on a list associated with the object (roughly analogous to how a bouncer at a private party would check your ID to see if your name is on the guest list); access is conveyed by editing the list. (Different ACL systems have a variety of different conventions regarding who or what is responsible for editing the list and how it is edited.)

Both capability-based and ACL-based models have mechanisms to allow access rights to be granted to all members of a *group* of subjects (often the group is itself modeled as a subject).

Access control systems provide the essential services of *identification and authentication (I&A)*, *authorization*, and *accountability* where:

- identification and authentication determine who can log on to a system, and the association of users with the software subjects that they are able to control as a result of logging in;
- authorization determines what a subject can do;
- accountability identifies what a subject (or all subjects associated with a user) did.

Identification and Authentication (I&A)

Identification and authentication (I&A) is the process of verifying that an identity is bound to the entity that makes an assertion or claim of identity. The I&A process assumes that there was an initial validation of the identity, commonly called identity proofing. Various methods of identity proofing are available ranging from in person validation using government issued identification to anonymous methods that allow the claimant to remain anonymous, but known to the system if they return. The method used for identity proofing and validation should provide an assurance level commensurate with the intended use of the identity within the system. Subsequently, the entity asserts an identity together with an authenticator as a means for validation. The only requirements for the identifier is that it must be unique within its security domain.

Authenticators are commonly based on at least one of the following four factors:

- *Something you know,* such as a password or a personal identification number (PIN). This assumes that only the owner of the account knows the password or PIN needed to access the account.
- *Something you have,* such as a smart card or security token. This assumes that only the owner of the account has the necessary smart card or token needed to unlock the account.
- *Something you are,* such as fingerprint, voice, retina, or iris characteristics.
- *Where you are,* for example inside or outside a company firewall, or proximity of login location to a personal GPS device.

Authorization

Authorization applies to subjects. Authorization determines what a subject can do on the system.

Most modern operating systems define sets of permissions that are variations or extensions of three basic types of access:

- Read (R): The subject can
  - o Read file contents
  - o List directory contents
- Write (W): The subject can change the contents of a file or directory with the following tasks:
  - o Add
  - o Create
  - o Delete
  - o Rename

- Execute (X): If the file is a program, the subject can cause the program to be run. (In Unix systems, the 'execute' permission doubles as a 'traverse directory' permission when granted for a directory.)

These rights and permissions are implemented differently in systems based on *discretionary access control* (*DAC*) and *mandatory access control* (*MAC*).

Accountability

Accountability uses such system components as *audit trails* (records) and *logs* to associate a subject with its actions. The information recorded should be sufficient to map the subject to a controlling user. Audit trails and logs are important for

- Detecting security violations
- Re-creating security incidents

If no one is regularly reviewing your logs and they are not maintained in a secure and consistent manner, they may not be admissible as evidence.

Many systems can generate automated reports based on certain predefined criteria or thresholds, known as clipping levels. *For example, a clipping level may be set to generate a report for the following:*

- More than three failed logon attempts in a given period
- Any attempt to use a disabled user account

These reports help a system administrator or security administrator to more easily identify possible break-in attempts.

Access Control Models

Access control models are sometimes categorized as either discretionary or non-discretionary. The three most widely recognized models are Discretionary Access Control (DAC), Mandatory Access Control (MAC), and Role Based Access Control (RBAC). MAC and RBAC are both non-discretionary.

Attribute-based Access Control

In attribute-based access control (ABAC), access is granted not based on the rights of the subject associated with a user after authentication, but based on attributes of the user. The user has to prove so called claims about his attributes to the access control engine. An attribute-based access control policy specifies which claims need to be satisfied in order to grant access to an object. For instance the claim could be "older than 18" . Any user that can prove this claim is granted access. Users can be anonymous as authentication and identification are not strictly required. One does however require means for proving claims anonymously. This can for instance be achieved using anonymous credentials or XACML (extensible access control markup language).

Discretionary Access Control

Discretionary access control (DAC) is an access policy determined by the owner of an object. The owner decides who is allowed to access the object and what privileges they have.

Two important concepts in DAC are

- *File and data ownership:* Every object in the system has an *owner*. In most DAC systems, each object's initial owner is the subject that caused it to be created. The access policy for an object is determined by its owner.
- *Access rights and permissions:* These are the controls that an owner can assign to other subjects for specific resources.

Access controls may be discretionary in ACL-based or capability-based access control systems. (In capability-based systems, there is usually no explicit concept of 'owner', but the creator of an object has a similar degree of control over its access policy.)

Mandatory Access Control

Mandatory access control (MAC) is an access policy determined by the system, not the owner. MAC is used in multilevel systems that process highly sensitive data, such as classified government and military information. A multilevel system is a single computer system that handles multiple classification levels between subjects and objects.

- *Sensitivity labels:* In a MAC-based system, all subjects and objects must have labels assigned to them. A subject's sensitivity label specifies its level of trust. An object's sensitivity label specifies the level of trust required for access. In order to access a given object, the subject must have a sensitivity level equal to or higher than the requested object.

- *Data import and export:* Controlling the import of information from other systems and export to other systems (including printers) is a critical function of MAC-based systems, which must ensure that sensitivity labels are properly maintained and implemented so that sensitive information is appropriately protected at all times.

Two methods are commonly used for applying mandatory access control:

- *Rule-based (or label-based) access control:* This type of control further defines specific conditions for access to a requested object. All MAC-based systems implement a simple form of rule-based access control to determine whether access should be granted or denied by matching:
  - o An object's sensitivity label
  - o A subject's sensitivity label
- *Lattice-based access control:* These can be used for complex access control decisions involving multiple objects and/or subjects. A lattice model is a mathematical structure that defines greatest lower-bound and least upper-bound values for a pair of elements, such as a subject and an object.

Few systems implement MAC; XTS-400 and SELinux are examples of systems that do. The computer system at the company in the movie *Tron* is an example of MAC in popular culture.

Role-based Access Control

Role-based access control (RBAC) is an access policy determined by the system, not the owner. RBAC is used in commercial applications and also in military systems, where multilevel security requirements may also exist. RBAC differs from DAC in that DAC allows users to control access to their resources, while in RBAC, access is controlled at the system level, outside of the user's control. Although RBAC is non-discretionary, it can be distinguished from MAC primarily in the way permissions are handled. MAC controls read and write permissions based on a user's clearance level and additional labels. RBAC controls collections of permissions that may include complex operations such as an e-commerce transaction, or may be as simple as read or write. A role in RBAC can be viewed as a set of permissions.

Three primary rules are defined for RBAC:

1. *Role assignment:* A subject can execute a transaction only if the subject has selected or been assigned a role.
2. *Role authorization:* A subject's active role must be authorized for the subject. With rule 1 above, this rule ensures that users can take on only roles for which they are authorized.
3. *Transaction authorization:* A subject can execute a transaction only if the transaction is authorized for the subject's active role. With rules 1 and 2, this rule ensures that users can execute only transactions for which they are authorized.

Additional constraints may be applied as well, and roles can be combined in a hierarchy where higher-level roles subsume permissions owned by sub-roles.

Most IT vendors offer RBAC in one or more products.

Telecommunication

In telecommunication, the term *access control* is defined in U.S. Federal Standard 1037C with the following meanings:

1. A service feature or technique used to permit or deny use of the components of a communication system.
2. A technique used to define or restrict the rights of individuals or application programs to obtain data from, or place data onto, a storage device.
3. The definition or restriction of the rights of individuals or application programs to obtain data from, or place data into, a storage device.
4. The process of limiting access to the resources of an AIS to authorized users, programs, processes, or other systems.

5. That function performed by the resource controller that allocates system resources to satisfy user requests.

This definition depends on several other technical terms from Federal Standard 1037C.

Public Policy

In public policy, access control to restrict access to systems ("authorization") or to track or monitor behavior within systems ("accountability") is an implementation feature of using trusted systems for security or social control.

Physical Security

Physical security describes measures that are designed to deny access to unauthorized personnel (including attackers or even accidental intruders) from physically accessing a building, facility, resource, or stored information; and guidance on how to design structures to resist potentially hostile acts. Physical security can be as simple as a locked door or as elaborate as multiple layers of barriers, armed security guards and guardhouse placement. Good physical security uses the concept of layered defense, in appropriate combinations to deter and delay intrusions (passive defense), and detect and respond to intrusions (active defense). Ultimately it should be too difficult, risky or costly to an attacker to even attempt an intrusion. However, strong security measures also come at a cost, and there can be no perfect security. It is up to a security designer to balance security features and a tolerable amount of personnel access against available resources, risks to assets to be protected, and even aesthetics. There are also life-cycle sustaining costs to consider.

Physical security is not a modern phenomenon. Physical security exists in order to deter or prevent persons from entering a physical facility. Historical examples of physical security include city walls, moats, etc.

The *technology* used for physical security has changed over time. While in past eras, there was no passive infrared (PIR) based technology, electronic access control systems, or video surveillance system (VSS) cameras, the essential methodology of physical security has not altered over time. Fundamentally, good physical security is a combination of defensive principles designed to:

- deter
- delay
- detect, and
- respond (and ultimately, deny access)

... to intrusions into critical physical spaces. The first two actions of deter and delay are considered passive defense, while the remaining are active in nature.

Elements and Design

The field of security engineering has identified the following elements to physical security:

- obstacles, to frustrate trivial attackers and delay serious ones; to include:
  - o explosion protection;
- detection systems, such as surveillance systems, alarms, security lighting, security guard patrols or closed-circuit television cameras, to make it likely that attacks will be noticed; and
- security response, to repel, catch or frustrate attackers when an attack is detected.

In a well designed system, these features must complement each other. There are at least four layers of physical security:

- Environmental design
- Mechanical, electronic and procedural access control
- Intrusion detection (with appropriate response procedures)
- Personnel Identification (authentication)

There may be many choices to consider and there is no "best" solution that will satisfy a broad class of situations. Each situation is unique. What is offered in this article are only proven techniques, but not always required or expected, or satisfactory for the end user.

The goal of physical security is to convince potential attackers that the likely costs of attack exceeds the value of making the attack, e.g. that consequences of a failed attack may well exceed the gain. The combination of layered security features establishes the presence of territoriality.

The initial layer of security for a campus, building, office, or other physical space uses crime prevention through environmental design to deter threats. Some of the most common examples are also the most basic - warning signs, fences, vehicle barriers, vehicle height-restrictors, restricted access points, site lighting and trenches. However, even passive things like hedgerows may be sufficient in some circumstances.

The next layer is *mechanical* and includes gates, doors, and locks. Key control of the locks becomes a problem with large user populations and any user turnover. Keys quickly become unmanageable, often forcing the adoption of electronic access control. *Electronic access control* easily manages large user populations, controlling for user lifecycles times, dates, and individual access points. For example a user's access rights could allow access from 0700h to 1900h Monday through Friday and expires in 90 days. Another form of access control (*procedural*) includes the use of policies, processes and procedures to manage the ingress into the restricted area. An example of this is the deployment of security personnel conducting checks for authorized entry at predetermined points of entry. This form of access control is usually supplemented by the earlier forms of access control (i.e. mechanical and electronic access control), or simple devices such as physical passes.

An additional sub-layer of mechanical/electronic access control protection is reached by integrating a *key management system* to manage the possession and usage of mechanical keys to locks or property within a building or campus.

The third layer is *intrusion detection* systems or alarms. Intrusion detection monitors for unauthorized access. It is less a preventative measure and more of a response trigger, although some would argue that it is a deterrent. Intrusion detection has a high incidence of false alarms. In many jurisdictions, law enforcement will not respond to alarms from intrusion detection systems. For example, a motion sensor near a door could trigger on either a person or a squirrel. The sensor itself does not do identification and as far as it is designed, anything moving near that door is unauthorized.

The last layer is *video monitoring* systems. Security cameras can be a deterrent in many cases, but their real power comes from incident verification and historical analysis. For example, if alarms are being generated and there is a camera in place, the camera could be viewed to verify the alarms. In instances when an attack has already occurred and a camera is in place at the point of attack, the recorded video can be reviewed. Although the term closed-circuit television (CCTV) is common, it is quickly becoming outdated as more video systems lose the closed circuit for signal transmission and are instead transmitting on computer networks. Advances in information technology are transforming video monitoring into video analysis. For instance, once an image is digitized it can become data that sophisticated algorithms can act upon.

As the speed and accuracy of automated analysis increases, the video system could move from a monitoring system to an intrusion detection system or access control system. It is not a stretch to imagine a video camera inputting data to a processor that outputs to a door lock. Instead of using some kind of key, whether mechanical or electrical, a person's visage is the key. FST21, an Israeli company that entered the US market this year, markets intelligent buildings that do just that. When actual design and implementation is considered, there are numerous types of security cameras that can be used for many different applications. One must analyze their needs and choose accordingly.

Note that video monitoring does not necessarily guarantee that a human response is made to an intrusion. A human must be monitoring the situation realtime in order to respond in a timely manner. Otherwise, video monitoring is simply a means to gather evidence to be analyzed at a later time - perhaps too late in some cases.

Intertwined in these four layers are people. Guards have a role in all layers, in the first as patrols and at checkpoints. In the second to administer electronic access control. In the third to respond to alarms. The response force must be able to arrive on site in less time than it is expected that the attacker will require to breach the barriers. And in the fourth to monitor and analyze video. Users obviously have a role also by questioning and reporting suspicious people. Aiding in identifying people as known versus unknown are identification systems. Often photo ID badges are used and are frequently coupled to the electronic access control system. Visitors are often required to wear a visitor badge.

Other Physical Security Tools

In recent times, new developments in information and communications technology, as well as new demands on security managers, have widened the scope of physical security apparatus.

Fire alarm systems are increasingly becoming based on Internet Protocol, thus leading to them being accessible via local and wide area networks within organizations. Emergency notification is now a new standard in many industries, as well as physical security information management (PSIM). A PSIM application integrates all physical security systems in a facility, and provides a single and comprehensive means of managing all of these resources. It consequently saves on time and cost in the effectual management of physical security.

Examples

Many installations, serving a myriad of different purposes, have physical obstacles in place to deter intrusion. This can be high walls, barbed wire, glass mounted on top of walls, etc.

The presence of PIR-based motion detectors are common in many places, as a means of noting intrusion into a physical installation. Moreover, VSS/CCTV cameras are becoming increasingly common, as a means of identifying persons who intrude into physical locations.

Businesses use a variety of options for physical security, including security guards, electric security fencing, cameras, motion detectors, and light beams.

ATMs (cash dispensers) are protected, not by making them invulnerable, but by spoiling the money inside when they are attacked. Money tainted with a dye could act as a flag to the money's unlawful acquisition.

Safes are rated in terms of the time in minutes which a skilled, well equipped safe-breaker is expected to require to open the safe. These ratings are developed by highly skilled safe breakers employed by insurance agencies, such as Underwriters Laboratories. In a properly designed system, either the time between inspections by a patrolling guard should be less than that time, or an alarm response force should be able to reach it in less than that time.

Hiding the resources, or hiding the fact that resources are valuable, is also often a good idea as it will reduce the exposure to opponents and will cause further delays during an attack, but should not be relied upon as a principal means of ensuring security. Not all aspects of Physical Security need be high tech. Even something as simple as a thick or thorny bush can add a layer of physical security to some premises, especially in a residential setting.

Bouncer (doorman)

A bouncer (also known as a doorman or cooler) is an informal term for a security guard employed at venues such as bars, nightclubs or concerts to provide security, check legal age, and refuse entry to a venue based on criteria such as intoxication, aggressive behavior, or attractiveness. Bouncers are often required where crowd size, clientele or alcohol consumption may make arguments or fights commonplace.

In the United States, civil liability and court costs related to the use of force by bouncers are "the highest preventable loss found within the [bar] industry..." and other countries have found similar issues related to the excessive use of force. Studies suggest that one of the reasons that some bouncers emphasis physical force is their self image as a strongly masculine group, which requires them to respond to aggression in violent ways. In many countries, federal or state governments have taken steps to professionalise the industry by requiring bouncers to have training, licensing, and/or a criminal records background check.

History

In the 1990s and 2000s, increased awareness of the risks of lawsuits and criminal charges (particularly in the United States and industrialized world) have led many bars and venues to train their bouncers to use communication and conflict resolution skills rather than brute force against troublemakers. However, the earlier history of the occupation suggests that the stereotype of bouncers as rough, tough, physical enforcers has indeed been the case in many countries and cultures throughout history. Historical references also suggest that the 'doorman' function of guarding a place and selecting who can have entry to it (the stereotypical task of the modern bouncer) could at times be a honorific and evolve into a relatively important position.

Ancient Times

The significance of the doorman as the person allowing (or barring) entry is found in a number of Mesopotamian myths (and later in Greek myths descended from them), including that of Nergal overcoming the seven doormen guarding the gates to the Underworld.

In 1 Chronicles 26 of the Old Testament, the Levitical Temple is described as having a number of 'gatekeepers' - amongst their duties are "protect[ing] the temple from theft", from "illegal entry into sacred areas" and "maintain[ing] order", all functions they share with the modern concept of the bouncer, though the described temple servants also serve as holy persons and administrators themselves (it is noted that some administrative function is still present in today's bouncing in the higher position of the supervisor).

The Romans had a position known as the 'Ostiarius' (doorkeeper), initially a slave or other such inferior personage, who guarded the door, and sometimes ejected unwanted people from the house whose gate he guarded. The term later become a low-ranking clergy title.

Plautus, in his play *Bacchides* (written approximately 194-184 BC), mentions a "large and powerful" doorman/bouncer as a threat to get an unwelcome visitor to leave.

Tertullian, an early Christian author living mainly in the 1st century AD, while reporting on the casual oppression of Christians in Carthage, noted that bouncers were counted as part of a semi-legal underworld, amongst other 'shady' characters such as gamblers and pimps.

Modern Times

During the late 19th and early 20th centuries, US saloon-keepers and brothel madams hired bouncers to remove troublesome, violent, or dead-drunk patrons, and protect the saloon girls and prostitutes. The word "bouncer" was first popularized in a novel by Horatio Alger, Jr., called The *Young Outlaw,* which was first published in 1875. Alger was an immensely popular author in the 19th century, especially with young people and his books were widely quoted. In Chapter XIV, entitled "Bounced", a boy is thrown out of a restaurant because he has no money to pay for his dinner:

> *An 1883 newspaper article stated that "'The Bouncer' is merely the English 'chucker out'. When liberty verges on license and gaiety on wanton delirium, the Bouncer selects the gayest of the gay, and - bounces him!"*

19th Century

In US Western towns in the 1870s, high-class brothels known as "good houses" or "parlour houses" hired bouncers for security and to prevent patrons from evading payment. "Good house"-style brothels "...considered themselves the cream of the crop, and [the prostitutes working there] scorned those who worked in (or out of) saloons, dance halls, and theatres." The best bordellos looked like respectable mansions, with attractively-decorated parlours, a game room and a dance hall. For security, "somewhere in every parlor house there was always a bouncer, a giant of a man who stayed sober to handle any customer who got too rough with one of the girls or didn't want to pay his bill." The "protective presence" of bouncers in high-class brothels was "...one of the reasons the girls considered themselves superior to [lower-class] free-lancers, who lacked any such shepherds."

In Wisconsin's lumberjack days, bouncers would physically remove drinkers who were too drunk to keep buying drinks, and thus free up space in the bar for new patrons. The slang term 'snake-room' was used to describe a "...room off a saloon, usually two or three steps down, into which a barkeeper or the bouncer could slide drunk lumberjacks head first through swinging doors from the barroom." In the late 19th century, until Prohibition, bouncers also had the unusual role of protecting the saloon's buffet. To attract business, "...many saloons lured customers with offers of a "free lunch"—usually well salted to inspire drinking, and the saloon "bouncer" was generally on hand to discourage [those with too] hearty appetites".

In the late 19th century, bouncers at small town dances and bars physically resolved disputes and removed troublemakers, without worrying about lawsuits. In the main bar in one Iowa town, "...there were many quarrels, many fights, but all were settled on the spot. There were no court costs [for the bouncers or the bar]; only some aches and pains [for the troublemakers]."

In the 1880s and 1890s, bouncers were used to maintain order in the "The Gut", the roughest part of New York's Coney Island, which was filled with "ramshackle groups of wooden shanties", bars, cabarets, fleabag hotels and brothels. Huge bouncers patrolled these venues of vice and "roughly ejected anyone who violated the loose rules of decorum" by engaging in pick-pocketing, jewelry thieving, or bloody fights.

During the 1890s, San Diego had a similarly rough waterfront area and redlight district called the 'Stingaree', where bouncers worked the door at brothels. Prostitutes worked at the area's 120 bawdy houses in small rooms, paying a fee to the procurer who usually was the bouncer or 'protector' of the brothel. The more expensive, higher-class brothels were called "parlour houses", and they were "run most decorously", and the "best of food and drink was served." To maintain the high-class atmosphere at these establishments, male patrons were expected to act like gentlemen; "...if any customer did or said anything out of line, he was asked to leave. A bouncer made sure he did".

20th century

Bouncers in pre-World War I United States were also sometimes used as the guardians of morality. As ballroom dancing was often considered as an activity which could lead to immoral conduct if the dancers got too close, some of the more reputable venues had bouncers to remind patrons not to dance closer than nine inches to their partners. The bouncers' warnings tended to consist of light taps on the shoulder at first, and then progressed to sterner remonstrations.

In the 1930s, bars in the bawdiest parts of Baltimore, Maryland docks hired bouncers to maintain order and eject aggressive patrons. The Oasis club, operated by Max Cohen, hired "...a lady bouncer by the name of Mickey Steele, a six-foot acrobat from the Pennsylvania coal fields. Mickey was always considerate of the people she bounced; first asking them where they lived and then throwing them in that general direction. She was succeeded by a character known as 'Machine-Gun Butch' who was a long-time bouncer at the club".

In the Weimar Republic in the Germany of the 1920s and early 1930s, doormen protected venues from the fights caused by Nazis and other potentially violent groups (such as Communists). Such scenes were fictionalized in the movie *Cabaret*. Hitler surrounded himself with a number of former bouncers such as Christian Weber; the SS originated as a group designated to protect party meetings.

In early Nazi Germany, some bouncers in underground jazz clubs were also hired to screen for Nazi spies, because jazz was considered a "degenerate" form of music by the Nazi party. Later during the Nazi regime, bouncers also increasingly barred non-German people (such as foreign workers) from public functions, such as 'German' dances at dance halls.

Bouncers also often come into conflict with football hooligans, due to the tendency of groups of hooligans to congregate at pubs and bars before and after games. In the United Kingdom for example, long-running series of feuds between fan groups like The Blades and groups of bouncers in the 1990s were described by researchers.

Bouncers have also been known to be associated with criminal gangs, especially in places like Russia, Hong Kong or Japan, where bouncers may often belong to these groups or have to pay the crime syndicates to be able to operate. In Hong Kong, triad-connected reprisal or intimidation attacks against bouncers have been known to occur.

Hong Kong also features a somewhat unusual situation where some bouncers are known to work for prostitutes, instead of being their pimps. Hong Kong police have noted that due to the letter of the law, they sometimes had to charge the bouncer for illegally extorting the women when the usually expected dominance situation between the sex worker and her 'protector' was in fact reversed.

In the 1990s and 2000s, a number of bouncers have written "tell-all" books about their experiences on the door. They indicate that male bouncers are respected by some club-goers as the ultimate 'hard men', while at the same time, these bouncers can also be lightning rods for aggression and macho posturing on the part of obnoxious male customers wanting to prove themselves. Bouncing has also started to attract some academic interest as part of ethnographic studies into violent subcultures. Bouncers were selected as one of the groups studied by several English researchers in the 1990s because their culture was seen as 'grounded in violence', as well as because the group had increasingly been 'demonized', especially in common liberal discourse.

Personality and Behaviour

Character

Although a common stereotype of bouncers is that of the thuggish brute, a good club security staff member requires more than just physical qualities such as strength and size: "The best bouncers don't "bounce" anyone... they talk to people" (and remind them of the venue rules).

An ability to judge and communicate well with people will reduce the need for physical intervention, while a steady personality will prevent the bouncer from being easily provoked by customers. Bouncers also profit from good written communication skills, because they are often required to document assaults in an incident log or using an incident form. Well-kept incident logs can "cover the employee's back" if criminal charges or a lawsuit later arise from an incident.

However, British research from the 1990s also indicates that a major part of both the group identity and the job satisfaction of bouncers is related to their self image as a strongly masculine person who is capable of dealing with – and dealing out – violence; their employment income plays a lesser role in their job satisfaction. Bouncer subculture is strongly influenced by perceptions of honour and shame, a typical characteristic of groups that are constantly in the public eye. Factors in enjoying work as a bouncer were also found in the general prestige and respect that was accorded to bouncers, sometimes bordering on hero worship. The camaraderie between bouncers (even of different clubs), as well as the ability to work "in the moment" and outside of the drudgery of typical jobs were also often cited.

The same research has also indicated that the decisions made by bouncers, while seeming haphazard to an outsider, often have a basis in rational logic. The decision to turn certain customers away at the door because of too casual clothing is for example often based on the perception that the person will be more willing to fight (compared to someone dressed in expensive attire). Many similar decisions taken by a bouncer during the course of a night are also being described as based on experience rather than just personality.

Use of Force : Excessive Force

Movies often depict bouncers physically throwing patrons out of clubs and restraining drunk customers with headlocks, which has led to a popular misconception that bouncers have (or reserve) the right to use physical force freely. However, in many countries bouncers have no legal authority to use physical force more freely than any other civilian—meaning they are restricted to reasonable levels of force used in self defense, to eject drunk or aggressive patrons refusing to leave a venue, or when restraining a patron who has committed an offence until police arrive. Lawsuits are possible if injuries occur, even if the patron was drunk or using aggressive language.

With civil liability and court costs related to the use of force as *"the highest preventable loss found within the industry..."* (US) and bars being "sued more often for using unnecessary or excessive force than for any other reason" (Canada), substantial costs may be incurred by indiscriminate violence against patrons—though this depends heavily on the laws and customs of the country. In Australia, the number of complaints and lawsuits against venues due to the behaviour of their bouncers has been credited with turning many establishments to using former police officers to head their in-house security, instead of hiring private firms.

According to statistical research in Canada, bouncers are as likely to face physical violence in their work as urban-area police officers. The research also found that the likelihood of such encounters increased (with statistical significance) with the number of years the bouncer had worked in his occupation. Despite popular misconceptions, bouncers in Western countries are normally unarmed. Some bouncers may carry weapons such as expandable batons for personal protection, but they may not have a legal right to carry a weapon even if they would prefer to do so.

Alternatives

Use of force training programs teach bouncers ways to avoid using force and explain what types of force are considered allowable by the courts. Some bars have gone so far as to institute policies barring physical contact, where bouncers are instructed to ask a drunk or disorderly patron to leave - if the patron refuses, the bouncers call police. However, if the police are called too frequently, it can reflect badly on the venue upon renewal of its liquor licence.

Another strategy used in some bars is to hire smaller, less threatening or female bouncers, because they may be better able to defuse conflicts than large, intimidating bouncers. The more 'impressive' bouncers, in the often tense environments they are supposed to supervise, are also often challenged by aggressive males wanting to prove their machismo. Large and intimidating bouncers, whilst providing an appearance of strong security, may also drive customers away in cases where a more relaxed environment is desired. In addition, female security staff, apart from having fewer problems searching female patrons for drugs or weapons, and being able to enter women's wash rooms to check for illegal activities, are also considered as better able to deal with drunk or aggressive women.

In Australia, for example, women comprise almost 20% of the security industry and increasingly work the door as well, using "a smile, chat and a friendly but firm demeanor" to resolve tense situations. Nearly one in nine of Britain's nightclub bouncers are also women, with the UK's 2003 Licensing Act giving the authorities "discretionary power to withhold a venue's licence if it does not employ female door staff." This is credited with having "opened the door for women to enter the profession.". However, female bouncers are still a rarity in many countries, such as in India, where two women who became media celebrities in 2008 for being "Punjabs first female bouncers" were soon sacked again after accusations of unbecoming behaviour.

Regulation and Training

In many countries, a bouncer must be licensed and lacking a criminal record to gain employment within the security/crowd control sector. In some countries or regions, bouncers may be required to have extra skills or special licenses and certification for first aid, alcohol distribution, crowd control, or fire safety.

Canada

In Canada, bouncers have the right to use reasonable force to expel intoxicated or aggressive patrons. First, the patron must be asked to leave the premises. If the patron refuses to leave, the bouncer can use reasonable force to expel the patron. This has been upheld in a number of court cases. Under the definition of 'reasonable force', "it is perfectly acceptable [for the bouncer] to grab a patron's arm to remove the patron from the premises." However, "Only in situations where employees reasonably believe that the conduct of the patron puts them in danger can they inflict harm on a patron and then only to the extent that such force is necessary for self defence."

In Alberta, bar and nightclub security staff will have to take a new, government-run training course on correct bouncer behaviour and skills before the end of 2008. The six-hour 'ProTect' course will, among other subjects, teach staff to identify conflicts before they become violent, and how to defuse situations without resorting to force.

In Ontario, courts have ruled that "a tavern owes a twofold duty of care to its patrons. It must ensure that it does not serve alcohol which would apparently intoxicate or increase the patron's intoxication. As well, it must take positive steps to protect patrons and others from the dangers of intoxication." Regarding the second requirement of protecting patrons, the law holds that "customers cannot be ejected from your premises if doing so would put them in danger [e.g., due to the patron's intoxication]. Bars can be held liable for ejecting a customer who they know, or should know, is at risk of injury by being ejected."

In Ontario, bartenders and servers have to have completed the Smart Serve Training Program, which teaches them to recognise the signs of intoxication. The Smart Serve program is also recommended for other staff in bars who have contact with potentially intoxicated patrons, such as bouncers, coat check staff, and valets. The Smart Serve certification program encourages bars to keep Incident Reporting Logs, to use as evidence if an incident gets to court. With the August 2007 *Private Security and Investigative Services Act*, Ontario law also requires security industry workers, including bouncers to be licensed.

New Zealand

In New Zealand, there is no national-level regulation of bouncers as of 2006. The New Zealand Security Association supports the Hospitality Association of New Zealand's efforts to introduce certification for bouncers, doormen and other people responsible for security at bars and sporting events. The association argues that security officers should be "...properly trained professionals, not just a 'big thug' to stand at the door.", decrying the practice of using "unlicensed, untrained security staff". The organisation has been lobbying the New Zealand government to introduce legislation on training requirements for bar security staff.

Singapore

Singapore requires all bouncers to undergo a background check and attend a 5-day 'National Skills Recognition System' course for security staff. However, many of the more professional security companies (and larger venues with their own dedicated security staff) have noted that the course is insufficient for the specific requirements of a bouncer and provide their own additional training.SIA

United Kingdom

In the UK, "door supervisors" - as they are termed - must hold a licence from the Security Industry Authority. The training for a door supervisor licence takes 30 hours, and includes issues such as behaviour, conflict management, civil and criminal law, search and arrest procedures, drug awareness, recording of incidents and crime scene preservation, licensing law, equal opportunities and discrimination, health and safety at work, physical intervention, and emergency procedures. One current provider of training is the British Institute of Innkeeping Awarding Body.

According to the BBC, a leaked government communication (Oct 2010) favours the abolition of the SIA as a further example of the Conservative Party's widespread cuts, with the SIA being an example of one of the many Quangos the Conservatives intend to disband. Whilst this may alleviate to some extent the financial burden on employers and individuals alike, the vast majority of the industry sees this as a retrograde step, fearing a return of the organized criminal element to the now regulated industry.

Republic of Ireland

In the Republic of Ireland all potential doormen (Bouncers) must complete a FETAC level 4 course in Door Security Procedures. This allows them to apply for a PSA license (Private Security Authority) The PSA vet all applicants before issuing a license, Subsequently some past convictions will disqualify an applicant from working in the security industry. The license issued by the PSA entitles the holder of the license to work on pubs, clubs and event security. It is to be noted that currently event security is an unlicensed sector in Ireland and one does not require a PSA license to provide a security service at an event. However the PSA in conjunction with some of the major security companies in Ireland are in the process of regulating the events sector, As a means for continuous development of standards.

United States

Requirements for bouncers vary from state to state, with some examples being:

California: In California, Senate Bill 194 requires any bouncer or security guard to be registered with the State of California Department of Consumer Affairs Bureau of Security and Investigative Services. These guards must also complete a criminal background check, including submitting their fingerprints to the California Department of Justice and the Federal Bureau of Investigation. Californians must undertake the "Skills Training Course for Security Guards" before receiving a security licence. Further courses allow for qualified security personnel to carry batons upon completion of training.

New York: In New York State, it is illegal for a bar owner to knowingly hire a felon for a bouncer position. Under Article 7 General Business Law, bars and nightclubs are not allowed to hire bouncers without a proper license. Under New York state law only a Private Investigator or Watch, Guard and Patrol Agency can supply security guards/bouncers to bars

Closed-circuit Television

Closed-circuit television (CCTV) is the use of video cameras to transmit a signal to a specific place, on a limited set of monitors.

It differs from broadcast television in that the signal is not openly transmitted, though it may employ point to point (P2P), point to multi-point, or mesh wireless links. Though almost all video cameras fit this definition, the term is most often applied to those used for surveillance in areas that may need monitoring such as banks, casinos, airports, military installations, and convenience stores. Videotelephony is seldom called "CCTV" but the use of video in distance education, where it is an important tool, is often so called.

In industrial plants, CCTV equipment may be used to observe parts of a process from a central control room, for example when the environment is not suitable for humans. CCTV systems may operate continuously or only as required to monitor a particular event. A more advanced form of CCTV, utilizing Digital Video Recorders (DVRs), provides recording for possibly many years, with a variety of quality and performance options and extra features (such as motion-detection and email alerts). More recently, decentralized IP-based CCTV cameras, some equipped with megapixel sensors, support recording directly to network-attached storage devices, or internal flash for completely stand-alone operation.

Surveillance of the public using CCTV is particularly common in the United Kingdom, where there are reportedly more cameras per person than in any other country in the world. There and elsewhere, its increasing use has triggered a debate about security versus privacy.

History

The first CCTV system was installed by Siemens AG at Test Stand VII in Peenemunde, Germany in 1942, for observing the launch of V-2 rockets. The noted German engineer Walter Bruch was responsible for the design and installation of the system.

In the U.S. the first commercial closed-circuit television system became available in 1949, called Vericon. Very little is known about Vericon except it was advertised as not requiring a government permit.

CCTV recording systems are still often used at modern launch sites to record the flight of the rockets, in order to find the possible causes of malfunctions, while larger rockets are often fitted with CCTV allowing pictures of stage separation to be transmitted back to earth by radio link.

In September 1968, Olean, New York was the first city in the United States to install video cameras along its main business street in an effort to fight crime. The use of closed-circuit TV cameras piping images into the Olean Police Department propelled Olean to the forefront of crime-fighting technology.

The use of CCTV later on became very common in banks and stores to discourage theft, by recording evidence of criminal activity. Their use further popularized the concept. The first place to use CCTV in the United Kingdom was King's Lynn, Norfolk.

In recent decades, especially with general crime fears growing in the 1990s and 2000s, public space use of surveillance cameras has taken off, especially in some countries such as the United Kingdom.

Uses

Crime Prevention and Prevalence

Experiments in the UK during the 1970s and 1980s (including outdoor CCTV in Bournemouth in 1985), led to several larger trial programs later that decade.

These were deemed successful in the government report "CCTV: Looking Out For You", issued by the Home Office in 1994, and paved the way for a massive increase in the number of CCTV systems installed. Today, systems cover most town and city centres, and many stations, car-parks and estates.

A more recent analysis by Northeastern University and the University of Cambridge, "Public Area CCTV and Crime

Prevention: An Updated Systematic Review and Meta-Analysis," examined 44 different studies that collectively surveyed areas from the United Kingdom to U.S. cities such as Cincinnati and New York. The analysis found that:

(1) Surveillance systems were most effective in parking lots, where their use resulted in a 51% decrease in crime;

(2) Public transportation areas saw a 23% decrease in crimes;

(3) Systems in public settings were the least effective, with just a 7% decrease in crimes overall.

When sorted by country, however, systems in the United Kingdom accounted for the majority of the decrease; the drop in other areas was insignificant.

The exact number of CCTV cameras in the UK is not known for certain because there is no requirement to register CCTV cameras. However, research published in CCTV Image magazine estimates that the number of cameras in the UK is 1.85 million. The number is based on extrapolating from a comprehensive survey of public and private cameras within the Cheshire Constabulary jurisdiction. This works out as an average of one camera for every 32 people in the UK, although the density of cameras varies from place to place to such a degree as to make this figure almost meaningless. The Cheshire report also claims that the average person on a typical day would be seen by 70 CCTV cameras, although many of these sightings would be brief glimpses from cameras in shops.

The Cheshire figure is regarded as more dependable than a previous study by Michael McCahill and Clive Norris of Urban Eye published in 2002. Based on a small sample in Putney High Street, McCahill and Norris estimated the number of surveillance cameras in private premises in London at around 500,000 and the total number of cameras in the UK at around 4,200,000. According to their estimate the UK has one camera for every 14 people. Although it has been acknowledged for several years that the methodology behind this figure is somewhat dubious, it has continued to be quoted in the absence of a better figure.

The CCTV User Group estimates that there are around 1.5 million CCTV cameras in city centres, stations, airports, major retail areas and so forth. This figure does not include the smaller surveillance systems such as those that may be found in local corner shops and is therefore broadly in line with the Cheshire report. Research conducted by the Scottish Centre for Crime and Justice Research and based on a survey of all Scottish local authorities, identified that there are over 2,200 public space CCTV cameras in Scotland.

There is little evidence that CCTV deters crime; in fact, there is considerable evidence that it does not. According to a Liberal Democrat analysis, in London "Police are no more likely to catch offenders in areas with hundreds of cameras than in those with hardly any." A 2008 Report by UK. Police Chiefs concluded that only 3% of crimes were solved by CCTV. In London, a Metropolitan Police report showed that in 2008 only one crime was solved per 1000 cameras. There are valid reasons for including CCTV as a component of a physical security program, but deterrence is not one of them.

Cameras have also been installed on public transport in the hope of deterring crime, and in mobile police surveillance vans, often with automatic number plate recognition. In some cases CCTV cameras have become a target of attacks themselves.

On July 22, 2005, Jean Charles de Menezes was shot dead by police at Stockwell tube station. According to brother Giovani Menezes, "The film showed that Jean did not have suspicious behaviour" .

Because of the bombing attempts the previous day, some of the tapes had been supposedly removed from CCTV cameras for study, and they were not functional. An ongoing change to DVR-based technology may in future stop similar problems occurring.

In October 2009, an "Internet Eyes" website was announced which would pay members of the public to view CCTV camera images from their homes and report any crimes they witnessed. The site aimed to add "more eyes" to cameras which might be insufficiently monitored, but civil liberties campaigners criticized the idea as "a distasteful and a worrying development".

Hacking and Video Art

Hackers and guerrilla artists have exposed the vulnerabilities of the video systems in an act dubbed "video sniffing" They have crossed feeds, uploaded their own video feeds and used the video footage for artistic purposes.

Industrial Processes

Industrial processes that take place under conditions dangerous for humans are today often supervised by CCTV. These are mainly processes in the chemical industry, the interior of reactors or facilities for manufacture of nuclear fuel. Special cameras for some of these purposes include line-scan cameras and thermographic cameras which allow operators to measure the temperature of the processes. The usage of CCTV in such processes is sometimes required by law.

Traffic Monitoring

Many cities and motorway networks have extensive traffic-monitoring systems, using closed-circuit television to detect congestion and notice accidents. Many of these cameras however, are owned by private companies and transmit data to drivers' GPS systems.

The UK. Highways Agency has a publicly-owned CCTV network of over 1,200 cameras covering the English motorway and trunk road network. These cameras are primarily used to monitor traffic conditions and are not used as speed cameras. With the addition of fixed cameras for the Active Traffic Management system, the number of cameras on the Highways Agency's CCTV network is likely to increase significantly over the next few years.

The London congestion charge is enforced by cameras positioned at the boundaries of and inside the congestion charge zone, which automatically read the license plates of cars. If the driver does not pay the charge then a fine will be imposed. Similar systems are being developed as a means of locating cars reported stolen.

Other surveillance cameras serve as traffic enforcement cameras.

Transport Safety

A CCTV system may be installed where an operator of a machine cannot directly observe people who may be injured by some unexpected machine operation. For example, on a subway train, CCTV cameras may allow the operator to confirm that people are clear of doors before closing them and starting the train.

Operators of an amusement park ride may use a CCTV system to observe that people are not endangered by starting the ride. A CCTV camera and dashboard monitor can make reversing a vehicle safer, if it allows the driver to observe objects or people not otherwise visible.

Outside the U.K.

The use of CCTV in the United States is less common, though increasing, and generally meets stronger opposition. In 1998, 3,000 CCTV systems were in use in New York City. There are more than 10,000 CCTV systems in Chicago.

In the last few years particularly, the percentage of people in the U.S. having installed a security-camera system has increased dramatically. Global Security Solutions with the help of Zone Tech Systems first announced the launch of IP surveillance in the U.S. security industry by partnering up with Axis Communications (an IP pioneer). Today's CCTV market has transformed the shift towards IP-based security products and systems.

In Latin America, the CCTV market is growing rapidly with the increase of property crime.

Criminal Use

Criminals may use surveillance cameras, for example a hidden camera at an ATM to capture people's PINs without their knowledge. The devices are small enough not to be noticed, and are placed where they can monitor the keypad of the machine as people enter their PINs. Images may be transmitted wirelessly to the criminal.

Privacy

A mobile closed-circuit TV van monitoring a street market.

Opponents of CCTV point out the loss of privacy of the people under surveillance, and the negative impact of surveillance on civil liberties. Furthermore, they argue that CCTV displaces crime, rather than reducing it. Critics often dub CCTV as "Big Brother surveillance", a reference to George Orwell's novel *Nineteen*

Eighty-Four, which featured a two-way telescreen in every home through which The Party would monitor the populace. Civil liberties campaign group Big Brother Watch have published several research papers into CCTV systems. In December 2009, they released a report documenting council controlled CCTV cameras.

More positive views of CCTV cameras have argued that the cameras are not intruding into people's privacy, as they are not surveilling private, but *public* space, where an individual's right to privacy can reasonably be weighed against the public's need for protection from presumptively innocent people . However, both the United States Supreme Court in Katz vs. The United States and anti-surveillance activists have held that there is a right to privacy in public areas.

The recent growth of CCTV in housing areas also raises serious issues about the extent to which CCTV is being used as a social control measure rather than simply a deterrent to crime. However, since the September 11 attacks of 2001, many studies have suggested that public opinion of CCTV has grown more favorable. Many proponents of CCTV cite the attacks of the 2005 London Underground bombings as one example of how effective surveillance led to swift progress in post-event investigations.

Quite apart from government-permitted use (or abuse), questions are also raised about illegal access to CCTV recordings. The Data Protection Act 1998 in the United Kingdom led to legal restrictions on the uses of CCTV recordings, and also mandated their registration with the Data Protection Agency. In 2004, the successor to the Data Protection Agency, the Information Commissioner's Office clarified that this required registration of all CCTV systems with the Commissioner, and prompt deletion of archieved recordings.

However, subsequent case law (Durant vs. FSA) has limited the scope of the protection provided by this law, and not all CCTV systems are currently regulated. Private sector personnel in the UK who operate or monitor CCTV devices or systems are now considered security guards and have been made subject to state licensing.

A 2007 report by the UK's Information Commissioner's Office, highlighted the need for the public to be made more aware of the "creeping encroachment" into their civil liberties created by the growing use of surveillance apparatus. A year prior to the report Richard Thomas, the Information Commissioner, warned that Britain was "sleepwalking into a surveillance society".

In 2007, the UK watchdog Camera Watch claimed that the majority of CCTV cameras in the UK are operated illegally or are in breach of privacy guidelines. In response, the Information Commissioner's Office denied the claim adding that any reported abuses of the Data Protection Act are swiftly investigated.

In the United States, there are no such data-protection mechanisms. It has been questioned whether CCTV evidence is allowable under the Fourth Amendment, which prohibits "unreasonable searches and seizures". The courts have generally not taken this view.

In Canada, the use of video surveillance has grown very rapidly. In Ontario, both the *municipal* and *provincial* versions of the Freedom of Information and Protection of Privacy Act outline very specific guidelines that control how *images* and *information* can be gathered by this method and/or released.

Technological Developments

Computer Controlled Analytics and Identification

Today's High-definition CCTV cameras have many computer controlled technologies that allow them to identify, track, and categorize objects in their field of view.

Video Content Analysis (VCA) is the capability of automatically analyzing video to detect and determine temporal events not based on a single image. As such, it can be seen as the automated equivalent of the biological visual cortex.

A system using VCA can recognize changes in the environment and even identify and compare objects in the database using size, speed, and sometimes color. The camera's actions can be programmed based on what it is "seeing". For example; an alarm can be issued if an object has moved in a certain area, or if a painting is missing from a wall, and if someone has spray painted the lens.

VCA analytics can also be used to detect unusual patterns in a videos environment. The system can be set to detect anomalies in a crowd of people, for instance a person moving in the opposite direction in airports where passengers are only supposed to walk in one direction out of a plane or in a subway where people are not supposed to exit through the entrances.

VCA also has the ability to track people on a map by calculating their position from the images. It is then possible to link many cameras and track a person through an entire building or area. This can allow a person to be followed without having to analyze many hours of film. Currently the cameras have difficulty identifying individuals from video alone, but if connected to a key-card system, identities can be established and displayed as a tag over their heads on the video.

There is also a significant difference in where the VCA technology is placed, either the data is being processed within the cameras (on the edge) or by a centralized server. Both technologies have their pros and cons.

Facial recognition system Is a computer application for automatically identifying or verifying a person from a digital image or a video frame from a video source. One of the ways to do this is by comparing selected facial features from the image and a facial database.

The combination of CCTV and facial recognition has been tried as a form of mass surveillance, but has been ineffective because of the low discriminating power of facial recognition technology and the very high number of false positives generated. This type of system has been proposed to compare faces at airports and seaports with those of suspected terrorists or other undesirable entrants.

Computerized monitoring of CCTV images is under development, so that a human CCTV operator does not have to endlessly look at all the screens, allowing an operator to observe many more CCTV cameras. These systems do not observe people directly. Instead, they track their behavior by looking for particular types of body-movement behavior, or particular types of clothing or baggage.

To many, the development of CCTV in public areas, linked to computer databases of people's pictures and identity, presents a serious breach of civil liberties. Critics fear the possibility that one would not be able to meet anonymously in a public place or drive and walk anonymously around a city. Demonstrations or assemblies in public places could be affected as the state would be able to collate lists of those leading them, taking part, or even just talking with protesters in the street.

Retention, Storage and Preservation

Most CCTV systems record and store digital video and images to a Digital Video Recorder or in the case of IP cameras directly to a server, either on-site or offsite.

The amount of data stored and the retention period of the video or pictures are subject to compression ratios, images stored per second, image size and duration of image retention before being overwritten.

Recordings are usually kept for a preset amount of time and then automatically archieved, overwritten or deleted. The amount of time the videos are kept allow retrieval and review in the event a crime was committed or the information needs to be studied for any number of reasons.

Closed-circuit Digital Photography (CCDP)

A development in the world of CCTV (October 2005) is in the use of megapixel digital still cameras that can take 1600 x 1200 pixel resolution images of the camera scene either on a time lapse or motion-detection basis. Images taken with a digital still camera have higher resolution than those taken with a typical video camera. Relatively low-cost digital still cameras can be used for CCTV purposes, using CCDP software that controls the camera from the PC.

Images of the camera scene are transferred automatically to a computer every few seconds. Images may be monitored remotely if the computer is connected to a network.

Combinations of PIR activated floodlights with 1.3Mpix and better digital cameras are now appearing. They save the images to a flash-memory card which is inserted into a slot on the device. The flash card can be removed for viewing on a computer if ever an incident happens. They are not intended for live viewing, but are a very simple and cheap "install and forget" approach to this issue.

Closed-circuit digital photography (CCDP) is more suited for capturing and saving recorded photographs, whereas closed-circuit television (CCTV) is more suitable for live-monitoring purposes.

IP Cameras

A growing branch in CCTV is *internet protocol* cameras (IP cameras). IP cameras use the Internet Protocol (IP) used by most Local Area Networks (LANs) to transmit video across data networks in digital form. IP can optionally be transmitted across the public internet, allowing users to view their camera(s) through any internet connection available through a computer or a 3G phone. For professional or public infrastructure security applications, IP video is restricted to within a private network or VPN.

Networking CCTV Cameras

The city of Chicago operates a networked video surveillance system which combines CCTV video feeds of government agencies with those of the private sector, installed in city buses, businesses, public schools, subway stations, housing projects etc. Even home owners are able to contribute footage. It is estimated to incorporate the video feeds of a total of 15,000 cameras.

The system is used by Chicago's Office of Emergency Management in case of an emergency call: it detects the caller's location and instantly displays the real-time video feed of the nearest security camera to the operator, not requiring any user intervention. While the system is far too vast to allow complete real-time monitoring, it stores the video data for later usage in order to provide possible evidence in criminal cases.

London also has a network of CCTV systems that allows multiple authorities to view and control CCTV cameras in real time. The system allows authorities including the Metropolitan Police Service, Transport for London and a number of London boroughs to share CCTV images between them. It uses a network protocol called Television Network Protocol to allow access to many more cameras than each individual system owner could afford to run and maintain.

The Glynn County Police Department uses a wireless mesh-networked system of portable battery-powered tripods for live megapixel video surveillance and central monitoring of tactical police situations. The systems can be used either on a stand-alone basis with secure communications to nearby police laptops, or within a larger mesh system with multiple tripods feeding video back to the command vehicle via wireless, and to police headquarters via 3G.

Integrated Systems

Integrated systems allow users to connect remotely from the internet and view what their cameras are viewing remotely, similar to that of IP cameras. In one incident, a lady from Boynton Beach, Florida was able to watch her house get robbed and contacted police directly from her office at work.

Wireless Security Camera

Many consumers are turning to wireless security cameras for home surveillance. Wireless cameras do not require a video cable for video/audio transmission, simply a cable for power. Wireless cameras are also easy and inexpensive to install. Previous generations of wireless security cameras relied on analog technology; modern wireless cameras use digital technology which delivers crisper audio, sharper video, and a secure and interference-free signal.

CCTV Camera Vandalism

Unless physically protected, CCTV cameras have been found to be vulnerable against a variety of (mostly illegal) tactics:

- Some people will deliberately destroy cameras. Some cameras can come with Dust-Tight, Pressurized, Explosion proof, and bullet-resistant housings.
- Spraying substances over the lens can make the image too blurry to be read.
- Lasers can blind or damage them. However, since most lasers are monochromatic, color filters can reduce the effect of laser pointers. However, filters will also impair image quality and overall light sensitivity of cameras (see laser safety article for details on issues with filters). Also, complete protection from infrared, red, green, blue

and UV lasers would require use of completely black filters, rendering the camera useless.

Security Smoke

Security smoke (sometimes called security fog or smoke screen) is thermally generated white smoke specifically used as a security measure. Current security smoke machines use glycol or glycerine mixed with distilled water to produce a dense white fog which obscures vision and presents a confrontational barrier to any intruders.

History of Security Smoke

Traditional Security Systems

The market for using security smoke as a theft prevention tool came about because of an increase in the ability of thieves to circumvent existing physical security measures, often by simply raising the level of violence utilised to gain entry. Burglar alarms often have a delay of several minutes before police or private security are able to respond, meaning a well organized criminal has a period of time in which to enter and take what he likes.

Closed-circuit television and recording devices have been nullified as thieves routinely hide their identities. The security smoke market developed as an alternative security method, designed not to deter entry, but to prevent loss if a thief did gain access.

Early Security Smoke Systems

The first security smoke system was designed, manufactured and installed by Concept Engineering in 1974 to protect gold bullion in specialised vaults. In 1993 Concept launched the *Smoke Screen* range, the first commercial security smoke system to be designed and manufactured under ISO 9000.

Composition of the Smoke

A smoke "simulant", usually a glycol or glycerine mixed with distilled water, is vaporized and then condensed in free air to produce the distinctive smoke-like effect. The particles produced are on average 0.2-2.0 micrometres in diameter, meaning that the fog settles very slowly (and therefore has excellent longevity). This also means that residue and contamination is highly unlikely.

Applications

Security smoke systems have been employed in a wide variety of industries, including banks, jewellers, retail premises, cash-handling chains, offices and private homes. Often businesses have turned to security smoke systems when other, more traditional, security methods have failed to prevent repeated break-ins and stock loss. It is estimated that as of January 2010 there are over 100,000 premises using security smoke systems in the UK.

Protecting High-value Products

Security smoke systems have been successfully used to protect high-value items from opportunistic smash and grab style raids, for example jewellers' window displays. Major retailers, such as Aurum Holdings – owner of Mappin & Webb, Goldsmiths and Watches of Switzerland – have installed security smoke systems and have seen a dramatic decrease in losses from such break-ins.

Cash Handling Chains

Security smoke machines have been successfully used in protecting personnel and currency during the delivery and collection of cash. The introduction of a portable security smoke generator was awarded best new physical product at IFSEC 2009, providing cash-carriers with a high-level of protection against an increased risk during out of hours cash deliveries.

Endorsement by Crime Prevention Organizations

Guidelines from the Association of Chief Police Officers approve security smoke devices, and the ACPO *Secured By Design* accreditation scheme endorses certain manufacturers of security smoke systems. UK insurers also recommend security smoke as an approved method of reducing stock loss and deterring break-ins.

Safety Considerations

One of the primary concerns raised is the possibility of contamination of premises, stock and personal possessions by the generated fog. Independent tests have shown that well installed, properly maintained security smoke systems leave no residue, and some security smoke installers offer a guarantee of this. Alternative concerns suggest that the confrontational nature of the smoke can cause some intruders to panic and put staff at risk. To minimize this risk, a great deal of care is taken in selecting where the smoke generators are installed. Security smoke now has its own European standard EN50131-8 which specifically states that it must not be used in such a way as to create a mantrap.

Alarm

An alarm gives an audible or visual warning about a problem or condition.

Alarms include:

- burglar alarms, designed to warn of burglaries; this is often a silent alarm: the police or guards are warned without indication to the burglar, which increases the chances of catching him or her.
- alarm clocks can produce an alarm at a given time
- distributed control manufacturing systems or DCSs, found in nuclear power plants, refineries and chemical facilities also generate alarms to direct the operator's attention to an important event that he or she needs to address.
- alarms in an operation and maintenance (O&M) monitoring system, which informs the bad working state of (a particular part of) the system under monitoring.
  - o first-out alarm
- safety alarms, which go off if a dangerous condition occurs. Common public safety alarms include:
  - o tornado sirens
  - o fire alarms
    - – "Multiple-alarm fire", a locally-specific measure of the severity of a fire and the fire-department reaction required.
  - o car alarms

- o community Alarm or autodialer alarm (medical alarms)
- o air raid sirens
- o personal alarm
- o tocsins – a historical method of raising an alarm

Alarms have the capability of causing a fight-or-flight response in humans; a person under this mindset will panic and either flee the perceived danger or attempt to eliminate it, often ignoring rational thought in either case. We can characterize a person in such a state as "alarmed".

With any kind of alarm, the need exists to balance between on the one hand the danger of false alarms (called "false positives") – the signal going off in the absence of a problem – and on the other hand failing to signal an actual problem (called a "false negative"). False alarms can waste resources expensively and can even be dangerous. For example, false alarms of a fire can waste firefighter manpower, making them unavailable for a real fire, and risk injury to firefighters and others as the fire engines race to the alleged fire's location. In addition, false alarms may acclimatise people to ignore alarm signals, and thus possibly to ignore an actual emergency: Aesop's fable of *The Boy Who Cried Wolf* exemplifies this problem.

Etymology

The word comes from the Old French *A l'arme* meaning "To the arms", "To the weapons", telling armed men to pick up their weapons and get ready for action, because an enemy may have suddenly appeared.

Alarm Management

Alarm management is the application of human factors (or ergonomics as the field is referred to outside the U.S.) along with instrumentation engineering and systems thinking to manage the design of an alarm system to increase its usability. Most often the major usability problem is that there are too many alarms annunciated in a plant upset, commonly referred to as alarm flood, since it is so similar to a flood caused by excessive rainfall input with a basically fixed drainage output capacity. However, there can also be other problems with an alarm system such as poorly designed alarms, improperly set alarm points, ineffective annunciation, unclear alarm messages, etc.

Alarm Problem History

From their conception, large chemical, refining, power generation, and other processing plants required the use of a control system to keep the process operating successfully and producing products. Due to the fragility of the components as compared to the process, these control systems often required a control room to protect them from the elements and process conditions.

In the early days of control rooms, they utilized what were referred to as "panel boards" which were loaded with control instruments and indicators. These were tied to sensors located in the process streams and on the outside of process equipment. The sensors relayed their information to the control instruments via 4-20 mA current loop in the form of twisted pair wiring. At first these systems merely yielded information, and a well-trained operator was required to make adjustments either by changing flow rates, or altering energy inputs to keep the process within its designed limits.

Alarms were added to alert the operator to a condition that was about to exceed a design limit, or had already exceeded a design limit. Additionally, Emergency Shut Down (ESD) systems were employed to halt a process that was in danger of exceeding either safety, environmental or monetarily acceptable process limits. Alarm were indicated to the operator by annunciator horns, and lights of different colors. (For instance, green lights meant OK, Yellow meant not OK, and Red meant BAD.) Panel boards were usually laid out in a manner that replicated the process flow in the plant.

So instrumentation indicating operating units with the plant was grouped together for recognition sake and ease of problem solution. It was a simple matter to look at the entire panel board, and discern whether any section of the plant was running poorly. This was due to both the design of the instruments and the implementation of the alarms associated with the instruments. Instrumentation companies put a lot of effort into the design and individual layout of the instruments they manufactured. To do this they employed behavioral psychology practices which revealed how much information a human being could collect in a quick glance. More complex plants had more complex panel boards, and therefore often more human operators or controllers.

Thus, in the early days of panel board systems, alarms were regulated by both real estate, and cost. In essence, they were limited by the amount of available board space, and the cost of running wiring, and hooking up an annunciator (horn), indicator (light) and switches to flip to acknowledge, and clear a resolved alarm. It was often the case that if you wanted a new alarm, you had to decide which old one to give up.

As technology developed, the control system and control methods were tasked to continue to advance a higher degree of plant automation with each passing year. Highly complex material processing called for highly complex control methodologies. Also, global competition pushed manufacturing operations to increase production while using less energy, and producing less waste. In the days of the panel boards, a special kind of engineer was required to understand a combination of the electronic equipment associated with process measurement and control, the control algorithms necessary to control the process (PID basics), and the actual process that was being utilized to make the products.

Around the mid 80's, we entered the digital revolution. Distributed control systems (DCS) were a boon to the industry. The engineer could now control the process without having to understand the equipment necessary to perform the control functions. Panel boards were no longer required, because all of the information that once came across analog instruments could be digitized, stuffed into a computer and manipulated to achieve the same control actions once performed with amplifiers and potentiometers.

As a side effect, that also meant that alarms were easy and cheap to configure and deploy. You simply typed in a location, a value to alarm on and set it to active. The unintended result was that soon people alarmed everything. Initial installers set an alarm at 80% and 20% of the operating range of any variable just as a habit. One other unfortunate part of the digital revolution was that what once covered several square yards of real estate, now had to be fit into a 17 inch computer monitor. Multiple pages of information was thus employed to replicate the information on the replaced panel board. Alarms were utilized to tell an operator to go look at a page he was not viewing.

Alarms were used to tell an operator that a tank was filling. Every mistake made in operations usually resulted in a new alarm. With the implementation of the OSHA 1910 regulations, HAZOPS studies usually requested several new alarms. Alarms were everywhere. Incidents began to accrue as a combination of too much data collided with too little useful information.

Alarm Management History

Recognizing that alarms were becoming a problem, industrial control system users banded together and formed the Alarm Management Task Force, which was a customer advisory board led by Honeywell in 1990. The AMTF included participants from chemical, petrochemical, and refining operations. They gathered and wrote a document on the issues associated with alarm management. This group quickly realized that alarm problems were simply a subset of a larger problem, and formed the Abnormal Situation Management Consortium (ASM is a registered trademeark of Honeywell).

The ASM Consortium developed a research proposal and was granted funding from the National Institute of Standards and Technology (NIST) in 1994. The focus of this work was addressing the complex human-system interaction and factors that influence successful performance for process operators. Automation solutions have often been developed without consideration of the human that needs to interact with the solution. In particular, alarms are intended to improve situation awareness for the control room operator, but a poorly configured alarm system does not achieve this goal.

The ASM Consortium has produced documents on best practices in alarm management, as well as operator situation awareness, operator effectiveness, and other operator-oriented issues. These documents were originally for ASM Consortium members only, but the ASMC has recently offered these documents publicly.

The ASM consortium also parcipated in development of an alarm management guideline published by the Engineering Equipment & Materials Users' Association (EEMUA) in the UK. The ASM Consortium provided data from their member companies, and contributed to the editing of the guideline. The result is EEMUA 191 "Alarm Systems- A Guide to Design, Management and Procurement".

Several institutions and societies are producing standards on alarm management to assist their members in the best practices use of alarms in industrial manufacturing systems. Among them are the ISA (ISA SP-18), API (API 1167) and NAMUR (Namur NA 102). Several companies also offer software packages to assist users in dealing with alarm management issues. Among them are DCS manufacturing companies, and third-party vendors who offer add-on systems.

Concepts

The fundamental purpose of alarm annunciation is to alert the operator to deviations from normal operating conditions, i.e. abnormal operating situations. The ultimate objective is to prevent, or at least minimize, physical and economic loss through operator intervention in response to the condition that was alarmed. For most digital control system users, losses can result from situations that threaten environmental safety, personnel safety, equipment integrity, economy of operation, and product quality control as well as plant throughput. A key factor in operator response effectiveness is the speed and accuracy with which the operator can identify the alarms that require immediate action.

By default, the assignment of alarm trip points and alarm priorities constitute basic alarm management. Each individual alarm is designed to provide an alert when that process indication deviates from normal. The main problem with basic alarm management is that these features are static. The resultant alarm annunciation does not respond to changes in the mode of operation or the operating conditions.

When a major piece of process equipment like a charge pump, compressor, or fired heater shuts down, many alarms become unnecessary. These alarms are no longer independent exceptions from normal operation. They indicate, in that situation, secondary, noncritical effects and no longer provide the operator with important information. Similarly, during start-up or shutdown of a process unit, many alarms are not meaningful. This is often the case because the static alarm conditions conflict with the required operating criteria for start-up and shutdown.

In all cases of major equipment failure, startups, and shutdowns, the operator must search alarm annunciation displays and analyze which alarms are significant. This wastes valuable time when the operator needs to make important operating decisions and take swift action. If the resultant flood of alarms becomes too great for the operator to comprehend, then the basic alarm management system has failed as a system that allows the operator to respond quickly and accurately to the alarms that require immediate action. In such cases, the operator has virtually no chance to minimize, let alone prevent, a significant loss.

In short, one needs to extend the objectives of alarm management beyond the basic level. It is not sufficient to utilize multiple priority levels because priority itself is often dynamic. Likewise, alarm disabling based on unit association or suppressing audible annunciation based on priority do not provide dynamic, selective alarm annunciation. The solution must be an alarm management system that can dynamically filter the process alarms based on the current plant operation and conditions so that only the currently significant alarms are annunciated.

The fundamental purpose of dynamic alarm annunciation is to alert the operator to relevant abnormal operating situations. They include situations that have a necessary or possible operator response to insure:

- Personnel and Environmental Safety,
- Equipment Integrity,
- Product Quality Control.

The ultimate objectives are no different than the previous basic alarm annunciation management objectives. Dynamic alarm annunciation management focuses the operator's attention by eliminating extraneous alarms, providing better recognition of critical problems, and insuring swifter, more accurate operator response.

The Need for Alarm Management

Alarm management is usually necessary in a process manufacturing environment that is controlled by an operator using a control system, such as a DCS or a programmable logic controller (PLC). Such a system may have hundreds of individual alarms that up until very recently have probably been designed with only limited consideration of other alarms in the system. Since humans can only do one thing at a time and can pay attention to a limited number of things at a time, there needs to be a way to ensure that alarms are presented at a rate that can be assimilated by a human operator, particularly when the plant is upset or in an unusual condition.

Alarms also need to be capable of directing the operator's attention to the most important problem that he or she needs to act upon, using a priority to indicate degree of importance or rank, for instance. A good example of this problem is from the old US sitcom *MASH*. A common scene was Radar O'Reilly slipping in a requisition for something that Hawkeye wanted in the stack of papers for Colonel Potter to sign. In much the same way, if alarms were unprioritized, the important ones can be mixed in with lower value nuisance ones.

Some Improvement Methods

The techniques for achieving rate reduction range from the extremely simple ones of reducing nuisance and low value alarms to redesigning the alarm system in a holistic way that considers the relationships among individual alarms.

Nuisance Reduction

The first step in a continuous improvement program is often to measure alarm rate, and resolve any chronic problems such as alarms that have no use (often described as one that does not require the operator to take an action). Note that the alarm rate, as measured by the alarms in a journal, is not necessarily the alarm rate seen by operators. This is because a chattering alarm will not update an unacknowledged alarm annunciator (and therefore looks like a single alarm to an operator), but will show up multiple times in a journal.

Design Guide

This step involves documenting the methodology or philosophy of how to design alarms. It can include things such as what to alarm, standards for alarm annunciation and text messages, how the operator will interact with the alarms, etc.

Documentation and Rationalization

This phase is a detailed review of all alarms to document their design purpose, and to ensure that they are selected and set properly and meet the design criteria. Ideally this stage will result in a reduction of alarms, but doesn't always.

Advanced Methods

The above steps will often still fail to prevent an alarm flood in an operational upset, so advanced methods such as alarm suppression under certain circumstances are then necessary. As an example, shutting down a pump will always cause a low flow alarm on the pump outlet flow, so the low flow alarm may be suppressed if the pump was shut down since it adds no value for the operator, because he or she already knows it was caused by the pump being shutdown. This technique can of course get very complicated and requires considerable care in design. In the above case for instance, it can be argued that the low flow alarm does add value as it confirms to the operator that the pump has indeed stopped.

Alarm management becomes more and more necessary as the complexity and size of manufacturing systems increases. A lot of the need for alarm management also arises because alarms can be configured on a DCS at nearly zero incremental cost, whereas in the past on physical control panel systems that consisted of individual pneumatic or electronic analog instruments, each alarm required expenditure and control panel real estate, so more thought usually went into the need for an alarm. Numerous disasters such as Three Mile Island and the Chernobyl accident have established a clear need for alarm management.

The Seven Steps to Alarm Management

Step 1: Create and adopt an alarm philosophy

A comprehensive design and guideline document that makes it clear "exactly how to do alarms right."

Step 2: Alarm performance benchmarking

Analyze the alarm system to determine its strengths and deficiencies, and effectively map out a practical solution to improve it.

Step 3: "Bad actor" alarm resolution

From experience, it is known that around half of the entire alarm load usually comes from a relatively few alarms. The methods for making them work properly are documented, and can be applied with minimum effort and maximum performance improvement.

Step 4: Alarm documentation and rationalization (D&R)

A full overhaul of the alarm system to ensure that each alarm complies with the alarm philosophy and the principles of good alarm management.

Step 5: Alarm system audit and enforcement

DCS alarm systems are notoriously easy to change and generally lack proper security. Methods are needed to ensure that the alarm system does not drift from its rationalized state.

Step 6: Real-time alarm management

More advanced alarm management techniques are often needed to ensure that the alarm system properly supports, rather than hinders, the operator in all operating scenarios. These include Alarm Shelving, State-Based Alarming, and Alarm Flood Suppression technologies.

Step 7: Control and maintain alarm system performance

Proper management of change and longer term analysis and KPI monitoring are needed, to ensure that the gains that have been achieved from performing the steps above do not dwindle away over time. Otherwise they will; the principle of "entropy" definitely applies to an alarm system.

Handling of Drunkard Guest

One of Mark Barnes's most memorable alcohol-fueled security incidents took place during a convention of 300 or so lawyers at the Kiawah Island Golf Resort in South Carolina. Barnes, the former director of safety and security, was on patrol with one of his staff when he received a report of a stolen "people mover," an oversized golf cart that holds six to eight people. When Barnes caught up with the cart, which was careening down the middle of a parkway, it was slightly over capacitya'a dozen or so lawyers were hanging off it.

After pulling the cart over, the driver, who obviously shouldn't have been behind the wheel of any vehicle, even a low-powered one, began rifling his hands around the dashboard, muttering, "I can't find the registration for this thing."

Dealing with drunk patrons in a hotel or resort takes more finesse than, say, bouncing someone out of a sleazy dive on 25-cent-beer night. Barnes agreed to provide some tips on dealing with the tipsy.

First, be prepared. "Before it even gets to the point of having security intervene, make sure your managers, bartenders and servers are aware of the warning signs," says Barnes. He educates Kiawah's staff using TIPS (Training for Intervention Procedures, a national program to teach bartenders, servers, sellers and consumers how to prevent the misuse of alcohol). On a more macro level, Barnes advises always establishing a rapport with the guest group's meeting planner, to make sure that that person knows the bar hours, the rules of the hospitality suites and so on. He also suggests checking out each group's itinerary, to know what they are doing each day and night. For example, if they are heading off-island for dinner, it's likely some members of the group will return to the resort already liquored up.

When that happens, it's not unusual to find an exaggeratedly happy (or angry) guest who may either be quietly drunk or drunk and bothering others. Servers are trained to gently inform such a guest that he cannot order more alcohol but is welcome to coffee or a soft drink. If the guest doesn't take kindly to that suggestion, the server calls a manager, who tries to deal with the situation in as friendly a way as possible. If the guest becomes loud or confrontational, the manager then informs the guest that security is being called (which he may have done already).

"You don't want to throw the cuffs on them and arrest them."

When the security person arrives, he introduces himself in a friendly manner and invites the guest to join him in a conversation away from the bar area. He'll even ask the guest to bring along a friend (sober friends can help calm down the drunk).

"Once you've removed them from [the bar], once you walk them away, you want to get them out of there," says Barnes. The goal is to escort the guest to his or her room and station a security person outside for a half-hour or so to make sure the person stays put. For guests staying in a villa, Barnes always makes sure that at least two security staffers transport the person, just in case the guest later makes accusations of mistreatment. If the guest is female, Barnes sends along a female security staffer too.

Celebrities pose an added challenge. In such cases, says Barnes, it's best to involve one of the celebrity's friends.

"They'll respond more to the person that's their friend than [to] a manager or security person." For convention guests, he advises contacting the meeting planner to help intervene. "A lot of the time, the guest's job could be on the line," he says.

In a worst-case scenario, in which an inebriated guest has assaulted someone or damaged property, security immediately gets the person out of the area through a back way (a fire exit for example). "You don't want to throw the cuffs on them and arrest them [in the bar area]; you grab them carefully and get them out of sight of the public. Their pride kicks in if it's in public view, and they'll try to fight you," says Barnes. In cases like this, local law enforcement should be summoned.

Fractures and its Treatment

Children are constantly bumping and bruising themselves. All it takes is one fall too hard, and your child just might end up with a broken bone. One out of five people has a fracture at some point of time in their lives, and the maximum of these fractures occur during childhood. Here are some first aid tips, which you should memories, just to be on the safe side.

How can you tell if it's a fracture or a sprain?

The pain is less intensive in a sprain than in a fracture, but never make the mistake of underestimating your child's pain. It takes a doctor to differentiate between the two, which is why the same kind of first aid is administered in both cases.

What is a dislocation?

A dislocation is when the bone has come out from the socket. This also results in acute pain, swelling, an inability to carry any weight and an inability to move the injured limb. The first aid administered in case of a dislocation is also the same.

Fractures are of two kinds:

Hairline fracture

A hairline fracture is just when the bone gets a CRACK that goes through it. Such fracture still cause immense pain, but at least chances of an operation are less.

Compound fracture

A compound fracture is one in which the bone completely breaks apart pops out through the skin. Ouch! This is the worst kind, and it may result in loss of blood as well.

If your child has had a bad fall, and you feel it may be a fracture, you should call a doctor, preferably an orthopedic surgeon, immediately. Here's what you can do by way of administering first aid.

Do NOT move the injured limb

The first step to be taken is to immobilize the limb. It should not be moved at all. Use any handy material to immobilize the limb. You could use a magazine or newspaper for support, and make a sling with the help of some cloth, a rope or shoelaces.

Leg Fracture

If your child has fractured his leg, carefully straighten it out. Call for an ambulance and in the meantime, secure the leg so it doesn't move. Apply two splints, one on the inner leg from the foot to the inner thigh, and the other, on the outside, from the foot to the armpit. Secure the splints well. Do NOT move your child until his leg has been completely immobilized. You could even tie both legs together for added support.

Hand Fracture

The hand should be moved to a 90-degree angle and kept close to the chest. It should be immobilized in this position. Move the hand as gently as possible, and if the pain is too intense, do not move it at all.

Bleeding

If your child is bleeding, you should treat the bleeding first. Stop the bleeding by first cleaning it carefully with an antiseptic, and then by applying a sterile dressing. Do not bandage tightly over the injury site. Apply a clean dressing gently over the wound.

Remember

Keep RICE in mind, as a first aid treatment for all fractures, sprains and dislocations. RICE stands for Rest, Ice, Compression and Elevation.

Rest

Give plenty of rest to the immobilsed limb. Move it as little as possible so that there is no strain.

Ice

Apply ice to the injured area. No heat treatment or massage should be given. Use an ice pack or wrap up some ice cubes in a damp towel and apply it to the injured area. You could also use anything frozen such as a packet of frozen peas.

Do not massage the injured area, and don't apply any ointments like Iodex.

Compression

Wrap up the injured area with a crepe bandage if possible, or use any clean, fresh cloth available. Wrap it as tight as is comfortable. However, ask the doctor before bandaging the area. This will relieve the pain somewhat.

Elevation

The injured limb should preferably be raised above the level of the heart. This could be done with the help of a pillow while sleeping.

Wounds and Hemorrhage

Wound is a break in the continuity of a tissue of the body either internal or external.

Classification of Wounds

1. Closed wound

Causes:

- Blunt object that may result in contusion or bruises
- Application of external forces

Signs and Symptoms

- Pain and tenderness
- Swelling
- Discoloration
- Hematoma
- Uncontrolled restlessness
- Thirst
- Symptoms of shock
- Vomiting or cough-up blood
- Passage of blood in the urine or feces
- Sign of blood along mouth, nose and ear canal

First Aid Management

- I- Iced application
- C- Compression
- E- Elevation
- S- Splinting

2. Open Wound- a break in the skin or mucous membrane; or the protective layer is damage.

Dangers

- Hemorrhage
- Infection
- Shock

Kinds of Bleeding

- Arterial bleeding
- Venous bleeding
- Capillary bleeding

First Aid Management

- C- Control bleeding
- C- Cover the wound
- C- Care for shock
- C- Consult or refer to physician

Home Care (Wounds with bleeding not severe)

- Clean the wound with soap and water.
- Apply mild antiseptics.
- Cover wounds with dressing and bandage.

Reminders:

1. All wounds must be thoroughly inspected and covered with a dry dressing to control bleeding and prevent further contamination.
2. Once bleeding is controlled by compression, the limb should be splinted to further control bleeding, stabilize the injured part, miniinize the victim's pain and facilitate the patient's transport to the hospital.
3. As with closed soft tissue injuries, the injured part should be elevated to just above the level of the victim's heart to minimize severity.
4. Amputated body parts should be saved, wrapped in a dry gauze, placed in a plastic bag, kept cool, and transported with the patient.
5. Don't induce further bleeding to clean the wound.
6. Don't use absorbent cottom as a dressing.

Dressings and Bandages

A bandage is a piece of material used either to support a medical device such as a dressing or splint, or on its own to provide support to the body, they can also be used to restrict a part of the body. During heavy bleeding or following a poisonous bite it is important to slow the flow of blood, tight bandages accomplish this task very well. Bandages are available in a wide range of types, from generic cloth strips, to specialized shaped bandages designed for a specific limb or part of the body, although bandages can often be improvised as the situation demands, using clothing, blankets or other material. In colloquial American English, the word "bandage" is often used to mean a dressing, which is used directly on a wound, whereas a bandage is technically only used to support a dressing, and not directly on a wound.

Gauze Bandage

The most common type of bandage is the gauze bandage, a simple woven strip of material, or a woven strip of material with a Telfa absorbent barrier to prevent adhering to wounds, which can come in any number of widths and lengths. A gauze bandage can be used for almost any bandage application, including holding a dressing in place.

Compression Bandage

The term 'compression bandage' describes a wide variety of bandages with many different applications.

Short stretch compression bandages are applied to a limb (usually for treatment of lymphedema or venous ulcers). This type of bandage that is capable of shortening around the limb after application and is therefore not exerting ever-increasing pressure during inactivity. This dynamic is called resting pressure and is considered safe and comfortable for long-term treatment. Conversely, the stability of the bandage creates a very high resistance to stretch when pressure is applied through internal muscle contraction and joint movement. This force is called working pressure.

Long stretch compression bandages have long stretch properties, meaning their high compressive power can be easily adjusted. However, they also have a very high resting pressure and must be removed at night or if the patient is in a resting position.

Triangular Bandage

Also known as a cravat bandage, a triangular bandage is a piece of cloth cut into a right-angled triangle, and often provided with safety pins to secure it in place. It can be used fully unrolled as a sling, folded as a normal bandage, or for specialized applications, as on the head. One advantage of this type of Bandage is that it can be makeshift and made from a fabric scrap or a piece of a t-shirt. The Boy Scouts popularized use of this bandage in many of their first aid lessons. They carry a cravat bandage with their uniform in the form of a neckerchief. When used to make a sling, for humerus or forearm fractures, it is best to tie the middle point. This goes under the elbow to help secure and restrict further movement of the arm. Next, take one of the long ends of the triangle bandage and tuck it under the arm.

Then pull it over the injured shoulder and behind the neck. The other long end should be placed over the opposite should and tied with the other end on the side of the neck (not the back of the neck because of the pressure it places on it). Make sure the sling covers the arm from the elbow to or a little beyond the hand. To be nice you can also place something round in their hand and place in functioning position.

Tube Bandage

A tube bandage is applied using an applicator, and is woven in a continuous circle. It is used to hold dressings or splints on to limbs, or to provide support to sprains and strains, and it stops the bleeding.

CISO/CSO Security- Securing the Hospitality Industry... What's the Hold-up?

With so much recent attention on the exploitation of major hotel and resort chains, we felt that we should take a closer look at the causes and potential solutions to the problem. We have had the opportunity to work with several resorts over the last 12 months and wanted to share some distinct commonalities related to security that we experienced. The objective of this article is to reveal the issues and present practical solutions to address them.

Issues and Concerns

The goal of almost any hotelier is to provide the best experience possible for their guests; from the moment they arrive to their time of departure. This is the overriding concern that drives the hospitality industry. Whether it is a speedy check-in, prompt and courteous delivery of room service, or simply the emptying of ash trays; everything is guest-centric with an emphasis on the speed and quality of delivery. This issue affects security in that the definition of this function, as understood by many within the industry, is mutually exclusive to fulfilling this primary objective. Many believe that security safeguards slow down the ability of the hotel staff to provide the aforementioned service.

The next issue is the industry specific applications that are available to support the resort in delivering service. Hotel specific applications such as property management, point of sale, spa, in room services, etc. are primarily produced by a small group of specialized product vendors that have access to a captive market. This has been primarily caused by the nature in which these various applications need to interact with each other at the resort to provide a seamless array of services to guests. Such specialty presents a barrier to entry for competition producing a limited number of vendors; many of which are not always motivated or capable to modernize their products with the inclusion of standard security controls. Additionally, many resorts highly customize these applications to provide their unique level of service making it difficult to upgrade their applications; even when the vendor has a new version.

Another factor with larger hospitality chains is the nature and structure of their information technology operations. The majority of IT operations are centralized with most of the critical technical functionality being housed at that one location. This functionality often includes e-mail, domain services, as well as the critical elements of hotel specific applications such as property management. With this centralized model, it is common for the majority of senior IT personnel to be congregated at the central location with more junior staff at each resort location.

The problem with this arrangement is that there are still critical systems and functions that are operated at the local resort level. The security of these items and the access they provide to sensitive data is usually left to junior IT personnel with little if any specific training in information security. This is compounded by the increase in the number of technical services that are offered to guests by most resorts. These items include services such as wireless internet, in-room account information systems, and robust business centers. Even when these systems are outsourced to third parties, which is common, their proximity to the resort and its infrastructure results in additional burden and risk to the local hotel network and support team. Lastly, many resorts do not have a structured security program with the associated policies and procedures that can be adhered to; leading these junior technicians and personnel to fend for themselves.

Under circumstances where a resort has a formal security program, they generally lack elements that would be required to have an affective security strategy; focusing on issues that are solely associated with the physical security. This returns us to the definition of security as understood by the hospitality industry. This limited view misses the three other required components to have a comprehensive security strategy: people, process, and technology.

The final issue that will complicate the ability of resorts to provide a secure environment is the increased technical capability of our society. This includes both the guests, as well as the perspective hacker community. The nature of business today mandates the use of technologies to extend the capabilities of the organization to anywhere that an employee travels. Internet connectivity is no longer considered a luxury, rather is an expectation of any business traveler within the United States. Nothing is worse for a resort than a bored business traveler, who has some technical capability, sitting in their room with a laptop. This circumstance will turn just about any of us to "The Dark Side." The other situation that is presented to resorts is the "Black Hat" Hacker.

Recent hacker conventions have focused on the lack of security within the hospitality space. It's no longer a secret, nor is it merely for a lark. This target has been identified as profitable and soft; low risk and high potential for reward. This is not the reputation that any industry needs!

What can be Done?

- The hospitality industry needs to understand that they have been targeted!
- Smaller hotels should employ a documented security strategy. Larger hotel chains need to develop a strategy along with a full security program to implement the

strategy that addresses risk reduction for people, process, technology, and facilities.

- Training & Awareness programs for all hotel employees.
- Take the time to perform a risk assessment prior to the deployment of any new technology.
- Hotels need to develop their own application security requirements and insist that the specialized software vendors meet them.
- Hotels need to stop treating back-office operations as an afterthought.
- Shorten the service life of antiquated hardware and software.

Conclusion

The exploitation of information systems for the hospitality industry has been highly prevalent in recent news. Resort chains that are household names have had to report that thousands of their guest's personal information has been exposed unintentionally. Unfortunately, this trend will continue until the industry demonstrates that it is ready to address security seriously.

6

Hotel Safety and Security

Recent events have turned the hospitality industry's focus on safety and security issues. With large corporate customers stepping up their requirements in terms of employee safety and data protection, the industry as a whole is challenged to increase safety and security levels, without impacting their day to day operations, or the guests' experience.

Electronic Security

Intrusion Detection

Naivety and carelessness help burglars just as much as inadequate security measures. Therefore, protection must be both passive and active:

- Passive through mechanical protection equipment
- Active with an electronic alarm system

The additional observance of simple security rules and the necessary everyday prudence are another significant contribution to minimize risk. Optimum protection of people and buildings is based on the following four pillars:

- Prudence as free-of-charge protection
- Mechanical protection equipment as the first line of defense
- Electronic robbery and burglar alarm systems for the reliable detection of dangers
- Forwarding alarms for the immediate notification of personnel providing assistance

Access Control

In the open hotel environment, ensuring that the right people have access to the right areas is crucial to safeguard guests, staff and assets. At Siemens, we know that the future of a company is also a question of security technology and therefore, the right technology for access control. The aim is to qualify access authorization and, at the same time, flexibly adapt the authentication of persons to the individual corporate requirements, as well as to be able to individually configure access rights both geographically and chronologically.

The requirements mentioned can only be resolved with the aid of modern systems for access control. Therefore, open system solutions with flexible networks are required. They are only configured under consideration of the intended use of the building and the organization involved. Its special structures and the specific workflows also have an effect. Factors such as the size of the company, the number of people, doors, elevator and access gate control as well as additional functions also have to be taken into account.

Future-oriented solutions include not only the linking of business management applications, but also the integration of other security systems. When linked to the building management systems, the information can also be optimally used under energy performance aspects. Our products and systems provide high levels of security and convenience, offering freedom of movement in a secure environment everywhere they are installed.

The products and systems are flexible, scalable and easy to use. They meet customer needs that range from providing security at a single entry point to overcoming the security challenges faced by large multinational corporations with thousands of doors and cardholders at different locations around the world.

Video Surveillance

Video surveillance has a proven a key element of any modern security system, acting both as a deterrent and a valuable asset in post-event analysis.

In sophisticated security concepts, the video system provides the visual basis for decisions and plays a central role – in addition to real-time monitoring of critical areas – in the identification of persons with the aid of biometric processes, and in the detection of dangers. Communication between the video system and the control center is performed using TCP/IP via any Ethernet, ATM or TN network structure. In conjunction with a video web client, operation, control and access is possible from anywhere in the world.

Mobile video systems

Whether for the monitoring of external installations, live coordination of service personnel or the management of mobile business activities, the high-speed availability of data and images is a task performed by mobile multimedia monitoring systems. Numerous detectors and cameras are grouped around a mobile digital system that can store multimedia information and quickly pass this on via modern communication networks.

Stationary digital room surveillance

Stationary systems are used for specific room surveillance using the existing IT infrastructures. These systems detect changes and monitor various alarm zones. If an alarm is triggered, the video sequences are recorded digitally and forwarded to higher-level management systems.

Recording alarm situations

Video surveillance not only detects incidents, but documents the entire process when an incident occurs – from the recording of the video images, the transmission and storage of this information, the initiation of automatic measures through to centralized data evaluation and archiving.

Video Control Centers

Communication between the video system and the control center is performed using TCP/IP via any Ethernet, ATM or TN network structure. In conjunction with a video web client, operation, control and access is possible from anywhere in the world.

Fire Safety

Fire safety refers to precautions that are taken to prevent or reduce the likelihood of a fire that may result in death, injury, or property damage, alert those in a structure to the presence of a fire in the event one occurs, better enable those threatened by a fire to survive, or to reduce the damage caused by a fire. Fire safety measures include those that are planned during the construction of a building or implemented in structures that are already standing, and those that are taught to occupants of the building.

Threats to fire safety are referred to as *fire hazards*. A fire hazard may include a situation that increases the likelihood a fire may start or may impede escape in the event a fire occurs.

Fire safety is often a component of building safety. Those who inspect buildings for violations of the Fire Code and go into schools to educate children on Fire Safety topics are fire department members known as *fire prevention officers*. The Chief Fire Prevention Officer or Chief of Fire Prevention will normally train newcomers to the Fire Prevention Division and may also conduct inspections or make presentations.

Key elements of a fire safety policy:

- Building a facility in accordance with the version of the local building code
- Maintaining a facility and conducting yourself in accordance with the provisions of the fire code. This is based on the occupants and operators of the building being aware of the applicable regulations and advice.

Examples of these include:

- Not exceeding the maximum occupancy within any part of the building.
- Maintaining proper fire exits and proper exit signage (e.g., exit signs pointing to them that can function in a power failure)
- Placing and maintaining fire extinguishers in easily accessible places.
- Properly storing/using, hazardous materials that may be needed inside the building for storage or operational requirements (such as solvents in spray booths).
- Prohibiting flammable materials in certain areas of the facility.

- Periodically inspecting buildings for violations, issuing Orders To Comply and, potentially, prosecuting or closing buildings that are not in compliance, until the deficiencies are corrected or condemning it in extreme cases.
- Maintaining fire alarm systems for detection and warning of fire.
- Obtaining and maintaining a complete inventory of firestops.
- Ensuring that spray fireproofing remains undamaged.
- Maintaining a high level of training and awareness of occupants and users of the building to avoid obvious mistakes, such as the propping open of fire doors.
- Conduct fire drills at regular intervals throughout the year.

Common Fire Hazards

Some common fire hazards are:

- Electrical systems that are overloaded, resulting in hot wiring or connections, or failed components
- Combustible storage areas with insufficient protection
- Combustibles near equipment that generates heat, flame, or sparks
- Candles
- Smoking (Cigarettes, cigars, pipes, lighters, etc.)
- Equipment that generates heat and utilizes combustible materials
- Flammable liquids
- Fireplace chimneys not properly or regularly cleaned
- Cooking appliances - stoves, ovens
- Heating appliances - wood burning stoves, furnaces, boilers, portable heaters
- Electrical wiring in poor condition
- Batteries
- Personal ignition sources - matches, lighters
- Electronic and electrical equipment

- Exterior cooking equipment - BBQ
- Campfires

Fire Code

In America, the Fire code (also Fire prevention code or Fire safety code) is a model code adopted by the state or local jurisdiction and enforced by fire prevention officers within municipal fire departments. It is a set of rules prescribing minimum requirements to prevent fire and explosion hazards arising from storage, handling, or use of dangerous materials, or from other specific hazardous conditions. It complements the building code.

The fire code is aimed primarily at preventing fires, ensuring that necessary training and equipment will be on hand, and that the original design basis of the building, including the basic plan set out by the architect, is not compromised. The fire code also addresses inspection and maintenance requirements of various fire protection equipment in order to maintain optimal active fire protection and passive fire protection measures.

A typical fire safety code includes administrative sections about the rule-making and enforcement process, and substantive sections dealing with fire suppression equipment, particular hazards such as containers and transportation for combustible materials, and specific rules for hazardous occupancies, industrial processes, and exhibitions.

Sections may establish the requirements for obtaining permits and specific precautions required to remain in compliance with a permit. For example, a fireworks exhibition may require an application to be filed by a licensed pyrotechnician, providing the information necessary for the issuing authority to determine whether safety requirements can be met. Once a permit is issued, the same authority (or another delegated authority) may inspect the site and monitor safety during the exhibition, with the power to halt operations, when unapproved practices are seen or when unforeseen hazards arise.

List of Some Typical Fire and Explosion Issues in a Fire Code

- fireworks, explosives, mortars and cannons, model rockets (licenses for manufacture, storage, transportation, sale, use)

- certification for servicing, placement, and inspecting fire extinguishing equipment
- general storage and handling of flammable liquids, solids, gases (tanks, personnel training, markings, equipment)
- limitations on locations and quantities of flammables (e.g., 10 liters of gasoline inside a residential dwelling)
- specific uses and specific flammables (e.g., dry cleaning, gasoline distribution, explosive dusts, pesticides, space heaters, plastics manufacturing)
- permits and limitations in various building occupancies (assembly hall, hospital, school, theater, elderly care, child care, prs that require a smoke detector, sprinkler system, fire extinguisher, or other specific equipment or procedures
- removal of interior and exterior obstructions to emergency exits or firefighters and removal of hazardous materials
- permits and limitations in special outdoor applications (tents, asphalt kettles, bonfires, etc.)
- other hazards (flammable decorations, welding, smoking, bulk matches, tire yards)
- Electrical safety code
- Fuel gas code

Public Fire Safety Education

Fire prevention programs may include distribution of smoke detectors, visiting schools to review key topics with the students and implementing nationally recognized programs such as NFPAs "Risk Watch" & "Learn not to burn."

Other programs or props can be purchased by fire departments or community organizations. These are usually entertaining and designed to capture children's attention and relay important messages. Props include those that are mostly auditory, such as puppets & robots. The prop is visually stimulating but the safety message is only transmitted orally. Other props are more elaborate, access more senses and increase the learning factor. They mix audio messages and visual queues with hands-on interaction. Examples of these include mobile trailer safety houses and tabletop hazard house simulators.

All programs tend to mix messages of general injury prevention, safety, fire prevention and escape in case of fire. In most cases the fire department representative is regarded as the expert and is expected to present information in a manner that is appropriate for each age group.

Fire Educator Qualifications

The US industry standard that outlines the recommended qualifications for fire safety educators is NFPA 1035: Standard for Professional Qualifications for Public Fire and Life Safety Educator, 2005 Edition. This standard is currently being revised and the newest edition is slated for release in 2010. According to NFPA, 1035 specifically covers the requirements for Fire and Life Safety Educator Levels I, II, and III; Public Information Officer; and Juvenile Firesetter Intervention Specialist Levels I and II.

Target Audiences

According to the United States Fire Administration, the very young and the elderly are considered to be "at risk" populations. These groups represent approximately 33% of the population.

Importance of Fire Safety at Hotels

- When you hear the words fire and hotel you may not get concerned, for hotels rarely catch fire. That maybe be true, but when a fire does occur the results can be overwhelming.
- In the summer of 1997, a resort hotel caught fire resulting in the death of 91 employees and guests. It is speculated that the high death toll was caused by insufficient extinguishing equipment and the violation of basis life safety and fire protection principals.
- The fire originated in the hotel kitchen where a gas leak in an oven caused an explosion.
- Some reports indicate that even though smoke alarms and automatic sprinkler systems were installed, they failed to function or provide any warning. Guests found exit doors blocked and chained shut.

- The leading cause of death in fires is smoke inhalation, not contact with the fire.
- The importance of fire safety in a hotel environment can't be overstated. The lives of guests and employees are at stake and the stakes are high.

Basic Fire Prevention Precautions

Fire prevention starts with good housekeeping.

- Mechanical and electrical rooms should not be used as storage areas. The storage of combustible materials such as boxes, towels and paper and flammable liquids such as paint, solvents and fuels should be avoided.
- A clear zone of 36 inches should be maintained around all electrical and mechanical equipment at all times.
- Store rooms, linen rooms and janitor closets can get very messy if you don't clean them after each use. All trash, empty boxes, etc. should be removed daily.
- The storage of paper, boxes and other materials can result in a potential fire hazard. Be sure to keep the storage at least 18 inches below sprinkler heads.
- Never store oily rags in anything but a metal can with a metal lid. The reason behind this is spontaneous combustion can occur. If soiled rags are just thrown in a corner or put in a nonmetal container, these rags can catch on fire.
- All flammable liquids should be stored in their original or UL-approved containers. The containers should then be placed in a flammable liquid storage cabinet.
- Be sure that all containers are closed and labeled with the contents and appropriate labels.
- Obey all smoking policies; never smoke in unauthorized areas. There have been many deaths attributed to smoking materials catching other materials on fire.
- If you work in the laundry facility, it's important that lint traps are cleaned at least once per shift and they may have to be cleaned more often depending on the linen.

Greasy Kitchen Rags

- A large number of hotel fires are caused by greasy kitchen rags. A few simple procedures will prevent this from happening at your hotel.
- First, kitchen rags should only be washed in the morning. The kitchen should deliver the rags prior to the laundry facility closing; the rags should be then placed in a bucket of degreaser and soaked overnight.
- In the morning the rags should be washed on the appropriate cycle, when complete, inspect them to ensure there is not a large build up of grease.
- Dry the linens; be sure that the kitchen rags complete the cool down cycle. Immediately remove and inspect the linens to be sure they have cooled, if not, lay them out on the table until all heat has dissipated.

Preventing Kitchen Fires

Kitchen hoods are another area where fire may occur. Grease-laden vapors rise from the cook line and are caught in the hood by filters or wash water. The residue left behind from these vapors is extremely flammable.

- The hood should be wiped out nightly to prevent the build up of grease; filters should be removed and washed at least weekly. This may need to be done as often as daily, depending on the type of kitchen equipment being used and how busy the kitchen is.
- The hood and duct work must be professionally cleaned at least every three months.
- Be sure that deep fat fryers are separated from open flame equipment by either distance or a baffle. Following these simple procedures will greatly reduce the chances that a fire will occur in your kitchen.

Emergency Planning

- To avoid being unprepared for an emergency, fire drills must be practiced. It requires time and effort, but it is a necessity.
- If you are not familiar with your responsibilities during a fire, please be sure to ask your supervisor.

- Emergency exits are identified throughout the hotel; everyone sees them but after awhile you don't pay any attention to them. Don't let these areas become a convenient storage area. In case of an emergency, this may be your only way to safety. Never block or stack materials in front of exit doors.
- Be familiar with your emergency evacuation plan, how and when to sound the alarm and know your evacuation routes and rally points.
- A rally point is designated outside the building, away from the building. The person in charge of this area will take a roll call and if someone is missing the person in charge can notify fire department officials that someone is missing and may still be in the building. These rallying points are very important so make sure you know where they are and how to get there.
- Do you know how to use fire extinguishers? Everyone says yes, but do they really know how to use an extinguisher? Have you ever discharged an extinguisher?
- The point we want to make here is not everyone is trained to use the fire extinguisher, but they should be. There are certain procedures that should be followed because if you do it wrong, it could be worse then not doing it at all.

Warning Systems

- When we think of early warnings we think alarms. Sometimes there are false alarms; sometimes it's the real thing. Every alarm should be taken seriously and action taken as require in your hotel policies and procedures.
- A manual pull station is designed to be activated when fire or smoke is spotted. It will activate the hotel fire alarm system and initiate the fire emergency procedures. You should know that manual pull stations are located next to every exit door.
- Smoke and heat detectors are early warning devices. Smoke alarms will activate when a certain amount of smoke enters the device.

- Heat detectors work a bit differently. They are activated by heat. At predetermined temperatures these detectors will sound an alarm.
- People hearing these alarms can't tell if they were activated by smoke or heat but it makes no difference—it's an early warning of the potential of a fire. There may be bells, horns, voice activation messages, again, all warning signs that something's wrong and action is required.
- Strobe lights are designed to warn hearing impaired people of possible fire or other emergency.

Fire Extinguishing Systems

- Automatic sprinkler systems are a bit different. These are pipes full of water with a temperature activation head. This means that if a fire reaches a predetermined temperature near a sprinkler head, the sprinklers fusible link will melt allowing the water to flow and extinguish the fire.
- In computer rooms, you may have a carbon dioxide system that floods the room with carbon dioxide. If this type of fire extinguisher system is activated, you should immediately leave the area.
- One of the ways a carbon dioxide system or fire extinguisher puts out a fire is to remove oxygen from the fire; it also reduces the amount of oxygen you have for breathing.

Responding to a Fire

- One of the most important rules about life safety is to honor all alarms. Don't think they are all false alarms, respond and take action, know what to do and when to do it.
- Reporting fires is also an important responsibility. In the event that you discover a fire, be sure to follow these procedures.
- First, sound the alarm by activating the manual pull station or break glass station; this will start the evacuation process.

- Second, call the hotel operator and report the exact location of the fire such as; third floor electrical room. Be specific.
- Third, if it's safe to do so, you can use a fire extinguisher to extinguish the fire. If you're in doubt, leave the firefighting to the professionals.
- The most important thing is life safety, so don't jeopardize your life or other people's lives by trying to extinguish a fire.
- Fourth, seal off the area and evacuate. Be sure to give proper directions.

Checking Equipment for Damage

- You should make it a habit everyday to look for signs of damaged or non-functioning life safety or fire protection devices.
- Are fire extinguishers in their proper places?
- Have bells, horns, sprinkler valves, pull stations, fire hoses or other items been damaged or tampered with?
- Are all of the fire doors closing and latching properly? It's your job to report damaged items so they can be repaired.
- It's an important job; it can be life or death in case of an emergency.

Smoke Inhalation

- As we said earlier smoke inhalation is the leading cause of death in fires; when a fire occurs, smoke rises. That's why you always hear safety professionals tell you to drop to the floor to find your way out of a smoke filled room.
- Don't be mistaken and believe that if you get down low the smoke won't affect you; that's not the case. In the early stages of a fire the smoke rises and you're able to see and breathe better near the floor, but eventually the smoke will fill the entire room.

Keeping Doors & Openings Closed

- Another prevention technique is to make sure all vertical

openings are closed and locked. This could be a laundry or trash shoot.

- Fire and smoke rises and if you have an open vent or opening, the fire is going to spread faster through that opening. Be sure all unprotected openings are closed, latched and locked.
- Generally, shoot doors are always kept closed. In some cases these shoot doors remain open, but they have a fusible link just like the sprinkler.
- If a fire melts the fusible link the door is automatically closed. It's a good idea to check these periodically to make sure they're in working condition.
- The same thing applies to electrical and pipe chase ways. The electrical wiring in pipes often run from floor to floor in an area called a chase way. The openings should be sealed with fire resistance insulation to prevent the transmission of smoke between floors. If you discover an unprotected opening, report it to engineering to be repaired.
- Atriums and open stairwells can be fire hazards for the very same reason. A small fire can easily be spread smoke throughout the stairwell or to multiply floors with an atrium. Many of these areas are equipped with smoke doors that close and seal off the area only when the fire alarm is activated.
- To protect the integrity of the exit stairwell, make sure all enclosed stairwell doors are self-closing and self-latching. These doors should never be propped open; it's a fire hazard to keep them open.

Fire, Smoke & Guest Doors

- Fire doors must always remain closed and latched, not locked but latched. This is of paramount importance. You don't want the doors to remain open and fill the stairways with smoke.
- Again, it's important to report any damage. This includes making sure fire doors operate as intended.
- Never allow storage or materials to be stacked near emergency exits or fire doors.

- In some corridors, additional doors which normally remain open and have been installed; these doors are called smoke doors and are designed to close automatically when the alarm sounds.
- They will compartmentalize the floor thereby helping to prevent the spread of smoke. These doors should be in good repair and should not be blocked open.
- Guest room doors are generally self-closing and self-latching, they're designed for that.
- It's everyone's job to report any door or other similar equipment that doesn't work properly.
- In case of fire, there may be smoke and fire dampers in specific parts of the building. You should be trained to identify these and to know how they operate. Again, make sure they're in serviceable condition.

Stairwell Pressurization & Corridor Egress

- Another safety factor is stairwell pressurization. Your hotel may be equipped with fans that are designed to create a positive pressure in stairwells which will prevent smoke from entering the stairwell. The pressurization will only function when the fire alarm is activated.
- When we discuss proper egress, we are talking about the method you use to exit the building. There should never be any storage in hotel corridors that impedes proper egress.
- There should never be any chairs or tables stored or placed in corridors; exit doors must be maintained in a clear and unobstructed manner—no storage, no chairs, no tables.
- Never lock or chain any emergency exit. This is a felony in almost every state and in many countries around the world. If you're having a security problem, report it to security or your manager but never lock or chain emergency exit doors.
- Of course, this applied to stairwells and other means of egress. Don't block emergency exits.

Preparing for an Emergency

Take a minute to think about an emergency. If you store materials in a stairwell or corridor, it may not be a problem for one or two people to exit, but what if fifty or one hundred people are trying to get out? That storage of material can cause people to panic and not get out.

- How about drapery and other materials? Most of these materials are combustible and can burn easily or melt and produce toxic smoke. Never place combustible materials in stairwells.
- Think about what happens in an emergency and prepare for it.
- Certainly, all exits must be clearly marked, lighted or illuminated. In case of an emergency, these will be your life line to safety.
- Report any damaged or non-functioning units so they can quickly be repaired or replaced. Check your signs. Are they in their proper place?
- Do arrows point the proper direction? In an emergency situation an arrow which directs someone away from an exit could mean much more than an inconvenience.
- Are emergency light provided? In case of an emergency and the hotel loses power will emergency lights come on and illuminate emergency exits and corridors?
- Emergency lights and exits should be inspected at least monthly; emergency generators should also be checked and tested frequently.

Risk Management

Risk management is the identification, assessment, and prioritization of risks (defined in ISO 31000 as *the effect of uncertainty on objectives*, whether positive or negative) followed by coordinated and economical application of resources to minimize, monitor, and control the probability and/or impact of unfortunate events or to maximize the realization of opportunities. Risks can come from uncertainty in financial markets, project failures (at any phase in development, production, or sustainment life-cycles), legal liabilities, credit risk, accidents, natural causes and disasters as well as deliberate attack from an adversary or events of uncertain root-cause. Several risk management standards have been developed including the Project Management Institute, the National Institute of Science and Technology, actuarial societies, and ISO standards.

Methods, definitions and goals vary widely according to whether the risk management method is in the context of project management, security, engineering, industrial processes, financial portfolios, actuarial assessments, or public health and safety.

The strategies to manage risk include transferring the risk to another party, avoiding the risk, reducing the negative effect or probability of the risk, ov even accepting some or all of the consequences of a particular risk.

Certain aspects of many of the risk management standards have come under criticism for having no measurable improvement on risk, whether the confidence in estimates and decisions seem to increase.

In ideal risk management, a prioritization process is followed whereby the risks with the greatest loss and the greatest probability of occurring are handled first, and risks with lower probability of occurrence and lower loss are handled in descending order. In practice the process can be very difficult, and balancing between risks with a high probability of occurrence but lower loss versus a risk with high loss but lower probability of occurrence can often be mishandled.

Intangible risk management identifies a new type of a risk that has a 100% probability of occurring but is ignored by the organization due to a lack of identification ability. For example, when deficient knowledge is applied to a situation, a knowledge risk materializes. Relationship risk appears when ineffective collaboration occurs.

Process-engagement risk may be an issue when ineffective operational procedures are applied. These risks directly reduce the productivity of knowledge workers, decrease cost effectiveness, profitability, service, quality, reputation, brand value, and earnings quality. Intangible risk management allows risk management to create immediate value from the identification and reduction of risks that reduce productivity.

Risk management also faces difficulties in allocating resources. This is the idea of opportunity cost. Resources spent on risk management could have been spent on more profitable activities. Again, ideal risk management minimizes spending and minimizes the negative effects of risks.

Method

For the most part, these methods consist of the following elements, performed, more or less, in the following order.

1. identify, characterize, and assess threats
2. assess the vulnerability of critical assets to specific threats
3. determine the risk (i.e. the expected consequences of specific types of attacks on specific assets)
4. identify ways to reduce those risks
5. prioritize risk reduction measures based on a strategy

Principles of Risk Management

The International Organization for Standardization (ISO) identifies the following principles of risk management:

Risk management should:

- create value
- be an integral part of organizational processes
- be part of decision making
- explicitly address uncertainty and assumptions
- be systematic and structured
- be based on the best available information
- be tailorable
- take into account human factors
- be transparent and inclusive
- be dynamic, iterative and responsive to change
- be capable of continual improvement and enhancement

Process

According to the standard ISO 31000 "Risk management—Principles and guidelines on implementation," the process of risk management consists of several steps as follows:

Establishing the Context

Establishing the context involves:

1. Identification of risk in a selected domain of interest
2. Planning the remainder of the process.
3. Mapping out the following:
   - o the social scope of risk management
   - o the identity and objectives of stakeholders
   - o the basis upon which risks will be evaluated, constraints.
4. Defining a framework for the activity and an agenda for identification.
5. Developing an analysis of risks involved in the process.
6. Mitigation or Solution of risks using available technological, human and organizational resources.

Identification

After establishing the context, the next step in the process of managing risk is to identify potential risks. Risks are about events that, when triggered, cause problems. Hence, risk identification can start with the source of problems, or with the problem itself.

- Source analysis Risk sources may be internal or external to the system that is the target of risk management. Examples of risk sources are: stakeholders of a project, employees of a company or the weather over an airport.
- Problem analysis Risks are related to identified threats. For example: the threat of losing money, the threat of abuse of privacy information or the threat of accidents and casualties. The threats may exist with various entities, most important with shareholders, customers and legislative bodies such as the government.

When either source or problem is known, the events that a source may trigger or the events that can lead to a problem can be investigated. For example: stakeholders withdrawing during a project may endanger funding of the project; privacy information may be stolen by employees even within a closed network; lightning striking an aircraft during takeoff may make all people on board immediate casualties.

The chosen method of identifying risks may depend on culture, industry practice and compliance. The identification methods are formed by templates or the development of templates for identifying source, problem or event. Common risk identification methods are:

- *Objectives-based risk identification:* Organizations and project teams have objectives. Any event that may endanger achieving an objective partly or completely is identified as risk.
- *Scenario-based risk identification:* In scenario analysis different scenarios are created. The scenarios may be the alternative ways to achieve an objective, or an analysis of the interaction of forces in, for example, a market or battle. Any event that triggers an undesired scenario alternative is identified as risk - see Futures Studies for methodology used by Futurists.
- *Taxonomy-based risk identification:* The taxonomy in taxonomy-based risk identification is a breakdown of possible risk sources. Based on the taxonomy and knowledge of best practices, a questionnaire is compiled. The answers to the questions reveal risks.
- *Common-risk checking:* In several industries, lists with known risks are available. Each risk in the list can be checked for application to a particular situation.
- *Risk charting:* This method combines the above approaches by listing resources at risk, threats to those resources, modifying factors which may increase or decrease the risk and consequences it is wished to avoid. Creating a matrix under these headings enables a variety of approaches. One can begin with resources and consider the threats they are exposed to and the consequences of each. Alternatively one can start with the threats and examine which resources they would affect, or one can begin with the consequences and determine which combination of threats and resources would be involved to bring them about.

Assessment

Once risks have been identified, they must then be assessed as to their potential severity of impact (generally a negative impact, such as damage or loss) and to the probability of occurrence. These quantities can be either simple to measure, in the case of the value of a lost building, or impossible to know for sure in the case of the probability of an unlikely event occurring. Therefore, in the assessment process it is critical to make the best educated decisions in order to properly prioritize the implementation of the risk management plan.

Even a short-term positive improvement can have long-term negative impacts. Take the "turnpike" example. A highway is widened to allow more traffic. More traffic capacity leads to greater development in the areas surrounding the improved traffic capacity.

Over time, traffic thereby increases to fill available capacity. Turnpikes thereby need to be expanded in a seemingly endless cycles. There are many other engineering examples where expanded capacity (to do any function) is soon filled by increased demand. Since expansion comes at a cost, the resulting growth could become unsustainable without forecasting and management.

The fundamental difficulty in risk assessment is determining the rate of occurrence since statistical information is not available on all kinds of past incidents. Furthermore, evaluating the severity of the consequences (impact) is often quite difficult for intangible assets. Asset valuation is another question that needs to be addressed.

Thus, best educated opinions and available statistics are the primary sources of information. Nevertheless, risk assessment should produce such information for the management of the organization that the primary risks are easy to understand and that the risk management decisions may be prioritized. Thus, there have been several theories and attempts to quantify risks. Numerous different risk formulae exist, but perhaps the most widely accepted formula for risk quantification is:

> *Rate (or probability) of occurrence multiplied by the impact of the event equals risk magnitude*

Composite Risk Index

The above formula can also be re-written in terms of a Composite Risk Index, as follows:

Composite Risk Index = Impact of Risk event x Probability of Occurrence

The impact of the risk event is commonly assessed on a scale of 1 to 5, where 1 and 5 represent the minimum and maximum possible impact of an occurrence of a risk (usually in terms of financial losses). However, the 1 to 5 scale can be arbitrary and need not be on a linear scale.

The probability of occurrence is likewise commonly assessed on a scale from 1 to 5, where 1 represents a very low probability of the risk event actually occurring while 5 represents a very high probability of occurrence.

This axis may be expressed in either mathematical terms (event occurs once a year, once in ten years, once in 100 years etc.) or may be expressed in "plain english" - event has occurred here very often; event has been known to occur here; event has been known to occur in the industry etc.). Again, the 1 to 5 scale can be arbitrary or non-linear depending on decisions by subject-matter experts.

The Composite Index thus can take values ranging (typically) from 1 through 25, and this range is usually arbitrarily divided into three sub-ranges. The overall risk assessment is then Low, Medium or High, depending on the sub-range containing the calculated value of the Composite Index. For instance, the three sub-ranges could be defined as 1 to 8, 9 to 16 and 17 to 25.

Note that the probability of risk occurrence is difficult to estimate, since the past data on frequencies are not readily available, as mentioned above. After all, probability does not imply certainty.

Likewise, the impact of the risk is not easy to estimate since it is often difficult to estimate the potential loss in the event of risk occurrence.

Further, both the above factors can change in magnitude depending on the adequacy of risk avoidance and prevention measures taken and due to changes in the external business environment. Hence it is absolutely necessary to periodically reassess risks and intensify/relax mitigation measures, or as necessary. Changes in procedures, technology, schedules, budgets, market conditions, political environment, or other factors typically require reassessment of risks.

Risk Options

Risk mitigation measures are usually formulated according to one or more of the following major risk options, which are:

1. Design a new business process with adequate built-in risk control and containment measures from the start.
2. Periodically reassess risks that are accepted in ongoing processes as a normal feature of business operations and modify mitigation measures.
3. Transfer risks to an external agency (e.g. an insurance company)
4. Avoid risks altogether (e.g. by closing down a particular high-risk business area)

Later research has shown that the financial benefits of risk management are less dependent on the formula used but are more dependent on the frequency and how risk assessment is performed.

In business it is imperative to be able to present the findings of risk assessments in financial, market, or schedule terms. Robert Courtney Jr. (IBM, 1970) proposed a formula for presenting risks in financial terms. The Courtney formula was accepted as the official risk analysis method for the US governmental agencies. The formula proposes calculation of ALE (annualized loss expectancy) and compares the expected loss value to the security control implementation costs (cost-benefit analysis).

Potential Risk Treatments

Once risks have been identified and assessed, all techniques to manage the risk fall into one or more of these four major categories:

- Avoidance (eliminate, withdraw from or not become involved)
- Reduction (optimize - mitigate)
- Sharing (transfer - outsource or insure)
- Retention (accept and budget)

Ideal use of these strategies may not be possible. Some of them may involve trade-offs that are not acceptable to the organization or person making the risk management decisions.

Another source, from the US Department of Defense, Defense Acquisition University, calls these categories ACAT, for Avoid, Control, Accept, or Transfer. This use of the ACAT acronym is reminiscent of another ACAT (for Acquisition Category) used in US Defense industry procurements, in which Risk Management figures prominently in decision making and planning.

Risk Avoidance

This includes not performing an activity that could carry risk. An example would be not buying a property or business in order to not take on the legal liability that comes with it. Another would be not flying in order not to take the risk that the airplane were to be hijacked. Avoidance may seem the answer to all risks, but avoiding risks also means losing out on the potential gain that accepting (retaining) the risk may have allowed. Not entering a business to avoid the risk of loss also avoids the possibility of earning profits.

Hazard Prevention

Hazard prevention refers to the prevention of risks in an emergency. The first and most effective stage of hazard prevention is the elimination of hazards. If this takes too long, is too costly, or is otherwise impractical, the second stage is mitigation.

Accident Chain

Every accident as a result of a hazard is preventable by breaking the accident chain before the last link. Breaking the chain is known as intervention, which is *reactive,* whereas reducing the potential for an accident chain at all is mitigation, which is *proactive.* An example of a reactive step is the creation of a collapse zone at a structure fire. An example of a proactive step is wearing personal protective equipment at a fire call.

The accident chain:

- The environment *such as weather or lighting*
- Human factors *such as training or attitude*
- Equipment *such as proper use and maintenance*
- Event *the unsafe junction of the previous three links*
- Accident *the actual injury or property damage*

Risk Reduction

Risk reduction or "optimization" involves reducing the severity of the loss or the likelihood of the loss from occurring. For example, sprinklers are designed to put out a fire to reduce the risk of loss by fire. This method may cause a greater loss by water damage and therefore may not be suitable. Halon fire suppression systems may mitigate that risk, but the cost may be prohibitive as a strategy.

Acknowledging that risks can be positive or negative, optimizing risks means finding a balance between negative risk and the benefit of the operation or activity; and between risk reduction and effort applied. By an offshore drilling contractor effectively applying HSE Management in its organisation, it can optimize risk to achieve levels of residual risk that are tolerable.

Modern software development methodologies reduce risk by developing and delivering software incrementally. Early methodologies suffered from the fact that they only delivered software in the final phase of development; any problems encountered in earlier phases meant costly rework and often jeopardized the whole project. By developing in iterations, software projects can limit effort wasted to a single iteration.

Outsourcing could be an example of risk reduction if the outsourcer can demonstrate higher capability at managing or reducing risks. For example, a company may outsource only its software development, the manufacturing of hard goods, or customer support needs to another company, while handling the business management itself. This way, the company can concentrate more on business development without having to worry as much about the manufacturing process, managing the development team, or finding a physical location for a call center.

Risk Sharing

Briefly defined as "sharing with another party the burden of loss or the benefit of gain, from a risk, and the measures to reduce a risk."

The term of 'risk transfer' is often used in place of risk sharing in the mistaken belief that you can transfer a risk to a third party through insurance or outsourcing. In practice if the insurance company or contractor go bankrupt or end up in court, the original risk is likely to still revert to the first party. As such in the terminology of practitioners and scholars alike, the purchase of an insurance contract is often described as a "transfer of risk."

However, technically speaking, the buyer of the contract generally retains legal responsibility for the losses "transferred", meaning that insurance may be described more accurately as a post-event compensatory mechanism. For example, a personal injuries insurance policy does not transfer the risk of a car accident to the insurance company.

The risk still lies with the policy holder namely the person who has been in the accident. The insurance policy simply provides that if an accident (the event) occurs involving the policy holder then some compensation may be payable to the policy holder that is commensurate to the suffering/damage.

Some ways of managing risk fall into multiple categories. Risk retention pools are technically retaining the risk for the group, but spreading it over the whole group involves transfer among individual members of the group. This is different from traditional insurance, in that no premium is exchanged between members of the group up front, but instead losses are assessed to all members of the group.

Risk Retention

Involves accepting the loss, or benefit of gain, from a risk when it occurs. True self insurance falls in this category. Risk retention is a viable strategy for small risks where the cost of insuring against the risk would be greater over time than the total losses sustained. All risks that are not avoided or transferred are retained by default.

This includes risks that are so large or catastrophic that they either cannot be insured against or the premiums would be infeasible. War is an example since most property and risks are not insured against war, so the loss attributed by war is retained by the insured. Also any amounts of potential loss (risk) over the amount insured is retained risk. This may also be acceptable if the chance of a very large loss is small or if the cost to insure for greater coverage amounts is so great it would hinder the goals of the organization too much.

Create a Risk Management Plan

Select appropriate controls or countermeasures to measure each risk. Risk mitigation needs to be approved by the appropriate level of management. For instance, a risk concerning the image of the organization should have top management decision behind it whereas IT management would have the authority to decide on computer virus risks.

The risk management plan should propose applicable and effective security controls for managing the risks. For example, an observed high risk of computer viruses could be mitigated by acquiring and implementing antivirus software. A good risk management plan should contain a schedule for control implementation and responsible persons for those actions.

According to ISO/IEC 27001, the stage immediately after completion of the risk assessment phase consists of preparing a Risk Treatment Plan, which should document the decisions about how each of the identified risks should be handled. Mitigation of risks often means selection of security controls, which should be documented in a Statement of Applicability, which identifies which particular control objectives and controls from the standard have been selected, and why.

Implementation

Implementation follows all of the planned methods for mitigating the effect of the risks. Purchase insurance policies for the risks that have been decided to be transferred to an insurer, avoid all risks that can be avoided without sacrificing the entity's goals, reduce others, and retain the rest.

Review and Evaluation of the Plan

Initial risk management plans will never be perfect. Practice, experience, and actual loss results will necessitate changes in the plan and contribute information to allow possible different decisions to be made in dealing with the risks being faced.

Risk analysis results and management plans should be updated periodically. There are two primary reasons for this:

1. to evaluate whether the previously selected security controls are still applicable and effective, and

2. to evaluate the possible risk level changes in the business environment. For example, information risks are a good example of rapidly changing business environment.

Limitations

If risks are improperly assessed and prioritized, time can be wasted in dealing with risk of losses that are not likely to occur. Spending too much time assessing and managing unlikely risks can divert resources that could be used more profitably. Unlikely events do occur but if the risk is unlikely enough to occur it may be better to simply retain the risk and deal with the result if the loss does in fact occur. Qualitative risk assessment is subjective and lacks consistency. The primary justification for a formal risk assessment process is legal and bureaucratic.

Prioritizing the *risk management processes* too highly could keep an organization from ever completing a project or even getting started. This is especially true if other work is suspended until the risk management process is considered complete.

It is also important to keep in mind the distinction between risk and uncertainty. Risk can be measured by impacts x probability.

Areas of Risk Management

As applied to corporate finance, risk management is the technique for measuring, monitoring and controlling the financial or operational risk on a firm's balance sheet. See value at risk.

The Basel II framework breaks risks into market risk (price risk), credit risk and operational risk and also specifies methods for calculating capital requirements for each of these components.

Enterprise Risk Management

In enterprise risk management, a risk is defined as a possible event or circumstance that can have negative influences on the enterprise in question. Its impact can be on the very existence, the resources (human and capital), the products and services, or the customers of the enterprise, as well as external impacts on society, markets, or the environment. In a financial institution, enterprise risk management is normally thought of as the combination of credit risk, interest rate risk or asset liability management, market risk, and operational risk.

In the more general case, every probable risk can have a preformulated plan to deal with its possible consequences (to ensure *contingency* if the risk becomes a *liability*).

From the information above and the average cost per employee over time, or cost accrual ratio, a project manager can estimate:

- the cost associated with the risk if it arises, estimated by multiplying employee costs per unit time by the estimated time lost (*cost impact,* C where C = *cost accrual ratio* * *S*).
- the probable increase in time associated with a risk (*schedule variance due to risk, Rs* where Rs = P * S):
  - o Sorting on this value puts the highest risks to the schedule first. This is intended to cause the greatest risks to the project to be attempted first so that risk is minimized as quickly as possible.
  - o This is slightly misleading as *schedule variances* with a large P and small S and vice versa are not equivalent. (The risk of the RMS *Titanic* sinking vs. the passengers' meals being served at slightly the wrong time).
- the probable increase in cost associated with a risk (*cost variance due to risk, Rc* where Rc = P*C = P*CAR*S = P*S*CAR)
  - o sorting on this value puts the highest risks to the budget first.
  - o see concerns about *schedule variance* as this is a function of it, as illustrated in the equation above.

Risk in a project or process can be due either to Special Cause Variation or Common Cause Variation and requires appropriate treatment. That is to reiterate the concern about external cases not being equivalent in the list immediately above.

Risk Management Activities as Applied to Project Management

In project management, risk management includes the following activities:

- Planning how risk will be managed in the particular project. Plans should include risk management tasks, responsibilities, activities and budget.

- Assigning a risk officer - a team member other than a project manager who is responsible for foreseeing potential project problems. Typical characteristic of risk officer is a healthy skepticism.
- Maintaining live project risk database. Each risk should have the following attributes: opening date, title, short description, probability and importance. Optionally a risk may have an assigned person responsible for its resolution and a date by which the risk must be resolved.
- Creating anonymous risk reporting channel. Each team member should have possibility to report risk that he/she foresees in the project.
- Preparing mitigation plans for risks that are chosen to be mitigated. The purpose of the mitigation plan is to describe how this particular risk will be handled – what, when, by who and how will it be done to avoid it or minimize consequences if it becomes a liability.
- Summarizing planned and faced risks, effectiveness of mitigation activities, and effort spent for the risk management.

Risk Management for Megaprojects

Megaprojects (sometimes also called "major programs") are extremely large-scale investment projects, typically costing more than US$1 billion per project. Megaprojects include bridges, tunnels, highways, railways, airports, seaports, power plants, dams, wastewater projects, coastal flood protection schemes, oil and natural gas extraction projects, public buildings, information technology systems, aerospace projects, and defence systems. Megaprojects have been shown to be particularly risky in terms of finance, safety, and social and environmental impacts. Risk management is therefore particularly pertinent for megaprojects and special methods and special education have been developed for such risk management.

Risk Management of Information Technology

Information technology is increasing pervasive in modern life in every sector.

IT risk is a risk related to information technology. This relatively new term due to an increasing awareness that information security is simply one facet of a multitude of risks that are relevant to IT and the real world processes it supports.

A number of methodologies have been developed to deal with this kind of risk.

ISACA's Risk IT framework ties IT risk to Enterprise risk management.

Risk Management Techniques in Petroleum and Natural Gas

For the offshore oil and gas industry, operational risk management is regulated by the safety case regime in many countries. Hazard identification and risk assessment tools and techniques are described in the international standard ISO 17776:2000, and organizations such as the IADC (International Association of Drilling Contractors) publish guidelines for HSE Case development which are based on the ISO standard. Further, diagrammatic representations of hazardous events are often expected by governmental regulators as part of risk management in safety case submissions; these are known as bow-tie diagrams. The technique is also used by organizations and regulators in mining, aviation, health, defence, industrial and finance.

Risk Management and Business Continuity

Risk management is simply a practice of systematically selecting cost effective approaches for minimizing the effect of threat realization to the organization. All risks can never be fully avoided or mitigated simply because of financial and practical limitations. Therefore all organizations have to accept some level of residual risks.

Whereas risk management tends to be preemptive, business continuity planning (BCP) was invented to deal with the consequences of realized residual risks. The necessity to have BCP in place arises because even very unlikely events will occur if given enough time. Risk management and BCP are often mistakenly seen as rivals or overlapping practices. In fact these processes are so tightly tied together that such separation seems artificial. For example, the risk management process creates important inputs for the BCP (assets, impact assessments, cost estimates etc.). Risk management also proposes applicable controls for the observed risks. Therefore, risk management covers several areas that are vital for the BCP process. However, the BCP process goes beyond risk management's preemptive approach and assumes that the disaster will happen at some point.

Risk Communication

Risk communication is a complex cross-disciplinary academic field. Problems for risk communicators involve how to reach the intended audience, to make the risk comprehensible and relatable to other risks, how to pay appropriate respect to the audience's values related to the risk, how to predict the audience's response to the communication, etc. A main goal of risk communication is to improve collective and individual decision making. Risk communication is somewhat related to crisis communication.

Bow Tie Diagrams

A popular solution to the quest to communicate risks and their treatments effectively is to use bow tie diagrams. These have been effective, for example, in a public forum to model perceived risks and communicate precautions, during the planning stage of offshore oil and gas facilities in Scotland. Equally, the technique is used for HAZID (Hazard Identification) workshops of all types, and results in a high level of engagement. For this reason (amongst others) an increasing number of government regulators for major hazard facilities (MHFs), offshore oil & gas, aviation, etc. welcome safety case submissions which use diagrammatic representation of risks at their core.

Communication advantages of bow tie diagrams:

- Visual illustration of the hazard, its causes, consequences, controls, and how controls fail.
- The bow tie diagram can be readily understood at all personnel levels.
- "A picture paints a thousand words."

Seven Cardinal Rules for the Practice of Risk Communication

(as first expressed by the U.S. Environmental Protection Agency and several of the field's founders)

- Accept and involve the public/other consumers as legitimate partners.
- Plan carefully and evaluate your efforts with a focus on your strengths, weaknesses, opportunities, and threats.

- Listen to the public's specific concerns.
- Be honest, frank, and open.
- Coordinate and collaborate with other credible sources.
- Meet the needs of the media.
- Speak clearly and with compassion.

Hotel Risk Management is Critical

One of the most important aspects of owning and operating a hotel is minimizing the various physical and liability risks associated with this type of business. Risk management is the process of evaluating a hotel's risk exposure and developing strategies for mitigating those. It incorporates a program for reducing exposure supplemented by insurance protection should an incident occur. A hotel owner and operator would be far better off if they could eliminate all the possibilities of an incident occurring on their property. Since this is not always possible, particularly incidents they have no control over, adequate insurance protection provides a way to reduce exposure to a financial loss.

When reviewing your hotel's risk management strategies, it is essential you understand all the potential areas of exposure and exactly how insurance policies are structured to handle the unfortunate incidents that could occur.

The primary areas of concern include the property itself, premises liability, automobile liability, worker's compensation, fidelity, boiler & machinery and umbrella. An effective risk management strategy will also reduce a hotel's insurance cost. Saving money on insurance requires not only a good broker who fully understands the unique risk exposure of a hotel, but one who can also advise on a strategy that will reduce the chance of an incident.

Let's look at some of the unique risks faced by hotels:

Property Risk

Property risk exposures in the industry are primarily due to the high combustibility of contents and multiple sources of ignition that exist in a hotel. Managing these as well as updating building electrical wiring, plumbing and heating systems must be a top priority to mitigate the potential for a fire loss.

Additionally, smoke alarms and sprinklers should be installed in all areas of the building and kitchen equipment must meet all National Fire Protection Association requirements. For resort areas, storm damage is always a concern and needs to be addressed.

It is always essential to insure a hotel's buildings and furniture, fixtures and equipment to replacement cost. Replacement cost is the cost to repair or rebuild to like kind and quality in today's dollars. Another major component of your property insurance is the BI (Business Interruption) exposure. BI exposure can be substantial due to lack of backup facilities and the seasonal natures of certain hotel operations. A hotel must be sure to complete a business income worksheet to ensure proper insurance proceeds for a loss of profits and continuing expenses. An accurate account of annual revenues by type such as room, food, and beverage will be advantageous for insurance brokers when they are researching the best and least expensive coverage.

Premises Liability

A hotel's premises liability exposure is high due to the number of guests typically in the property at any given time. High-rise hotels pose unique life-safety issues. Hotels should implement every safety code possible to ensure guest safety. Stairways, elevators, railings and floor coverings should all be in good condition. Exits should be clearly marked, and lighting should be available in the event of a power outage. Balconies should be regularly inspected and maintained. Guestrooms should be accessed by magnetic keys or other similar systems that are unique for each new guest. Services and recreational facilities, such as exercise rooms, swimming pools, laundry facilities, gift shops, barber, beauty and other personal services, require separate review. It is important to identify all the potential liabilities and develop a risk management strategy to reduce the chance of an incident.

Products Liability

Products liability exposures can be high if the hotel has a restaurant or lounge serving alcohol. Employees should be trained in the proper handling of food to prevent food poisoning or the spread of other transmissible diseases. Liquor liability exposures can be high if employees are not property trained to recognize the effects of excessive alcohol consumption.

Automobile Liability

Automobile liability exposure is also high for some properties, like airport hotels, when it is necessary to pick up and deliver guests to and from the hotel. Valet services present garage-keepers exposure for damages to guest's vehicles. With automobile exposures, pre-approval of acceptable MVR's (driving history report), and restricting driving duties to those between the ages of 18-65, are effective methods in managing this type of risk.

Workers Compensation

Workers compensation exposure is also high within the hospitality industry. Cleaning and maintenance operations can cause workers to experience lung, eye or skin irritations and reactions. Slip and falls, as well as lifting, back injury, hernia, sprain and strain, are all common occurrences.

Every hotel should have a risk management strategy that works to reduce the exposure and then provides adequate insurance to cover unfortunate incidents that were not prevented. Your hotel insurance broker can assist in finding an insurance company that has the extensive experience in evaluating unique hotel risks so you don't end up paying more for your coverage because the company overestimated the exposure and charged too much. The broker should also find you an insurance company with a hotel-oriented loss-control department, which will survey your hotel and assist in identifying areas of risk that can be addressed in your strategy.

When shopping for insurance, your broker will assist in obtaining adequate underwriting information to get you the best insurance at the lowest rate. COPE (Construction Occupancy Protection Information) should be organized per location, and include items such as buildings' square footage, construction materials, year built, number of stories, swimming pools, sprinklers, smoke alarms, key system, buildings contents, business income, hotel receipts, food receipts, liquor receipts and total receipts. Along with this information, obtaining up to five years of loss history is crucial for your broker to get your insurance program the best coverage, at the best price and with the best terms and conditions.

Hotel Motel Security

When traveling on business or pleasure, it may become necessary to stay overnight in a hotel or motel. Your hotel room becomes your home for the night and is your sanctuary while you sleep. It is important to give some thought about security planning. What hotel or motel are you going to select, and what room you are willing to accept? The cost of the hotel room is not always the best predictor of how safe the room will be. There are a few security rules of thumb that should apply to any hotel room you rent.

Higher Floors are Safer

Upper floors are safer from crime, but worse for fire rescue. Emergency rescue is best below the fifth floor. I compromise by picking a modern fire-safe hotel and always request a room on an upper floor to reduce crime exposure. Ground floor rooms are more vulnerable to crime problems because of access and ease of escape. In a high-rise building, rooms above the fifth-floor are usually safer from crime than those below because of lesser accessibility and ease of escape. Also, rooms not adjacent to fire stairs are safer from room invaders because they use them for escape. Criminals do not want to be trapped on an upper floor inside a high-rise hotel. By design, high-rise buildings usually have fewer ground level access points and are easier for the hotel staff to monitor who passes through the lobby after hours.

Door Security Hardware

Hotel or motel rooms should be equipped with a solid-core wood or metal door for best protection. Doors should be self-closing and self-locking. Room doors should have a deadbolt lock with at least a one-inch throw bolt. If the lock appears worn or there are pry marks around the lock area, get another room or move to another hotel. The knob-lock should be hotel-style where you can push a button on the inside knob and block out all keys. This feature is designed to prevent a former guest or housekeeper from entering the room once you are safely inside. Hotels with electronic card access have the advantage of being able to disable former keycards issued to previous guests and unauthorized employees. Electronic locks also will block out most room service keys when you set the deadbolt. The room door should have a wide-angle peephole so you can view who is at the door before opening.

Access Control

Do not open your door to someone who knocks unannounced. Some criminals will pretend to be a bellman, room service, maintenance, or even hotel security to gain admittance to your room. See my web pages on Hotel Room Invasion. Always call the front desk to confirm their status with the hotel and only open the door if you requested the service. Do not rely on door chains or swing bars to secure the doors while you partially open the door to speak someone. These are unreliable security devices. Teach your children not to open the door of any hotel room without knowing the person on the other side and without your permission.

Other Entry Points

Make sure all windows and sliding doors are secured, if they are accessible from the ground. It is a good idea to test all windows and glass doors to see if they are secure. Beware of balconies where someone can climb from one to another and enter through an open window or sliding door. If the windows or sliding doors are not securable, ask for another room or find another hotel. If your room has an adjoining door to an adjacent room, check it to see that it is secured with a deadbolt lock. If it is questionable, ask for another room.

Beware the Parking Lot

If you are a woman traveling alone or with small children, take advantage of car valet service, if available to avoid the parking lot. After checking-in, ask the bellman or desk clerk to escort you to your room. After unlocking the room, quickly inspect the closets, under the bed, and bathroom including behind the shower curtain before the bellman leaves. Tip the bellman for his efforts.

Occupancy Cues

Put the Do-Not-Disturb sign on the doorknob even when you are away, this deters room burglars (it may affect housekeeping service, however). Turn on the TV or radio just loud enough to hear through the door to give the appearance that the room is occupied. Leave one light on inside the room if you will return after dark.

This helps you see upon reentry and gives the room the appearance of occupancy from the outside. Always go through the same room inspection routine every time you re-enter. Women travelling alone should use caution when using the breakfast order doorknob hanger card. This card lists your name and number of persons in the room. A smart crook can knock on the door posing as room service and use your name as a ruse to gain entry.

When you find a suitable hotel that meets your safety standards and will cater to your security needs try to stick with it or with the same hotel chain. Don't be afraid to complain to management to get the safe room you deserve.

- Always request a room on an upper floor, if possible
- A solid door with a good deadbolt lock is best
- Electronic card access locks help limit access
- Make sure your door has a peephole and night latch and use it
- Turn on the TV or radio just loud enough to hear through the door
- Turn on a single light in the room if you plan to return after dark
- Inspect the room hiding places upon entering and check all locks
- Ask the bellman for an escort and use valet parking if alone

Hotel Security as a Guest Amenity

Hotel safety and security is a growing concern among travelers throughout the world. Let's face it; traveling is stressful enough without having to worry about becoming a crime victim while away from home. One only has to look at the negative impact on hotel bookings, following a highly publicized tourist attack, to see how important the perception of security is to the traveler.

When there is a choice, frequent travelers will seek out a hotel property that has superior security amenities. Initially, savvy travelers will select a property that satisfies their criteria and balance of location, price, business facilities, and food service. However, after visiting the property, it's the security features that might determine the continued loyalty of a guest.

Design Factors

The first opportunity to present a positive impression about the relative safety of a hotel or motel property is at the perimeter. For maximum effectiveness, there must be an obvious and distinct design transition as you enter the property from the public street. Solid deterrent cues include significant barriers like perimeter walls, decorative fencing, landscaped terraces, and a well-defined driveway and main entrance. A strong transition sends a subliminal message to the criminal that this hotel is private property and for use by hotel guests only.

Lighting

Good exterior lighting is designed to fill the gap between the property boundary and the hotel entrance and is the most important nighttime security feature. Public areas, when bathed in light, are both inviting to the guest and a powerful deterrent to crime. Good exterior lighting will allow you to see a potential threat at 100 feet. This minimum level of visibility gives you time to respond to the threat before being confronted by it. Exterior lighting must be even and balanced. Balanced lighting appears warm and comfortable and makes a property feel safe.

To achieve a balanced lighting effect, more fixtures are often necessary to fill the lighting gaps. Huge floodlights are not the best choice because they are not energy-efficient and tend to create glare and heavy shadows between fixtures. A surprising benefit of adding more and smaller light fixtures are that the total wattage can be reduced, which will save significant amounts of energy. Many properties have been able to pay for their entire lighting fixture upgrade in just one year, based on their energy savings alone.

Curbside Deterrence

Parking lot security is often the most overlooked area on a hotel property. Stranger-to-stranger crimes against persons are more likely to occur in the parking lot than in any other location. This is because parking lots offer the criminal the best hiding places, the fewest witnesses, and the quickest escape route. Parking lot surveillance can be relatively inexpensive by installing video cameras, but nothing beats a highly visible, uniformed security patrol that is capable of responding to a criminal incident and can call for help. Besides, a hotel guest would rather see a "live person" on the job that is paid to look out for their welfare.

Highly visible doormen and valet parking attendants are a great crime deterrent, especially on smaller hotel properties. Nothing instills more confidence in a hotel guest than a capable doorman who greets and makes eye contact with them as they enter the property. Criminals don't like doormen for two reasons: First, they don't want to be identified, and second, they don't want to be captured should they have to escape in a hurry. Without competent curbside security, crimes like purse snatches, car thefts, and luggage thefts would increase substantially on most urban properties.

A doorman can monitor a property better if the number of entrances is limited, especially at night. This design philosophy gives the hotel the advantage of making the criminal feel "out of place" and therefore more likely to be deterred.

Access control cues must continue inside the property to be totally effective and to foster that "safe and secure feeling" within a guest. As for the criminal, access control is like peeling an onion...the more layers they penetrate...the more uncomfortable it should feel.

Interior Access Control

In addition to physical barriers, access control involves the use of electronic equipment, personnel, and procedures. For example, the entire hotel staff should be trained to be attentive to all persons and report suspicious activity to the manager-on-duty. Hotel guests love this high level of courtesy and staff attentiveness, while criminals hate it. Hotel criminals prefer to remain unnoticed and anonymous. Multiple staff contacts will make them feel very uncomfortable and is usually enough to make them go elsewhere to ply their trade.

In a high-rise hotel, the ground floor lobby presents another major opportunity to deter crime. The best security designs position the registration, bellman, and concierge desks in a position to view critical access points. Important access points include the front, back, or side entrances, elevator banks, lounge, and restaurant entrances. In large metropolitan hotels, extra attention needs to be paid to guest luggage, briefcases, and handbags left casually on the lobby floor.

Guestroom Security

The guestroom represents the inner-circle of a hotel security plan. The guestroom is the sanctuary for the weary traveler where they expect to be safe. The guestroom doors and windows must be fortified to prevent forced entry, especially at the ground level. Doors must be nothing less than solid-core wood or metal, and be self-closing and self-locking. The door lock must consist of a high quality deadbolt with at least a one-inch bolt. The lock strike-plate must be bolted securely to the metal doorframe or by using three-inch screws when attached to a wood doorjamb. Accessible sliding windows must have secondary security devices attached to prevent forced entry or lifting out of the frame.

Visible signs of door lock maintenance are important to travelers. Doors must be tight fitting and the locks must be in good condition and should give a distinctive "clunk" as the deadbolt slides and locks in place. Guestroom doors must be equipped with a wide-angle peephole so a guest can see who is outside before opening the door.

A much appreciated guest amenity is the personal in-room lock-box. I especially appreciate the large ones that can secure my laptop computer. Electronic and keyless lock-boxes are best, as long as they are securely anchored. Although not designed to replace the hotel safe deposit box, in-room lock-boxes provide extra peace of mind for storing small valuables and personal documents.

Key Control

Metal room keys are being replaced by electronically coded key-cards. There is nothing more unsettling than checking into an upscale hotel and being issued a metal room key with the correct room number stamped on the key. Metal keys require a hotel to maintain an elaborate key control system with daily inventories of master key and E-Key checkout logs for the staff. The guest has no way of knowing that an adequate key control system is in place. If a room key or master key turns up missing, the affected locks must be changed. This event creates an on-going maintenance expense for a hotel.

Metal room keys do not make the same "security statement" as coded plastic key-cards. Key-cards have the capability of being randomly coded at the point of registration, which re-emphasizes the guest perception of room security. Key-card control is computer-based and therefore creates the necessary audit trail automatically. Master keys can be changed in a matter of a few keystrokes and lost key-cards are easily removed from the system. One of the best security features is the ability of the computer to interrogate each door lock and get a printout of everyone who accessed a particular room. This dramatically cuts down on theft from the rooms by hotel employees.

Predictions

Traveler demand for hotels that promote enhanced security will increase in the coming especially with the added fear of terrorism. Security amenities are important to travelers, especially the elderly and women traveling alone. I predict security conscious properties will gain advantage over competing hotels that fail to recognize this important new trend.

Family Security

Our family is at the center of our personal universe. Most people would do almost anything for the sake of their family. That includes protecting them from known dangers and harm while lodging at hotels or motels. This becomes increasing difficult, at times, because we live in an open society where we share the same public places as the violent criminals like at hotels and motels..

Family Security Plan

Whenever your family walks out the front door they leave that zone of protection that you have created. The secret to keeping your family reasonable safe once they leave home is to have a family security plan. To develop a family security plan you must give careful thought to the public routines of each family member and think of ways to make them safer from the violent people in the world. The best way to accomplish this is to hold a family meeting to discuss this plan and play *what if* using different scenarios.

For example, *what if* we need to stay overnight in a hotel? What steps should we take to make the process safer? *What if* we want to go to the swimming pool or gym? What precautions can we take to be safer in the parking lot? *What if* someone approaches to rob us while walking to our car on the street at night? What would we do and how would we react? Where would we go and who would we notify in case of emergency?

Most people have no such family plan and have not met as a family to discuss what if situations. When or if a criminal assault does occur, the family will not be prepared and will have to rely on instinct in response to the incident. What if their response instincts are wrong or their reactions inappropriate, under the circumstances? We read about these all the time in the newspaper or hear about them on television, for example, where a child was walking in an unfamiliar place and was tricked into a car of a total stranger and kidnapped.

Hotels and Motels

When traveling on business or pleasure with your family, it may become necessary to stay overnight in a hotel or motel. Your hotel room becomes your home for the night and is your sanctuary while you sleep. It is important to give some thought to what hotel or motel you select and what room you are willing to accept. The cost of the hotel room is not always a good predictor of how safe the room or property will be. There are a few rules of thumb that should apply to any hotel room you rent.

Room Location

Always request a room on an upper floor, if possible. Ground floor rooms are more vulnerable to crime problems because of access and ease of escape. In a high rise building, rooms above the fifth floor are usually safer than those below, again because of accessibility and ease of escape. Criminals do not want to be trapped on an upper floor inside a high-rise hotel. High-rise buildings usually have fewer ground level access points and are easier for the hotel staff to monitor who passes through the lobby after hours.

Room Security Features

Hotel or motel rooms should be equipped with a solid-wood or a metal door for best protection. Room doors should have a deadbolt lock with a one-inch throw bolt. If the lock looks worn or there are pry marks around the lock area, get another room or move to another hotel. The knob lock should be hotel-style where you can push a button on the inside knob and block out all keys.

This feature is designed to prevent a former guest or housekeeper from entering the room once you are inside. Hotels with electronic card-access have the advantage of being able to disable former key-cards issued to other guests. The room door should have a wide-angle peephole so you can view who is at the door before opening. Do not rely on door chains or swing bars to secure the doors when you peek out to speak someone. Teach your children not to open the door to any hotel room without knowing the person on the other side.

Make sure all windows and sliding doors are secured if they are accessible from the ground. It is a good idea to pull on all windows and glass doors to test if they are secure. Beware of balconies where someone can climb from one to another and enter through an open window or sliding door. If the windows or sliding doors are not securable, ask for another room or find another hotel.

Supervise Children

Children should not be allowed to wander the hotel grounds unsupervised. Everyone at a hotel is a stranger and it is difficult to discern who is a registered guest or who has criminal intentions. Do not leave a child at the pool or gym unsupervised. These are prime targets for predators.

If you are a woman traveling alone or with small children, take advantage of car valet service, if available to avoid the parking lot. After checking in at the desk, ask the bellman or desk clerk to escort you to your room. After unlocking the room, quickly inspect the closets, under the bed, and bathroom including behind the shower curtain before the bellman leaves. When you find a suitable hotel that meets your standards and will cater to your needs, try to stick with it or with the same hotel chain.

- Always request a room on an upper floor, if possible
- A solid core door with a good deadbolt lock is best
- Electronic card-access locks minimize key control questions
- Make sure your door has a peephole and night latch and use it
- Use your do not disturb sign whenever you are in the room
- Inspect the room hiding places upon entering and check all locks
- Supervise children at al times especially at the pool or gym
- Ask the bellman for an escort and use valet parking, if alone

Health and Safety in Hotels and Catering

Health and Safety in the catering sector covers restaurants, hotels, takeaways, public houses and night clubs. This sector employs in excess of 1.2 million people with the pubic in regular contact with businesses in the sector be them residents at a hotel or eating in food outlets.

Health and Safety in Hotels and Catering should be treated as a priority. Quantum, when undertaking a health and safety risk assessment will consider risks including Slips, Trips and Falls, Obstructions, Spillages, Lighting, Staff Clothing and Footwear and Space Requirements to name just a few.

Tailoring our approach to the catering industry we may choose to examine the adequacy of floor coverings; positioning of equipment in relation to work processes and storage.

Consider the following specific risks we may look for in the hotel and catering industry. Please note this list is not exhaustive:

- Drainage of hot oil from catering equipment
- Diluting/mixing/decanting cleaning chemicals
- Dismantling/cleaning dangerous equipment, e.g. food slicers/mixers etc.
- Manual handling of heavy/awkward loads
- Cleanliness and waste management
- Good housekeeping standards maintained

Swimming Pool

A swimming pool, swimming bath, wading pool, or simply a pool, is a container filled with water intended for swimming or water-based recreation. There are many standard sizes; the largest and deepest is the Olympic-size swimming pool. A pool can be built either above or in the ground, and from materials such as concrete (also known as gunite), metal, plastic or fiberglass.

The innovation of a composite construction of fibreglass, with an epoxy coating and porcelain ceramic tiles has led to the Pre-form, Composite-type with significant advantages over older methods; however, it also has increased sensitivity to metal staining.

Pools that may be used by many people or by the general public are called public, while pools used exclusively by a few people or in a home are called private. Many health clubs, fitness centers and private clubs have public pools used mostly for exercise. Many hotels and massage parlors have public pools for relaxation. Hot tubs and spas are pools with hot water, used for relaxation or therapy, and are common in homes, hotels, clubs and massage parlors. Swimming pools are also used for diving and other water sports, as well as for the training of lifeguards and astronauts.

Chemical disinfectants such as chlorine, bromine or mineral sanitizers, and additional filters are often used in swimming pools to prevent growth and spread of bacteria, viruses, algae and insect larvae. Alternatively, pools can be made without chemical disinfectants by using a biofilter with additional carbon filters and UV disinfection. In both cases, pools need to be fitted with an adequate flow rate.

Safety

Pools present a significant risk of infant and toddler death due to drowning. In regions where residential pools are common, drowning is a major cause of childhood fatalities. As a precaution, many municipalities have by-laws that require that residential pools be enclosed with fencing to restrict unauthorized access. The Virginia Graeme Baker Pool And Spa Safety Act regulates pools to reduce the risk of entrapment.

Many products exist, such as removable baby fences, floating alarms and window/door alarms. Some pools are equipped with computer-aided drowning prevention or other forms of electronic safety and security systems.

Suspended ceilings in indoor swimming pools are safety-relevant components. The selection of materials under tension should be done with care. Especially the selection of unsuitable stainless steels can cause problems with stress corrosion cracking.

First Aid

First aid is the provision of initial care for an illness or injury. It is usually performed by non-expert, but trained personnel to a sick or injured person until definitive medical treatment can be accessed. Certain self-limiting illnesses or minor injuries may not require further medical care past the first aid intervention. It generally consists of a series of simple and in some cases, potentially life-saving techniques that an individual can be trained to perform with minimal equipment.

While first aid can also be performed on all animals, the term generally refers to care of human patients.

History

The instances of recorded first aid were provided by religious knights, such as the Knights Hospitaller, formed in the 11th century, providing care to pilgrims and knights, and training other knights in how to treat common battlefield injuries. The practice of first aid fell largely in to disuse during the High Middle Ages, and organized societies were not seen again until in 1859 Henry Dunant organized local villagers to help victims of the Battle of Solferino, including the provision of first aid. Four years later, four nations met in Geneva and formed the organization which has grown into the Red Cross, with a key stated aim of "aid to sick and wounded soldiers in the field". This was followed by the formation of St. John Ambulance in 1877, based on the principles of the Knights Hospitaller, to teach first aid, and numerous other organization joined them with the term first aid first coined in 1878 as civilian ambulance services spread as a combination of "first treatment" and "national aid" in large railway centres and mining districts as well as with police forces.

First aid training began to spread through the empire through organizations such as St. John, often starting, as in the UK, with high risk activities such as ports and railways.

Many developments in first aid and many other medical techniques have been driven by wars, such as in the case of the American Civil War, which prompted Clara Barton to organize the American Red Cross. Today, there are several groups that promote first aid, such as the military and the Scouting movement. New techniques and equipment have helped make today's first aid simple and effective.

Aims

The key aims of first aid can be summarized in three key points:

- *Preserve life:* the overriding aim of all medical care, including first aid, is to save lives
- *Prevent further harm:* also sometimes called prevent the condition from worsening, or danger of further injury, this covers both external factors, such as moving a patient away from any cause of harm, and applying first aid techniques to prevent worsening of the condition, such as applying pressure to stop a bleed becoming dangerous.
- *Promote recovery:* first aid also involves trying to start the recovery process from the illness or injury, and in some cases might involve completing a treatment, such as in the case of applying a plaster to a small wound

First aid training also involves the prevention of initial injury and responder safety, and the treatment phases.

Key Skills

Certain skills are considered essential to the provision of first aid and are taught ubiquitously. Particularly the "ABC"s of first aid, which focus on critical life-saving intervention, must be rendered before treatment of less serious injuries. ABC stands for *Airway, Breathing,* and *Circulation*. The same mnemonic is used by all emergency health professionals. Attention must first be brought to the airway to ensure it is clear. Obstruction (choking) is a life-threatening emergency.

Following evaluation of the airway, a first aid attendant would determine adequacy of breathing and provide rescue breathing if necessary. Assessment of circulation is now not usually carried out for patients who are not breathing, with first aiders now trained to go straight to chest compressions (and thus providing artificial circulation) but pulse checks may be done on less serious patients.

Some organizations add a fourth step of "D" for *Deadly bleeding* or *Defibrillation,* while others consider this as part of the *Circulation* step. Variations on techniques to evaluate and maintain the ABCs depend on the skill level of the first aider. Once the ABCs are secured, first aiders can begin additional treatments, as required. Some organizations teach the same order of priority using the "3Bs": *Breathing, Bleeding,* and *Bones* (or "4Bs": *Breathing, Bleeding, Brain,* and *Bones*). While the ABCs and 3Bs are taught to be performed sequentially, certain conditions may require the consideration of two steps simultaneously. This includes the provision of both artificial respiration and chest compressions to someone who is not breathing and has no pulse, and the consideration of cervical spine injuries when ensuring an open airway.

Preserving Life

In order to stay alive, all persons need to have an open airway—a clear passage where air can move in through the mouth or nose through the pharynx and down in to the lungs, without obstruction. Conscious people will maintain their own airway automatically, but those who are unconscious (with a GCS of less than 8) may be unable to maintain a patent airway, as the part of the brain which automatically controls breathing in normal situations may not be functioning.

If the patient was breathing, a first aider would normally then place them in the recovery position, with the patient leant over on their side, which also has the effect of clearing the tongue from the pharynx. It also avoids a common cause of death in unconscious patients, which is choking on regurgitated stomach contents.

The airway can also become blocked through a foreign object becoming lodged in the pharynx or larynx, commonly called choking. The first aider will be taught to deal with this through a combination of 'back slaps' and 'abdominal thrusts'.

Once the airway has been opened, the first aider would assess to see if the patient is breathing. If there is no breathing, or the patient is not breathing normally, such as agonal breathing, the first aider would undertake what is probably the most recognized first aid procedure—cardiopulmonary resuscitation or CPR, which involves breathing for the patient, and manually massaging the heart to promote blood flow around the body.

Promoting Recovery

The first aider is also likely to be trained in dealing with injuries such as cuts, grazes or bone fracture. They may be able to deal with the situation in its entirety (a small adhesive bandage on a paper cut), or may be required to maintain the condition of something like a broken bone, until the next stage of definitive care (usually an ambulance) arrives.

Training

Basic principles, such as knowing to use an adhesive bandage or applying direct pressure on a bleed, are often acquired passively through life experiences. However, to provide effective, life-saving first aid interventions requires instruction and practical training. This is especially true where it relates to potentially fatal illnesses and injuries, such as those that require cardiopulmonary resuscitation (CPR); these procedures may be invasive, and carry a risk of further injury to the patient and the provider. As with any training, it is more useful if it occurs *before* an actual emergency, and in many countries, emergency ambulance dispatchers may give basic first aid instructions over the phone while the ambulance is on the way.

Training is generally provided by attending a course, typically leading to certification. Due to regular changes in procedures and protocols, based on updated clinical knowledge, and to maintain skill, attendance at regular refresher courses or recertification is often necessary. First aid training is often available through community organizations such as the Red Cross and St. John Ambulance, or through commercial providers, who will train people for a fee. This commercial training is most common for training of employees to perform first aid in their workplace. Many community organizations also provide a commercial service, which complements their community programmes.

Australia

In Australia, Nationally recognized First Aid certificates may only be issued by Registered training organizations who are accredited on the National Training Information System (NTIS). Courses are based on the delivery and assessment of Unit's of Competency from various Training Packages. Most First Aid certificates are issued at one of three levels::

- Provide Basic Emergency Life Support. Formerly Level 1 (or "Basic First Aid", or "Basic Life Support") this is a 1-day course covering primarily life-threatening emergencies. It involves the training and assessment of HLTFA201A from the HLT07 Health Training Package
- Apply First Aid. Formerly Level 2 ("Senior First Aid") is either a 2 day face to face course or 1 day face to face combined with 4 - 8 theory work at home or online. It involves the delivery and assessment of HLTFA301B Apply First Aid. It covers all the aspects of training in "Provide Basic Emergency Life Support, as well as specialized training for treatment of burns, bites, stings, electric shock and poisons and the use of an AED. Apply First Aid must be re-accredited every three years to remain current for use in the workplace Reaccreditation of the CPR component (HLTFACPR201 is generally required annually, although individual states set the specific requirements.
- Apply Advanced First Aid. Formerly Level 3 ("Occupational First Aid") is a three or four day course

covering advanced first aid, use of oxygen and automated external defibrillators and documentation. It is suitable for workplace First Aiders and those who manage First Aid facilities. It is based on the training and assessment of a group of units of competency - HLTFA301B Apply first aid, HLTFA402B Apply advanced first aid and HLTFA403A Manage first aid in the workplace - that are generally delivered together.

Other courses outside these levels are commonly taught, including CPR-only courses, Advanced Resuscitation, Remote Area or Wilderness First Aid, Administering Medications (such as salbutamol or the Epi-Pen) and specialized courses for parents, school teachers, community first responders or hazardous workplace first aiders. CPR Reaccreditation courses are sometimes required yearly, regardless of the length of the overall certification.

Canada

In Canada, first aid certificates are awarded by one of several national organizations including the Red Cross, the Lifesaving Society and St. John Ambulance. Or they can also be issued by sub-national organizations such as Certified Emergency Response Training. The terms "Emergency First Aid" and "Standard First Aid" are generic and based on a Health Canada (a federal department of the Government of Canada) review and approval of a training organization's curriculum/syllabus (training content), standards and other factors. Workplace safety regulations and standards for first aid vary by province depending on occupation. However, as some occupations are governed by federal, not provincial, workplace safety regulations, such as the transportation industry (marine, aviation, rail), trainees need to confirm with their employer as to exactly what specific training and certification standards comply with the applicable regulatory agencies, federal or provincial.

- *Emergency First Aid:* is an 8-hour course covering primarily life-threatening emergencies: CPR, bleeding, choking and other life-threatening medical emergencies.
- *Standard First Aid:* is a 16-hour course that covers the same material as Emergency First Aid and will include training for some, but not all, of the following: breaks;

burns; poisons, bites and stings; eye injuries; head and neck injuries; chest injuries; wound care; emergency child birth; and multiple casualty management.

- Medical First Responder (BTLS—known by different names among different Canadian organizations): is a 40 hour course. It requires Standard First Aid certification as a prerequisite. Candidates are trained in the use of oxygen, automated external defibrillators, airway management, and the use of additional emergency equipment.

CPR certification in Canada is broken into several levels. Depending on the level, the lay person will learn the basic one-person CPR and choking procedures for adults, and perhaps children, and infants. Higher-level designations also require two-person CPR to be learned. Depending on provincial laws, trainees may also learn the basics of automated external defibrillation (AED).

- Level A is the lowest level of CPR training. Trainees learn how to perform the standard one-rescuer CPR and choking procedures on adults.
- Level B requires the same procedures as Level A, but trainees learn to perform these maneuvers on children and infants in addition to adults.
- Level C requires the same maneuvers as Level B, and trainees are also taught how to perform two-person CPR.
- Level HCP (Health Care Professional) was introduced in Canada in response to new guidelines set by the International Liaison Committee on Resuscitation. In addition to the techniques taught in Level C, artificial resuscitation, AED use (to certification standards), and bag-valve-mask use is taught. Anyone with CPR-HCP certification is considered AED certified.

France

In France, first aid certificates are delivered by organizations that are approved by the Minister of the Interior, following the official national reference document (*Referentiel national*, RN). There are about 20 approved associations (Croix-rouge francaise,

Federation national de protection civile, Federation des securities francais Croix-Blanche, Ceuvres hospitalieres francaises de l'ordre de Malte, Union national de protection civile, Association national des premiers secours, ...); many administrations – army, fire services, national education, ... – are also approved.

- at school: basics must be taught at the primary school
  - o *grande section de maternelle* (5 years old): to detect a danger, to look for an adult,
  - o *cours elementaire 1* (CE1, 7 years old): to protect oneself, to call for help,
  - o *cours moyen* 2 (CM2, 10 years old): to make a complete phone call, to place a casualty in an adapted position (sitting, lying, recovery position);
- at the *Journee defense et citoyennete* (Information to the army careers): IAPS, *Initiation A l'alerte et aux premiers secours* (initiation to call for help and first aid)

1. Securing.
2. Calling for help.
3. The casualty is not alert (recovery position).
4. The casualty is not breathing (CPR, AED).

- PSC1: *Prevention et secours civiques de niveau 1* (Prevention and civic aid, level 1): 10 hours,
  0. Securing (including emergency casualty movement).

1. Calling for help.
2. The casualty is choking.
3. The casualty bleeds deadly.
4. The casulaty is not alert (recovery position).
5. The casulaty is not breathing (CPR, AED, including children and babies).
6. The casualty complains about illness (including strokes and heart infarction).
7. The casulaty complains after a trauma (burns, wounds, broken bones, joint sprains and dislocations).

- SST: *Sauvetage-secourisme du travail* (first aid at work):

similar to PSC1, with a study of the specific risks of the activity of the worker;

- PSE: *premiers secours en equipe* (team first aid, certified first responders):
  - o PSE1 (level 1): 35 hrs, general principles (managing stress, relationships to the casualty and the bystanders, hygiene, being part of a team, security, basic anatomy), complete assessment (check pupils, check pulse, pain assessment), cervical collar, suction, oxygen first aid, bandages and tourniquets, methods with two team members (emergency movements, recovery position, removal of a helmet, jaw thrust, CPR), specific cases (amputations, casualty in a car, drowning), simple patient transport (walking, sitting in a chair);
  - o PSE2 (level 2): 35 hrs,

Ireland

In Ireland, the workplace qualification is the Occupational First Aid Certificate. The Health and Safety Authority issue the standards for first aid at work and hold a register of qualified instructors, examiners and organizations that can provide the course. A FETAC Level 5 certificate is awarded after passing a three day course and is valid for two years from date of issue. Occupational First Aiders are more qualified than Cardiac First Responders (Cardiac First Response and training on the AED is now part of the OFA course) but less qualified than Emergency First Responders but strangely Occupational First Aid is the only one of the three not certified by PHECC. Organizations offering the certificate include, Ireland's largest first aid organisation, the Order of Malta Ambulance Corps, the St John Ambulance Brigade, and the Irish Red Cross. The Irish Red Cross also provides a Practical First Aid Course aimed at the general public dealing primarily with family members getting injured. Many other (purely commercially run) organizations offer training.

Singapore

In Singapore, the workplace qualification is the Occupational First Aid Certificate. The Ministry of Manpower (Singapore) issue the standards for first aid at work and qualifies first aid instructors, occupational nurses and doctors and registered safety officers as examiners and organizations that can provide the course. Instructors are required to undergo an ACTA certification, a nationally recognized training standard endorsed by the Workforce Development Agency. Workplaces with more than 25 employees are required to have certified Occupational First Aiders.

The Occupational First Aid Course recently incorporated a CPR and AED segment which is accredited by the National Resuscitation Council of Singapore and is valid for 2 years. Occupational First Aiders learn more workplace related topics than Cardiac First Responders and is the industry standard in Singapore. However, they may be less qualified than EMTs. The Singapore First Aid Training Centre conducts the Occupational First Aid Certification approved by the Ministry of Manpower (Singapore).

The Netherlands

In the Netherlands basic level lay firstaid training is mostly provided by specialised (commercial) first aid training companies or volunteer instructors and first aiders are mostly certified by the "Dutch Red Cross" and the foundation "Het Oranje Kruis". The foundation "LPEV" certifies mainly advanced and first responder level' firstaid training.

Medical firstaid must always be provided by certified ambulance crews, physicians and hospital staff.

United Kingdom

In the U.K., there are two main types of first aid courses offered. An "Emergency First Aid at Work" course typically lasts one day, and covers the basics, focusing on critical interventions for conditions such as cardiac arrest and severe bleeding, and is usually not formally assessed. A "First Aid at Work" course is usually a three-day course (two days for a re-qualification) that covers the full spectrum of first aid, and is formally assessed by recognized Health and Safety Executive assessors. Certificates for the "First Aid at Work" course are issued by the training organization and are valid for a period of three years from the date the delegate passes the course. Other courses offered by training organizations such as St. John Ambulance, St Andrew's First Aid or the British Red Cross include Baby and Child Courses, manual handling, people moving, and courses geared towards more advanced life support, such as defibrillation and administration of medical gases such as oxygen and entonox.

The British Forces use First Aid ranging from levels 1–3, to assist the medical staff on their Ship, Squadron, Section, Base or any other purpose required. They are trained in both Military and Civilian First Aid and often utilize their knowledge in aid stricken regions around the world. First Aid is vital on board HM Ships because of the number of people in a small area and the space given to perform their task, it is also vital for the Army and Royal Marines to know basic first aid to help the survival rate of the soldiers when in combat.

United States

In the United States, there is no universal schedule of First Aid levels that are applicable to all agencies that provide first aid training. Training is provided typically through the American Red Cross, but may also be completed by local fire departments and the American Heart Association (AHA) in terms of CPR. The American Red Cross, however, offers the following courses:

- CPR
  - CPR-Adult (CPR-A)
  - CPR-Child and Infant (CPR-CI)
  - CPR-Adult and Child (CPR-AC)
  - CPR-Adult, Child, and Infant (CPR-ACI)
- CPR/Automated External Defibrillator (AED)
  - CPR/AED-Adult (CPR/AED-A)
  - CPR/AED-Adult and Child (CPR/AED-AC)
- First Aid
  - Standard First Aid (SFA)
  - Standard First Aid plus any of the above CPR or CPR/AED courses
- Specialty
  - Babysitter's Training
  - Lifeguarding (Lifeguard training)

- o Dog, Cat, and Dog/Cat First Aid
- o Professional Rescuer Training (CPR, First Aid, and AED to meet Lifeguard, EMT, and Nursing regulations)
- o Bloodborne Pathogens Training
- o Wilderness Training
- o First Responder in the Workplace training (CPR/AED/ First Aid)
- o Instructor Certification

Red Cross training programs may vary by Chapter and season. Layman First Responders in the United States are subject to Good Samaritan law protections as long as their treatment does not extend beyond training or certification. First Aid training in the United States is limited to basic life support functions needed to sustain life, and training instills the importance of activating the Emergency Medical System before beginning assistance (through the Three C's: Check, Call, Care). Training classes range from a few hours for a specific course, or several days for combination, specialty, and instructor courses. Red Cross volunteers are required to be Standard First Aid plus CPR/ACI certified (AED is encouraged but not required as of 2009), as well as passing the FEMA NIMS Introductory certification.

Specific Disciplines

There are several types of first aid (and first aider) which require specific additional training. These are usually undertaken to fulfill the demands of the work or activity undertaken.

- Aquatic/Marine first aid—Usually practiced by professionals such as lifeguards, professional mariners or in diver rescue, and covers the specific problems which may be faced after water-based rescue and/or delayed MedEvac.
- Battlefield first aid—This takes in to account the specific needs of treating wounded combatants and noncombatants during armed conflict.
- Hyperbaric first aid—Which may be practiced by SCUBA diving professionals, who need to treat conditions such as the bends.

- Oxygen first aid—Providing oxygen to casualties who suffer from conditions resulting in hypoxia.
- Wilderness first aid is the provision of first aid under conditions where the arrival of emergency responders or the evacuation of an injured person may be delayed due to constraints of terrain, weather, and available persons or equipment. It may be necessary to care for an injured person for several hours or days.
- Hydrofluoric Acid first aid—taught to first aiders in the chemical industry where hydrofluoric acid may be used. Instructs the first aider how to initially treat (with calcium gluconate) any skin that has been splashed with the acid.

Symbols

Although commonly associated with first aid, the symbol of a red cross is an official protective symbol of the Red Cross. According to the Geneva Conventions and other international laws, the use of this and similar symbols is reserved for official agencies of the International Red Cross and Red Crescent, and as a protective emblem for medical personnel and facilities in combat situations. Use by any other person or organization is illegal, and may lead to prosecution.

The internationally accepted symbol for first aid is the white cross on a green background shown at the start of the page.

Some organizations may make use of the Star of Life, although this is usually reserved for use by ambulance services, or may use symbols such as the Maltese Cross, like the Order of Malta Ambulance Corps and St John Ambulance. Other symbols may also be used.

Conditions that often require first aid:

- Altitude sickness, which can begin in susceptible people at altitudes as low as 5,000 feet, can cause potentially fatal swelling of the brain or lungs.
- Anaphylaxis, a life-threatening condition in which the airway can become constricted and the patient may go into shock. The reaction can be caused by a systemic allergic reaction to allergens such as insect bites or

peanuts. Anaphylaxis is initially treated with injection of epinephrine.

- Battlefield first aid—This protocol refers to treating shrapnel, gunshot wounds, burns, bone fractures, etc. as seen either in the 'traditional' battlefield setting or in an area subject to damage by large scale weaponry, such as a bomb blast.
- Bone fracture, a break in a bone initially treated by stabilizing the fracture with a splint.
- Burns, which can result in damage to tissues and loss of body fluids through the burn site.
- Cardiac Arrest, which will lead to death unless CPR preferably combined with an AED is started within minutes. There is often no time to wait for the emergency services to arrive as 92 percent of people suffering a sudden cardiac arrest die before reaching hospital according to the American Heart Association.
- Choking, blockage of the airway which can quickly result in death due to lack of oxygen if the patient's trachea is not cleared, for example by the Heimlich Maneuver.
- Childbirth.
- Cramps in muscles due to lactic acid build up caused either by inadequate oxygenation of muscle or lack of water or salt.
- Diving disorders, drowning or asphyxiation.
- Gender-specific conditions, such as dysmenorrhea and testicular torsion.
- Heart attack, or inadequate blood flow to the blood vessels supplying the heart muscle.
- Heat stroke, also known as sunstroke or hyperthermia, which tends to occur during heavy exercise in high humidity, or with inadequate water, though it may occur spontaneously in some chronically ill persons. Sunstroke, especially when the victim has been unconscious, often causes major damage to body systems such as brain, kidney, liver, gastric tract. Unconsciousness for more than two hours usually leads to permanent disability.

Emergency treatment involves rapid cooling of the patient.

- Hair tourniquet a condition where a hair or other thread becomes tied around a toe or finger tightly enough to cut off blood flow.
- Heat syncope, another stage in the same process as heat stroke, occurs under similar conditions as heat stroke and is not distinguished from the latter by some authorities.
- Heavy bleeding, treated by applying pressure (manually and later with a pressure bandage) to the wound site and elevating the limb if possible.
- Hyperglycemia (diabetic coma) and Hypoglycemia (insulin shock).
- Hypothermia, or Exposure, occurs when a person's core body temperature falls below 33.7°C (92.6°F). First aid for a mildly hypothermic patient includes rewarming, but rewarming a severely hypothermic person could result in a fatal arrhythmia, an irregular heart rhythm.
- Insect and animal bites and stings.
- Joint dislocation.
- Poisoning, which can occur by injection, inhalation, absorption, or ingestion.
- Seizures, or a malfunction in the electrical activity in the brain. Three types of seizures include a grand mal (which usually features convulsions as well as temporary respiratory abnormalities, change in skin complexion, etc.) and petit mal (which usually features twitching, rapid blinking, and/or fidgeting as well as altered consciousness and temporary respiratory abnormalities).
- Muscle strains and Sprains, a temporary dislocation of a joint that immediately reduces automatically but may result in ligament damage.
- Stroke, a temporary loss of blood supply to the brain.
- Toothache, which can result in severe pain and loss of the tooth but is rarely life threatening, unless over time the infection spreads into the bone of the jaw and starts osteomyelitis.

- Wounds and bleeding, including lacerations, incisions and abrasions, Gastrointestinal bleeding, avulsions and Sucking chest wounds, treated with an occlusive dressing to let air out but not in.

General Hazards

Manual Handling

Manual handling may require repetitive or forceful movement or awkward postures. They may be activities in which a person has to lift, lower, push, pull, carry, move or restrain an object.

Injuries related to manual handling are generally caused by physical stress and strain over a long period of time.

In the hospitality and entertainment industry, manual handling risks include:

- carrying boxes;
- stacking shelves;
- cleaning and cooking equipment;
- stretching for pots and pans; and
- bending and balancing while serving.

Ways to control hazards:

- Arrange for deliveries to be unloaded directly to where they are needed.
- Use forklifts or pallet jacks to unload deliveries.
- Buy smaller, lighter cartons of stock.
- Use smaller pots and pans.
- Provide easy access shelving, or store heavier items in middle shelves and lighter items up higher.
- Ensure workers are trained in safe lifting methods.
- Share lifting tasks.
- Install a rubbish chute.
- Use smaller, lighter rubbish bins and move them by trolley.
- Place regularly-used items and equipment in easy-to-reach places.

- Use smaller trays and baskets for clearing tables.
- Carry only a limited number of plates and glasses at any time.
- Introduce buffet style service instead of table service.
- Redesign drive-through or servery windows to reduce the need to stretch. Provide a chute if possible.
- Fix tables and chairs in permanent positions so they don¿t have to be stacked, moved or set up daily. If this is not possible, use chair trolleys or light/collapsible furniture.
- Provide loading areas close to storage areas.

Slips, Trips and Falls

There is always a risk of slips and falls where food and beverages are prepared and served. These can be caused by cluttered walkways, poor lighting or busy work areas.

Ways to control hazards:

- Clean up spills and dropped food immediately.
- Erect warning signs if floors are freshly mopped.
- Use floor cleaning products that remove oil and grease.
- Minimize moisture buildup on floors.
- Cover normal flooring with a non-slip material (if possible) or use non-slip mats.
- Wear non-slip shoes.
- Keep walkways free of clutter.
- Replace steps with ramps.
- Install food lowering devices.
- Restrict the number of people entering the kitchen (for example, install a servery between the kitchen and dining room).
- Install adequate lighting, especially in delivery and storage areas.
- Install roofing in the unloading area to keep rain off workers.
- Design the delivery area so unloading is done as close as possible to the storage area.

Plant, Equipment and Machinery

The term 'plant' refers mainly to machinery with moving parts that may cause injuries. These include mixers, slicers and mincers. In the hospitality and entertainment industry, knives are also considered to be kitchen plant.

Employers have a duty to provide training on how to use any plant, equipment or machinery in the workplace.

Ways to control hazards:

- Purchase pre-made salads and sliced foods.
- Fix machines firmly to benches.
- Fit guards to plant with moving parts.
- Display operating instructions and safety information near plant.
- Regularly maintain appliances and machines in good working conditions. Tag and do not use a faulty appliance or machine.
- Check electrical equipment is safe to use.
- Use the right knife for the task, and cut away from the body. Secure cutting boards before use and use correct knife sharpening and carrying techniques.
- Be careful when using pressure vessels, for example espresso machines.
- Wear appropriate personal protective equipment such as mesh gloves or gauntlets.

Burns and Scalds

There is always a risk of burning or scalding where hot food and beverages are prepared and served.

Ways to control hazards:

- Place warning signs or stickers near hot equipment or surfaces.
- Add a gravity feed chute from the deep fryer to an external receptacle to eliminate the need to handle hot cooking oil waste.
- Use automatic food lowering devices where available.
- Cover equipment containing hot fat or fluids, when not in use.

- Use a tray or trolley to serve hot liquids, plates or utensils.
- Warn serving staff or customers if plates are hot.
- Follow safe working practices (for example, when using an espresso machine or deep frying food).
- Implement routine safety checks (for example, check that deep fryers and grills are turned off before closing time).
- Wear appropriate personal protective equipment such as heat resistant gloves and aprons.
- Use a waiter's cloth to protect arms while carrying hot plates or trays.
- Ensure workers are trained in the use of hot beverage machinery such as espresso machines.
- Take notice of warning signs regarding hot equipment.
- Train workers in preferred techniques for handling hot items such as:
    - o opening doors and lids of steam heated equipment away from the body;
    - o keeping saucepan or pot handles pointing away from the edge of a stove and make sure the handles are not over hotplates;
    - o using dry cloths to pick up hot items in order to avoid scalding; and
    - o removing all utensils from pans.
- Install windows in the kitchen door to help prevent accidents involving workers carrying hot foods or beverages. Alternatively, provide entrance and exit doors.
- Redesign the kitchen so work areas are away from heat sources.

Heat Stress

Workers are at risk of heat stress when unloading supplies, working in kitchens or during service delivery.

Ways to control hazards:

- Wear a hat, sunglasses and sunscreen when unloading outside.

- Install a roof over the delivery and unloading area to keep heat off workers.
- Take frequent breaks away from a hot kitchen.
- Wear cool clothing in the kitchen.
- Take regular breaks in a cool area with a glass of water.
- Maintain a comfortable temperature in the kitchen using ventilation, extraction or air conditioning.
- Install a serving counter between the kitchen and dining area to reduce the need for people to enter the kitchen.
- Redesign the kitchen so work areas are away from heat sources.
- Ensure workers are educated about the risks of heat stress.

Noise

The hospitality and entertainment industry can be a noisy work environment.

Sources of noise can include:

- beeping signals in food processes
- radios
- two-way headsets used in drive-through services
- kitchen noises
- coffee grinders
- dishwashers

Modern restaurants often do not have good acoustics due to minimalist interior design. For example hard reflecting surfaces do not reduce noise.

You may have a noise problem in your workplace if you have to raise your voice to talk to someone standing 1m away.

Ways to control hazards:

- In a drive-through, position speakers so they are close to the drivers and can be operated at a low volume.
- Play recorded or live music at a comfortable volume.
- Contain kitchen noise.

Electricity

The hospitality and entertainment industry uses electrical appliances extensively. Electric carving knives, toasters, sandwich presses, ovens, food warmers, coffee machines and milk shake makers are just a few examples.

Because these appliances are continuously and heavily used, they must be cleaned, maintained and checked regularly; otherwise their electrical safety may be compromised. Remember¿ electric shock may be fatal.

Electrical accidents at work are usually caused by:

- using faulty equipment
- working with damaged leads
- unsafe work practices
- a combination of all these

Ways to control hazards:

- Avoid using electrical appliances if possible.
- Use splashproof or waterproof appliances wherever possible.
- Install safety switches.
- Arrange for a qualified electrician to regularly test equipment.
- Continually check that electrical leads are not frayed or damaged. If they are, do not use the appliance.
- Be trained in electrical safety and the correct use of appliances.
- Avoid using double adapters or extension leads.
- Install more power points in the kitchen.
- Keep leads away from hot plates, hot equipment and walkways.
- Wear appropriate personal protective equipment such as rubber soled shoes.
- Guards or restrictor plates should be fitted to equipment where appropriate.
- Ensure leads and cables are not running across hot surfaces or walkways where they could be easily damaged.

- Ensure any pressure vessels (such as espresso machines) are fitted with low level cut-off devices.
- Make sure equipment is fitted with safety valves, water level and pressure gauges where required.

Hazardous Substances

Many cleaning products, like oven cleaners, contain substances that may cause adverse health effects. Any hazardous substance used in a workplace must be managed according to the Hazardous Substances Regulation and *Hazardous Substances Code of Practice 2003*.

Skin irritation is a very common health problem resulting from exposure to a hazardous substance. Other problems include occupational asthma, chemical poisoning, chemical burns and long term serious diseases such as cancer. People can breathe in a hazardous substance, accidentally swallow it, or absorb it through their skin.

An employer is legally obliged to assess the risk of every hazardous substance used or produced in the workplace; and if necessary, take steps to control the risk. Carry out an assessment every five years unless there are significant changes to the workplace or methods of work.

Note: Employers should also be aware that occasionally workers may develop skin sensitivity or allergy to certain foodstuffs, e.g. seafood. Although these are not hazardous substances, you may need to provide gloves for these workers or remove them from exposure when that food is being prepared.

To identify hazardous substances:

- Check container labels for signal words such as ¿poison¿, ¿hazardous¿ and ¿warning¿.
- Check that you have a Material Safety Data Sheet (MSDS) from the suppliers. The MSDS details hazards associated with the substance and recommends safety measures.
- Inspect the workplace to see if people are exposed to the hazardous substances, if safety precautions are in place, and if the precautions are effective.
- Record the date of the assessment, the product containing the hazardous substance, the degree of risk, control

measures and the type and timing of monitoring and/or health surveillance (if required).

- If there is a significant health risk, you must keep the following records for 30 years: the risk assessment report, monitoring results and health surveillance reports.
- If there is no significant health risk and exposure is controlled, keep the risk assessment for at least five years.

Ways to control hazards:

- Keep a copy of every relevant MSDS in a central register for quick access by staff. In a large workplace, have more than one register.
- Check that all containers are labelled with the product name and information about safe handling.
- If possible, substitute hazardous substances with less hazardous substances.
- Do not use drink containers to store hazardous substances.
- Train workers in safe handling procedures.
- Use correct storage facilities.
- Introduce control measures according to the degree of risk (for example, use full arm length rubber cloves when cleaning the oven; or do not continue to use a particular product).
- Wear appropriate personal protective equipment (for example, gloves, face shield or cotton overalls).

Parking Management Systems

Parking is the act of stopping a vehicle and leaving it unoccupied for more than a brief time. Parking on one or both sides of a road is commonly permitted, though often with restrictions. Parking facilities are constructed in combination with most buildings, to facilitate the coming and going of the buildings' users.

Parking Facilities

Parking facilities include indoor and outdoor private property belonging to a house, the side of the road where metered or laid-out for such use, a parking lot (American English) or car park (British English), indoor and outdoor multilevel structures, shared underground parking facilities, and facilities for particular modes of vehicle such as dedicated structures for cycle parking.

In the U.S., after the first public parking garage for motor vehicles was opened in Boston, May 24, 1898, livery stables in urban centers began to be converted into garages. In cities of the Eastern US, many former livery stables, with lifts for carriages, continue to operate as garages today.

The following terms give regional variations. All except *carport* refer to outdoor multilevel parking facilities. In some regional dialects, some of these phrases refer also to indoor or single-level facilities.

- *Parking ramp* (used in some parts of the upper Midwestern United States, especially Minneapolis, but sometimes seen as far east as Buffalo, New York). Elsewhere, the term "ramp" would apply to the inclines between floors of a parking garage, but not to the entire structure itself.
- *Multi-storey car park*
- *Car park* (UK, Hong Kong, South Africa)
- *Parking structure* (Western U.S.)
- *Parking garage* (Canada and USA, where this term does not always distinguish between outdoor above-ground multilevel parking and indoor underground parking.
- *Parking deck* (Eastern USA, an outdoor above-ground multilevel parking facility)
- *Carport* (open-air single-level covered parking)
- *Cycle park* (UK)
- *Parkade* (Canada)

In addition to basic car parking/parking lots variations of serviced parking types exist. Common serviced parking types are:

- *Park and ride*
- *Valet Parking*
- *Airport Parking*
- *Meet and Greet Parking*
- *Park and Fly Parking*

Modes of Parking

For most motorized vehicles, there are three basic modes of parking, based on the arrangement of vehicles — parallel parking, perpendicular parking, and angle parking. These are self-park configurations where the vehicle driver is able to access the parking independently.

Parallel Parking

With parallel parking of cars, these are arranged in a line, with the front bumper of one car facing the back bumper of an adjacent one. This is done parallel to a curb, when one is provided. Parallel parking is the most common mode of streetside parking for cars. It may also be used in parking lots and parking structures, but usually only to supplement parking spaces that use the other modes.

Perpendicular Parking

With perpendicular parking of cars, these are parked side to side, perpendicular to an aisle, curb, or wall. This type of car parking is more scalable than parallel parking and is therefore commonly used in car parking lots and car parking structures.

Often, in car parking lots using perpendicular parking, two rows of parking spaces may be arranged front to front, with aisles in between. If no other cars are blocking, a driver may perform a "pullthrough" by driving through one parking space into the connecting space to avoid having to reverse out of a parking space upon their return.

Sometimes, a single row of perpendicular car parking spaces is marked in the center of a street. This arrangement eliminates reversing from the manoeuvre; cars are required to drive in forwards and drive out forwards.

Angle Parking/echelon Parking

Angle parking of cars is similar to perpendicular parking for these vehicles, except that cars are arranged at an angle to the aisle (an acute angle with the direction of approach). The gentler turn allows easier and quicker parking, narrower aisles, and thus higher density than perpendicular parking. While in theory the aisles are one-way, in practice they are typically wide enough to allow two cars to pass slowly when drivers go down the aisles the wrong way.

Angle parking is very common in car parking lots. It may also be used in streetside car parking in the U.S. when there is more width available for car parking than would be needed for parallel parking of cars, as it creates a larger number of parking spaces. Some cities have utilized angled parking on-street (as compared to off-street parking facilities). This has been done mostly in residential, retail and mixed use areas where additional parking compared to parallel parking is desired and traffic volumes are lower.

Most angled parking is design in a *head-in* configuration while a few cities (Seattle, Portland, Baltimore, and Indianapolis are examples) have some *back-in* angled parking (typically on hills or low traffic volume streets).

Angle parking, known as *echelon parking* in Britain, is considered dangerous by cycling organizations, especially in the *head-in* configuration, but unwelcome in either form. When comparing to parallel parking:

1. There is a significant risk to cyclists from vehicles reversing out, as approaching bicycles are in the blind spot of the reversing and turning vehicles.
2. Longer vehicles project further into the road; this can inconvenience/endanger other road users,
3. The "surplus" road space which enables angle parking could also be used for bicycle lanes.

Hence organizations such as the Cyclists Touring Club are usually opposed to all proposed echelon parking schemes.

Other Parking Methods

Besides these basic modes of motor vehicle parking, there are instances where a more *ad hoc* approach to arranging motor vehicles is appropriate. For example, in parts of some large cities, such as Chicago, where land is expensive and therefore parking space is at a premium, there are parking lots for motor vehicles where the driver leaves the keys to the vehicle with an attendant who arranges vehicles so as to maximize the number of vehicles that can be parked in the lot. Vehicles may be packed up to five vehicles deep in combinations of perpendicular and/ or parallel parking with limited circulation aisles for the parking attendant. Such arrangements are known as *attendant parking*.

When the lot or facility is provided to serve the customers of a business, it is considered valet parking.

Inner city parking lots are often temporary, the operators renting land which is vacant pending the construction of a new office building. Some inner city lots are equipped with individual lifts, allowing cars to be stored above each other.

Another *ad hoc* arrangement is *tandem parking*. This is sometimes done with residential motor vehicle parking where two motor vehicles park nose-to-end in tandem. The first motor vehicle does not have independent access, and the second motor vehicle must move to provide access. As with attendant parking, the purpose is to maximize the number of motor vehicles that can park in a limited space.

Economics of Parking

In congested urban areas parking of motor vehicles is time consuming and sometimes expensive. Urban planners must consider whether and how to accommodate or 'demand manage' potentially large numbers of motor vehicles in small geographic areas. Usually the authorities set minimum, or more rarely maximum, numbers of motor vehicle parking spaces for new housing and commercial developments, and may also plan its location and distribution to influence its convenience and accessibility. The costs or subsidies of such parking accommodations can become a heated point in local politics. For example, in 2006 the San Francisco Board of Supervisors considered a controversial zoning plan to limit the number of motor vehicle parking spaces available in new residential developments.

In the graph to the right the value above the line represents the out-of-pocket cost per trip, per person for each mode of transportation, the value below the line accounts for subsidies, environmental impact, social and indirect costs. When cities charge market rates for on street parking and municipal parking garages for motor vehicles, and when bridges and tunnels are tolled for these modes, driving becomes less competitive in terms of out-of-pocket costs than other modes of transportation. When municipal motor vehicle parking is underpriced and roads are not tolled, the shortfall in tax expenditures by drivers, through gas tax and other taxes amounts to a very large subsidy for automobile use. The size of this subsidy for cars dwarfs the federal, state, and local subsidies for the maintenance of infrastructure and discounted fares for public transportation.

Where car parking spaces are a scarce commodity, and owners have not made suitable arrangements for their own parking, *ad hoc* overspill parking often takes place along sections of road where there is no planned scheme by a municipal authority to formally allocate roadspace to the car. Heated social discourse sometimes revolves around the sense of "ownership" that informally arises amongst individuals displaying overspill parking behaviour.

For example, during the winter of 2005 in Boston, the practice of some people saving convenient overspill roadway for themselves became controversial. At that time, many Boston regions had a tradition that if a person shoveled the snow out of a roadspace, that person could claim ownership of that space with some kind of marker (e.g. a chair or orange cone) in the space. However, city government defied that custom and cleared markers out of spaces. Indeed, parking space in Boston is such a rare commodity that in 2009 a single parking space in the Back Bay neighborhood sold for $300,000.

Festivals and sporting events often spawn a cottage industry of parking. Homeowners, schools, and businesses often make extra money by charging a flat rate fee for all-day parking during the event. In some countries, such 'cottage industry parking has transcended to large scale business. The UK airport parking industry is currently estimated to be worth 1.3 billion GBP per year.

According to the International Parking Institute, "parking is a $25 billion industry and plays a pivotal role in transportation, building design, quality of life and environmental issues"

Performance Parking

Donald C. Shoup in 2005 argued in his *The High Cost of Free Parking* book against the large consumption of land and other resources in urban and suburban areas for motor vehicle parking. Shoup's work has been popularized along with market-rate parking and performance parking, both of which raise the price of metered street parking with the goal of reducing cruising for parking and double parking.

'Performance parking' or variable-rate parking is based on Dr. Shoup's ideas. Electronic parking meters are used so that parking spaces in desirable locations and at desirable times are more expensive than less desirable locations. Other variations also include rising rates based on duration of parking. More modern ideas use networked parking meters which "bid up" (or down) the price of parking automatically with the goal of keeping 85–90% of the spaces in use at any given time to ensure perpetual parking availability. These ideas have been implemented in Redwood City, California and are being implemented in San Francisco.

Fringe Parking

Fringe parking is an area for parking usually located outside the central business district and most often used by suburban residents who work or shop downtown.

Entry Control System

The SIPARK PMA car park management system made by Siemens is one of the most advanced systems of its kind on the market.

SIPARK PMA is a system of modular design.

It allows flexible combinations of various components and offers optimum solutions that satisfy individual customer needs:

- Ticket vending machine for entry (for short- and long-term parkers) - SIPARK PMA ENT
- Ticket vending machine for exit (for short- and long-term parkers) - SIPARK PMA EXT
- Automatic and manual cashiers - SIPARK PMA APS/ SIPARK PMA MPS
- Long-term parker terminals - SIPARK PMA SPT
- Car park entry barriers - SIPARK PMA PB Servers/ operator stations

The system is based on barcode or magnetic stripe technology, and the central server ensures control, supervision and administration of the parking system. SIPARK PMA WinOperate - the user interface - affords access to all monitoring functions of the system and offers a host of statistical and administrative functions.

Another feature of the system is the SIPARK PMA LPR licence plate recognition. It facilitates automatic identification of car number plates, thus enhancing the security for the cars parked.

Parking Management Strategies, Evaluation and Planning

Parking is an essential component of the transportation system. Vehicles must park at every destination. A typical automobile is parked 23 hours each day, and uses several parking spaces each week. Parking convenience affects the ease of reaching destinations and therefore affects overall accessibility.

Parking facilities are a major cost to society, and parking conflicts are among the most common problems facing designers, operators, planners and other officials. Such problems can be often defined either in terms of *supply* (too few spaces are available, somebody must build more) or in terms of *management* (available facilities are used inefficiently and should be better managed). Management solutions tend to be better than expanding supply because they support more strategic planning objectives:

- Reduced development costs and increased affordability.
- More compact, multi-modal community planning (smart growth).
- Encourage use of alternative modes and reduce motor vehicle use (thereby reducing traffic congestion, accidents and pollution).
- Improved user options and quality of service, particularly for non-drivers.
- Improved design flexibility, creating more functional and attractive communities.
- Ability to accommodate new uses and respond to new demands.
- Reduced impervious surface and related environmental and aesthetic benefits.

Parking management refers to policies and programs that result in more efficient use of parking resources. Parking management includes several specific strategies; nearly two dozen are described in this report. When appropriately applied parking management can significantly reduce the number of parking spaces required in a particular situation, providing a variety of economic, social and environmental benefits. When all impacts are considered, improved management is often the best solution to parking problems.

Parking Management Principles

These ten general principles can help guide planning decision to support parking management.

1. *Consumer choice.* People should have viable parking and travel options.
2. *User information.* Motorists should have information on their parking and travel options.
3. *Sharing.* Parking facilities should serve multiple users and destinations.
4. *Efficient utilization.* Parking facilities should be sized and managed so spaces are frequently occupied.
5. *Flexibility.* Parking plans should accommodate uncertainty and change.
6. *Prioritization.* The most desirable spaces should be managed to favor higher-priority uses.
7. *Pricing.* As much as possible, users should pay directly for the parking facilities they use.
8. *Peak management.* Special efforts should be made to deal with peak-demand.
9. *Quality vs. quantity.* Parking facility quality should be considered as important as quantity, including aesthetics, security, accessibility and user information.
10. *Comprehensive analysis.* All significant costs and benefits should be considered in parking planning.

Parking Management Benefits

- *Facility cost savings.* Reduces costs to governments, businesses, developers and consumers.
- *Improved quality of service.* Many strategies improve user quality of service by providing better information, increasing consumer options, reducing congestion and creating more attractive facilities.

- *More flexible facility location and design.* Parking management gives architects, designers and planners more ways to address parking requirements.
- *Revenue generation.* Some management strategies generate revenues that can fund parking facilities, transportation improvements, or other important projects.
- *Reduces land consumption.* Parking management can reduce land requirements and so helps to preserve greenspace and other valuable ecological, historic and cultural resources.
- *Supports mobility management.* Parking management is an important component of efforts to encourage more efficient transportation patterns, which helps reduce problems such as traffic congestion, roadway costs, pollution emissions, energy consumption and traffic accidents.
- *Supports Smart Growth.* Parking management helps create more accessible and efficient land use patterns, and support other land use planning objectives.
- *Improved walkability.* By allowing more clustered development and buildings located closer to sidewalks and streets, parking management helps create more walkable communities.
- *Supports transit.* Parking management supports transit oriented development and transit use.
- *Reduced stormwater management costs, water pollution and heat island effects.* Parking management can reduce total pavement area and incorporate design features such as landscaping and shading that reduce stormwater flow, water pollution and solar heat gain.
- *Supports equity objectives.* Management strategies can reduce the need for parking subsidies, improve travel options for non-drivers, provide financial savings to lower-income households, and increase housing affordability.
- *More livable communities.* Parking management can help create more attractive and efficient urban environments by reducing total paved areas, allowing more flexible

building design, increasing walkability and improving parking facility design.

Examples

Below are three illustrative examples of parking management programs.

Reducing Building Development Costs

A mixed-use building is being constructed in an urban or suburban area that will contain 100 housing units and 10,000 square feet of commercial space. By conventional standards this requires 200 parking spaces (1.6 spaces per housing unit plus 4 spaces per 1,000 square feet of commercial space), costing from $2 million for surface parking (about 9% of the total development costs), up to $6 million for underground parking (about 25% of total development costs). However, because the building is in a relatively accessible location (on a street that has sidewalks, with retail business and public transit services located nearby) and onstreet parking is available nearby to accommodate occasional overflows, the building owners argue that a lower standard should be applied, such as 1.2 parking spaces per housing unit and 3 spaces per 1,000 square feet of commercial space, reducing total requirements to 150 spaces. To further reduce parking requirements the developer proposes the following:

- *Unbundle parking,* so parking spaces are rented separately from building space. For example, rather than paying $1,000 per month for an apartment with two parking spaces renters pay $800 per month for the apartment and $100 per month for each parking space. This typically reduces parking requirements by 20%.
- Encourage businesses to implement *commute trip reduction programs* for their employees, including *cashing out* free parking (employees are offered $50 per month if they don't use a parking space). This typically reduces automobile commuting by 20%.
- *Regulate* the most convenient parking spaces to favor higher-priority uses, including delivery vehicles and short errands, and handicapped users.

- Include four *carshare vehicles* in the building. Each typically substitutes for 5 personal vehicles, reducing 4 parking spaces.
- Incorporate excellent *walking facilities*, including sidewalk upgrades if needed to allow convenient access to nearby destinations, overflow parking facilities and transit stops.
- Incorporate *bicycle parking* and changing facilities into the building.
- Provide *information* to resident, employees and visitors about transit, rideshare and taxi services, bicycling facilities, and overflow parking options.
- Develop a contingency-based *overflow parking plan* that indicates where is available nearby if on-site facilities are full, and how and *spillover impacts* will be addressed. For example, identify where additional parking spaces can be rented if needed.

This management program allows total parking requirements to be reduced to 100 spaces, providing $100,000 to $500,000 in annualized parking facility capital and operating cost savings (compared with $20,000-$50,000 in additional expenses for implementing these strategies), as well as providing improved options to users and reduced vehicle traffic.

Increasing Office Building Profits and Benefits

An office building has 100 employees and 120 surface parking spaces, providing one space per employee plus 20 visitor spaces. The building earns $1,000,000 annually in rent, of which $900,000 is spent on debt servicing and operating expenses, leaving $100,000 annual net profit.

Parking management begins when a nearby restaurant arranges to use 20 spaces for staff parking during evenings and weekends for $50 per month per space, providing $12,000 in additional annual revenue. After subtracting $2,000 for walkway improvements between the sites, and additional operating costs, this increases profits 10%. Later a nearby church arranges to use 50 parking spaces Sunday mornings for $500 per month, providing $6,000 in annual revenue. After subtracting $1,000 for additional operating costs, this increases profits by another 5%. Next, a commercial parking operator arranges to rent the building's unused parking to general public during evenings and weekends.

This provides $10,000 in net annual revenue, an additional 10% profit. Inspired, the building manager develops a comprehensive management plan to take full advantage of the parking facility's value. Rather than giving each employee a reserved space, spaces are shared, so 80 spaces can easily serve the 100 employees. A commute trip reduction program is implemented with a $40 per month cash-out option, which reduces parking requirements by another 20 spaces. As a result, employees only need 60 parking spaces.

The extra 40 parking spaces are leased to nearby businesses for $80 per month, providing $32,000 in annual revenue, $9,600 of which is used to fund cash-out payments and $2,400 to cover additional costs, leaving $20,000 net profits. Because business is growing, the tenant wants additional building space for 30 more employees. Purchasing land for another building would cost approximately $1 million, and result in two separate work locations, an undesirable arrangement. Instead, the building manager stops leasing daytime parking and raises the cash-out rate to $50 per month, which causes an additional 10 percentage point reduction in automobile commuting.

With these management strategies, 87 parking spaces are adequate to serve 130 employees plus visitors, leaving the land currently used by 33 parking spaces available for a building site. To address concerns that this parking supply may be insufficient sometime in the future, a contingency plan is developed which identifies what will be done if more parking is needed, which might involve an overflow parking plan, providing additional commuter incentives during peak periods, leasing nearly parking, or building structured parking if necessary.

This parking management plan saves $1 million in land costs, a $50,000 annualized value. Parking spaces can still be rented on weekends and evenings, bringing in an additional $25,000. These parking management strategies increased total building profits about 75%, allow a business to locate entirely at one location, and provide parking to additional users during off-peak periods. Other benefits include increased income and travel options for employees, reduced traffic congestion and air pollution, and reduced stormwater runoff.

Downtown – Addressing Parking Problems

A growing downtown is experiencing parking problems. Most downtown parking is unpriced, with 2-hour limits for on-street parking. During peak periods 90% of core-area parking spaces are occupied, although there is virtually always parking available a few blocks away, and many of the core spaces are used by commuters or long-term visitors, who moved their vehicles every two hours to avoid citations.

Local businesses asked the city to build a $5 million parking structure, which would either require about $500,000 in annual subsidies or would require user charges. Experience in similar downtowns indicates that if most public parking is unpriced, few motorists will pay for parking so the structure would be underutilized and do little to alleviate parking problems. Local officials decide to first implement a management program, to defer or avoid the need for a parking structure.

Parking surveys are performed regularly to track utilization and turnover rates, in order to identify problems. The program's objectives are to encourage efficient use of parking facilities, insure that parking is convenient for priority uses (deliveries, customers and short errands), and maintain parking utilization at about 85%. It includes the following strategies:

- Increase enforcement of regulations, particularly during busy periods, but insure that enforcement is friendly and fair.
- Reduce on-street time limits (e.g., 2-hours to 90 minutes) where needed to increase turnover.
- Expand core area boundaries to increase the number of spaces managed for short-term use.
- Encourage businesses to share parking, so for example, a restaurant allows its parking spaces to be used by an office building during the weekdays in exchange for using the office parking during evenings and weekends.
- Encourage use of alternative modes. The city may partner with the downtown business organization to support

commute trip reduction programs and downtown shuttle service.

- Develop special regulations as needed, such as for disabled access, delivery and loading areas, or to accommodate other particular land uses.
- Implement a residential parking permit program if needed to address spillover problems in nearby residential areas, but accommodate non-residential users as much as possible.
- Provide signs and maps showing motorists where they may park.
- Have an overflow parking plan for occasionally special events that attract large crowds.
- Establish high standards for parking facility design, including aesthetic and safety features, to enhance the downtown environment.
- Price parking, using convenient pricing methods. Apply the following principles:
  - o Adjust rates as needed to maintain optional utilization (i.e., 85% peak occupancy).
  - o Structure rates to favor short-term uses in core areas and encourage longer-term parkers to shift to other locations.
  - o Provide special rates to serve appropriate uses, such as for evening and weekend events.
  - o Use revenues to improve enforcement, security, facility maintenance, marketing, and mobility management programs that encourage use of alternative modes.

Paradigm Shift

Parking planning is undergoing a *paradigm shift,* a fundamental change in how a problem is perceived and solutions evaluated. The old paradigm assumes that parking should be abundant and free at most destinations. It strives to maximize supply and minimize price. The old paradigm assumes that parking lots should almost never fill, that parking facility costs should be incorporated into the costs of buildings or subsidized by governments, and that every destination should satisfy its own parking needs.

The new paradigm strives to provide *optimal* parking supply and price. It considers too much supply as harmful as too little, and prices that are too low as harmful as those that are too high. The new paradigm strives to use parking facilities efficiently. It considers full lots to be acceptable, provided that additional parking is available nearby, and that any spillover problems are addressed. It emphasizes sharing of parking facilities between different destinations.

It favors charging parking facility costs directly to users, and providing financial rewards to people who reduce their parking demand. The old paradigm tends to resist change. It places a heavy burden of proof on innovation. The new paradigm recognizes that transport and land use conditions evolve so parking planning practices need frequent adjustment. It shifts the burden of proof, allowing new approached to be tried until their effectiveness (or lack thereof) is proven.

How Much is Optimal?

Optimal parking supply is the amount that motorists would purchase if they paid all costs directly and had good parking and transport options. But conventional planning practices reflect an assumption that it is desirable to maximize parking supply and minimize user charges. They consider parking management a measure of last resort, to be applied only where it is infeasible to expand supply.

Conventional planning determines how much parking to provide at a particular site planners based on recommended minimum parking standards published by various professional organizations. This provides an *index* or *parking ratio* used to calculate the number of spaces to supply at a particular location. These are *unconstrained* and *unadjusted* values, which generally reflect the maximum supply that could be needed.

These standards are often excessive and can usually be adjusted significantly downward (Topp 2009). To appreciate why it is helpful to know a little about how parking standards are developed. Conventional parking standards are based on parking demand surveys, the results of which are collected and published in technical reports such as ITE's *Parking Generation*. This process implies a higher degree of accuracy than is actually justified. Fewer than a dozen demand surveys are used to set standards for many land use categories. The analysis does not usually take into account geographic, demographic and economic factors that can affect parking demand, such as whether a site is urban or suburban, and whether parking is free or priced.

These standards err toward oversupply in many ways. They are derived from parking demand studies that were mostly performed in automobile-dependent locations. They are generally based on 85th percentile demand curves (which means that 85 out of 100 sites will have unoccupied parking spaces even during peak periods), an 85th occupancy rate (a parking facility is considered full if 85% of spaces are occupied) and a 10th design hour (parking facilities are sized to fill only ten hours per year). Applying these standards results in far more parking supply than is usually needed at most destinations, particularly where land use is mixed, there are good travel options, parking is managed for efficiency or priced.

Most people planning apply parking standards have little understanding of the biases and errors they contain, and the problems created by excessive parking supply. The application of generous and inflexible parking standards is often defended as being *conservative,* implying that this approach is cautious and responsible. Use of the word *conservative* in this context is confusing because it results in the opposite of what is implied. Excessive parking requirements waste resources, both directly, by increasing the money and land devoted to parking facilities, in indirectly, by increasing automobile use and sprawl. Better parking management actually tends to be more *conservative* overall.

Alternative Ways to Determine How Much Parking to Supply

There are better ways to determine how much parking to supply at a particular site. *Efficiency-based standards* size facilities for optimal utilization. This means that most parking lots are allowed to fill, provided that management strategies can insure user convenience and address any problems. For example, parking facilities at a store can be sized to fill daily or weekly, provided that overflow parking is available nearby, motorists have information about available parking options, and regulations are adequately enforced to address any spillover problems that develop.

Efficiency-based standards take into account geographic, demographic and economic factors that affect parking demand. They also reflect the relative costs and benefits of different options, so less parking is supplied where parking supply is relatively costly to provide or where management programs easy to implement. Efficiency-based standards should also reflect strategic planning objectives such as a desire for more compact development, or to reduce traffic.

Because it is not possible to predict exact parking demand and management program effectiveness, efficiency-based standards rely on *contingency-based planning*, which means that planners identify solutions that can be deployed if needed in the future. For example, if a new building is predicted to need 60 to 100 parking spaces, the conventional approach is to supply either the middle value (80 spaces), or the maximum value (100 spaces). With contingency-based planning, the lower-bound value (60 spaces) is initially supplied, conditions are monitored, and various strategies are identified for implementation if needed. This may include banking land for additional parking supply and various parking management programs. This allows planners to use lower parking standards with the confidence that any resulting problems can be easily solved.

Parking Facility Costs

A major benefit of parking management is its ability to reduce facility costs (Parking Costs," Litman, 2003). Parking facility costs are usually borne indirectly through rents, taxes and as a component of retail goods, so most people have little idea of parking facility costs and the potential savings from more efficient management. A typical parking space is 8-10 feet (2.4-3.0 meters) wide and 18-20 feet (5.5-6.0 meter) deep, totaling 144-200 square feet (13-19 sq. meters). Off-street parking requires driveways and access lanes, and so typically requires 300-400 square feet (28-37 square meters) per space, allowing 100-150 spaces per acre (250-370 per hectare).

The direct, annualized costs of providing parking (not including indirect costs such as stormwater management, environmental impacts, aesthetic degradation, etc.). This varies from about $250 per space if otherwise unused land is available, and construction and operating costs are minimal, to more than $2,250 for structured parking with attendants. On-street parking spaces require less land per space than off-street parking, since they do not require access lanes, but their opportunity costs can be high if they use road space needed for traffic lanes or sidewalks.

The *Parking Cost, Pricing and Revenue Calculator* can be used to calculate these costs for a particular situation. In addition to these direct costs, generous parking supply imposes indirect costs, including increased sprawl, impervious surface and associated stormwater management costs, reduced design flexibility, reduced efficiency of alternative modes (walking, ridesharing and public transit use), and increased traffic problems. Put more positively, parking management can help solve a variety of economic, social and environmental problems, increase economic productivity, and make consumers better off overall.

Parking Management Strategies

This section describes a variety of specific parking management strategies. For more information see Litman (2006a) and related chapters in VTPI (2005).

Shared Parking

Shared Parking means that a parking facility serves multiple users or destinations ("Shared Parking," VTPI, 2005). This is most successful if destinations have different peak periods, or if they share patrons so motorists park at one facility and walk to multiple destinations. Parking facilities can be shared in several ways.

- *Shared Rather Than Reserved Spaces.* Motorists share parking spaces, rather than being assigned a reserved space. For example, 100 employees can usually share 60-80 parking spaces, since at any particular time some are on leave, commuting by an alternative mode, in the field, or working another shift. Hotels, apartments, condominiums and dormitories can share parking spaces among several units, since the number of vehicles per unit varies over time. Sharing can be optional, so for example, motorists could choose between $60 per month for a shared space or $100 for a reserved space.

- *Share Parking Among Destinations.* Parking can be shared among multiple destinations. For example, an office building can share parking with a restaurant or theater, since peak demand for offices occurs during weekdays, and on weekend evenings for restaurants and theaters. Sharing can involve mixing land uses on single site, such as a mall or campus, or by creating a sharing arrangement between sites located suitably close together.
- *Public Parking Facilities.* Public parking, including on-street, municipal off-street, and commercial (for profit) facilities generally serve multiple destinations. Converting from free, single-use to paid, public parking allows more efficient, shared use.
- *In Lieu Fees.* "In lieu fees" mean that developers help fund public parking facilities instead of providing private facilities serving a single destination. This tends to be more cost effective and efficient. It can be mandated or optional.
- *Special Parking Assessment.* Businesses in an area can be assessed a special assessment or tax to fund parking facilities in their area, as an alternative to each business supplying its own facilities. This is often implemented through a downtown business improvement district.

Parking Regulation

Parking regulations control who, when and how long vehicles may park at a particular location, in order to prioritize parking facility use. The describes common regulations and the type of parking activity they favor.

Parking Maximums

Parking Maximums means that an upper limit is placed on parking supply, either at individual sites or in an area. Area-wide limits are called *Parking Caps.* These can be in addition to or instead of minimum parking requirements. Excessive parking supply can also be discouraged by reducing public parking supplies, imposing a special parking tax, and by enforcing regulations that limit temporary parking facilities. Maximums often apply only to certain types of parking, such as long-term, single-use, free, or surface parking, depending on planning objectives.

Remote Parking and Shuttle Service

Remote Parking (also called *Satellite Parking*) refers to the use of off-site parking facilities. This often involves shared facilities, such as office workers parking at a restaurant parking lot during the day, in exchange for restaurant employees using the office parking lot evenings and weekends. It can involve use of public facilities, such as commercial parking lots. Remote parking can also involve use of parking facilities located at the periphery of a business district or other activity center, and use of overflow parking during a special event that attracts large crowds. Special shuttle buses or free transit service may be provided to connect destinations with remote parking facilities, allowing them to be farther apart than would otherwise be acceptable. Another type of remote parking is use of *Park & Ride* facilities, often located at the urban fringe where parking is free or significantly less expensive than in urban centers.

Remote parking requires providing adequate use information and incentives to encourage motorists to use more distant facilities. For example, signs and maps should indicate the location of peripheral parking facilities, and they should be significantly cheaper to use than in the core. Without such incentives, peripheral parking facilities are often underused while core parking is congested.

Smart Growth

Smart growth (also called *New Urbanism, Location Efficient Development* and *Transit Oriented Development*) is a general term for development policies that result in more efficient transportation and land use patterns, by creating more compact, development with multi-modal transportation systems ("Smart Growth," VTPI 2005). Smart growth supports and is supported by parking management. Parking management reduces the amount of land required for parking facilities, reduces automobile use and increases infill affordability. These land use patterns, in turn, tend to reduce vehicle ownership and use, and so reduce parking requirements. They allow more sharing of parking facilities, shifts to alternative modes, and various types of parking pricing. Smart growth usually incorporates specific parking management strategies. Effective parking management is a key component of smart growth.

Increase Capacity of Existing Parking Facilities

Increase capacity of existing parking facilities means that parking supply increases without using more land or major construction. There are various ways to do this: Use currently wasted areas (corners, edges, undeveloped land, etc.). This can be particularly appropriate for small car spaces, motorcycle and bicycle parking.

- Where there is adequate street width, change from parallel to angled on-street parking.
- Maximize the number of on-street parking spaces, for example, by using a curb lane for parking rather than traffic during off-peak periods, and designating undersized spaces for small cars or motorcycles.
- Provide special, small parking spaces for motorcycles. Allow and encourage motorcycles to share parking spaces when possible.
- Reduce parking space size. Shorter-term parking requires larger spaces, but employee and residential parking spaces can be somewhat smaller. A portion of spaces can be sized for compact vehicles, which require about 20% less space than full-size stalls.
- Use car stackers and mechanical garages. These can significantly increase the number of vehicles parked in an area. However, they are only suitable for certain applications. They generally require an attendant to move lower-level vehicles when needed to access upperlevel vehicles, and stackers may be unable to accommodate larger vehicles such as SUV, vans and trucks.
- Use valet parking, particularly during busy periods. This can increase parking capacity by 20-40% compared with users parking their vehicles. Commercial lots often have attendants park vehicles during busy periods, but not off-peak.

- Remove or consolidate non-operating vehicles, equipment, material and junk stored in parking facilities, particularly in prime locations.

Mobility Management

Mobility Management (also called *Transportation Demand Management* or *TDM*) is a general term for strategies that increase transportation system efficiency by changing travel behavior (VTPI 2005). It may affect travel frequency, mode, destination or timing (for example, shifting from peak to off-peak).

Parking Pricing

Parking Pricing means that motorists pay directly for using parking facilities ("Parking Pricing," VTPI 2005; Shoup 2005). This may be implemented as a parking management strategy (to reduce parking problems), as a mobility management strategy (to reduce transport problems), to recover parking facility costs, or to raise revenue for any purpose (such as funding local transport programs or downtown improvements). It is often intended to achieve a combination of objectives.

Currently, most parking is inefficiently priced; it is provided free, significantly subsidized, or bundled (automatically included) with building purchases and rents, forcing consumers to pay for parking facilities regardless of whether or not they want it. When motorists do pay directly for parking, it is often a flat annual or monthly fee, providing little incentive to use an alternative mode occasionally. Rates should be set to optimize parking facility use, called *performance-based pricing,* which means that about 15% of parking spaces are vacant and available at any time (Shoup 2006 and 2008).

Bibliography

Burns, P., : *From Communist to Common-weal: Reflections on Tourism Training in Romania,* Tourism Recreation Research, 1998.

Chalazion, P: *Tourism and Cultural Change, Sunderland,* Business Education Publishers Ltd, 1996.

Conroy, B. : *Quality in Education and Training for Tourism,* London, Tourism Society, 1997.

Cooper, Chris: *Geography of Travel and Tourism,* The, London, Heinemann, 1987.

Cukier, J. : *Tourism Employment in Bali: Trends and Implications,* London: Thompson, 1996.

Douglas C: *Practical Tourism Forecasting,* Oxford, Butterworth Heinemann, 1996.

Elio, C.: *The Hospitality Law Desk Reference,* Miami, Southern Beverage Journal, 1994.

Foster, Douglas: *Travel and Tourism Management,* London, Macmillan Educational, 1985.

Fowler, Peter: *Heritage and Tourism: In the Global Village,* London, Retailed, 1993.

Ghimire, Krishna: *The Native Tourist*: Mass Tourism within Developing Regions, London, Earthscan, 2001.

Hoffman, Edward: *Project Management Success Stories: Lessons of Project Leaders,* New York, John Wiley & Son, 2000.

Holloway, J. C. : *Labour, Vocational Education and Training, in W. Pompl and P. Lavery,* Tourism in Europe - Structures and Developments, Oxford, CAB International, 1993.

Ireland, Lewis: *Quality Management for Projects and Programs,* Upper Darby, PMI, 1991.

Jennings, Gayle: *Tourism Research,* Chichester, Wiley, 2001.

Judy A: *Tourism: Management of Facilities*, London, Pitman: M & E, 1993.

Kotler, Philip: *Marketing for Hospitality and Tourism*: New Jersey, Prentice-Hall, 1998.

Larkham, P J: *Building a New Heritage: Tourism, Culture & Identity in the New Europe*, London, Routledge,1994.

Laws, Eric: *Tourist Destination Management: Issues, Analysis & Policies*, London, Routledge, 1995.

Lock, Dennis: *Project Management*, New York, Wiley, 1996.

Medlik, S: *Management of Tourism*, The, London, Heinemann, 1975.

Nancy N.: *Choosing a Career in Hotels, Motels, and Resorts*, New York, Rosen Pub. Group, 1997.

Nightingale, M. : *Tourism Occupations, Career Profile and Knowledge*, Annals of Tourism Research, 1981.

Nijkamp, Peter: *Sustainable Tourism Development*, Aldershot, Avebury, 1995.

Peters, M: *International Tourism*, London, Hutchinson, 1969.

Phipps, A: *Tourism and Intercultural Exchange: Why Tourism Matters*, Clevedon, Channel View, 2005.

Prentice, R: *Conceptualising The Experiences of Heritage Tourists*, 1997.

Ritchie, J. R. B. : *Alternative Approaches to Teaching Tourism*, Guildford, University of Surrey, 1988.

Robert C.: *Cases in Hospitality Marketing and Management*, New York, John Wiley, 1997.

Rocco, M.: *An Introduction to Hospitality Today*, Orlando, Educational Institute, 1998.

Ruddy, J. : *Education and Human Resource Development for the Hospitality and Tourism Industry*, Hong Kong, Hong Kong, 1992.

Schwaninger, M: *Trends in Leisure and Tourism for 2000 - 2010*, Prentice Hall, 1989.

Stear, L. : *Design of a Curriculum for Destination Studies*, Annals of Tourism Research, 1981.

Swarbrooke, J. : *Tourism and Leisure Education in the United Kingdom*, Tilberg, Netherlands, Tilberg University Press, 1995.

Thomas F. : *Introduction to the Hospitality Industry*, New York, Wiley, 1995.

Index

I

J

K

L

M

N

P

R

S

T

W

❑❑❑